BUCKEYE MADNESS

The Glorious, Tumultuous, Behind-the-Scenes Story of Ohio State Football

JOE MENZER

Simon & Schuster
New York   London   Toronto   Sydney

SIMON & SCHUSTER
Rockefeller Center
1230 Avenue of the Americas
New York, NY 10020

SIMON & SCHUSTER and colophon are registered trademarks
of Simon & Schuster, Inc.

For information about special discounts for bulk purchases,
please contact Simon & Schuster Special Sales at
1-800-456-6798 or business@simonandschuster.com

Designed by Karolina Harris

Manufactured in the United States of America

10 9 8 7 6 5 4 3 2 1

Library of Congress Cataloging-in-Publication Data
Menzer, Joe.
    Buckeye madness : the glorious, tumultuous, behind-the-scenes story of
Ohio State football / Joe Menzer.
        p.   cm.
    Includes bibliographical references and index.
    1. Ohio State Buckeyes (Football team)—History. 2. Ohio State Univer-
sity—Football—History. I. Title.

GV958.O35M46 2005
796.332'63'0977157—dc22

                                                    2005044103

ISBN-13: 978-0-7432-5788-6
ISBN-10:   0-7432-5788-X

All photos courtesy of © Brockway Sports Photos

Acknowledgments

GROWING UP as a sports nut in Ohio, you cannot escape the shadow of Ohio State University football. It fits that the Ohio State mascot is a nut—but a dangerous one. If eaten, the buckeye nut can be detrimental to your health, so it's better to look at it rather than to consume it. Ohio State football, on the other hand, is all-consuming once one chooses to enter the world of these beloved Buckeyes. I grew up in Hamilton, Ohio, between Dayton and Cincinnati, but had relatives in Columbus who actually would dress me up in Ohio State football gear when I would visit as a small child. I still have at least one picture in my possession to offer as proof. I'm still not sure if I should thank my Uncle Bill and Aunt Louise and all my older cousins for that, or not. The outfit came complete with helmet and even one of those oversized OSU parka-type coats that the actual players sometimes wore on the sidelines, and it dwarfed me. But I felt big in it, even at age six or seven or whatever I was at the time, and like every other kid in Ohio, at some time or another, I pretended to be an Ohio State football player throttling Michigan whenever I was in it.

My idea for this book came as I watched the 2002 Buckeyes win the national championship with an improbable upset of the heavily favored Miami Hurricanes in the Tostitos Fiesta Bowl. It seemed to me that they had reached back into the past to land a coach in Jim Tressel, who was an unabashed Woody Hayes disciple, after wandering in the college football wilderness under a coach who appeared to be a decent guy, but simply never understood the traditions of Ohio State football.

This book could not have come about if not for the generosity of men like Archie Griffin, Jim Karsatos, and Chris Spielman, who willingly gave time from their busy lives for interviews. Griffin, the only two-time Heisman Trophy winner in the history of college football, has been described as one of the nicest men in sports—and he did not disappoint during an interview that ran long because he didn't want to stop telling stories. The candid Karsatos, a former Ohio State quarterback, is a member of the respected radio broadcast team. Spielman now serves as head coach of the Arena Football League's Columbus Destroyers, but has never stopped bleeding scarlet and gray. Like Karsatos, he may disagree with some of what goes on with the Buckeyes now and then—and he's free in expressing his opinions on a local Columbus radio show—but he also fervently believes in the integrity of the program and its traditions.

This book is the story of how the program evolved in the years between Woody Hayes's last true national championship in 1968 and the championship run in 2002, and beyond. It is the story of all the young men who played at Ohio State during that time, and all the extraordinary and sometimes eccentric men who coached them. It is the story of Hayes, one of the most fascinating and complex men in sports during the twentieth century; of Earle Bruce and his struggle to follow in the legendary Hayes's football cleats; of John Cooper and his pitfalls against Michigan, plus his failure to understand the true depth of college football's greatest rivalry; of Jim Tressel and the current state of college football, filled with challenges away from the field that Hayes never could have comprehended.

There are stories both humorous and sad, sometimes heroic and occasionally tragic. They encompass the truly glorious, though often tumultuous, behind-the-scenes story of Ohio State football.

In addition to those listed above, my heartfelt thanks go out to Steve Snapp of the OSU sports information office, Curt Hunter of the Columbus Destroyers, and a long list of former Buckeye players and coaches too numerous to list here. I do want to offer a special thanks, though, to Dave Foley, Mark Lang, Dom Capers, Fred Pagac, Scott Zalenski, Drew Carter, Chris Gamble, and Ed Sidwell. All were most helpful in piecing certain stories together and placing bits of history in proper context and order. There also were many others who helped from the "enemy" perspective as well, including Pro Football Hall of Famer Joe DeLamiellure, Mike Trgovac, Rodney Peete, and Richard Williamson. Several members of the Ohio State 2002, 2003, and 2004 teams also deserve thanks for their cooperation. And as always I must thank the public relations staffs of several NFL teams, but especially that of the Carolina Panthers. I am proud to call Charlie Dayton, the Panthers' director of communications, a friend. Thanks also to Chance Brockway and Chance Brockway Jr. of Brockway Sports Photos for providing the terrific photos inside this book.

There have been many previous books written about the Buckeyes that proved helpful in my research. All are listed in the bibliography, but there is perhaps no better book about Woody Hayes than *Woody Hayes: A Reflection* written in 1991 by former *Columbus Dispatch* sports editor Paul Hornung, who shares a last name and a passion for football with his namesake who starred at Notre Dame and for the Green Bay

Packers. Also useful was Jerry Brondfield's *Woody Hayes and the 100-Yard War* and a number of other books, including *What It Means To Be a Buckeye,* edited by Jeff Snook.

I also owe thanks to sports editor Terry Oberle at the *Winston-Salem Journal* for allowing me to continue my book pursuits when not covering the Panthers for the newspaper. And I hope that this book meets the high expectations of my colleague at the *Journal,* one of the biggest Buckeye fans I know, John Delong, who also happens to be related to a darn good former OSU tight end, Ben Hartsock.

No book I do could take shape without the always encouraging words and never-ending assistance of my agent, Shari Wenk. And I have never had an easier or more effective editing team to work with than Bob Bender and Johanna Li at Simon & Schuster.

Finally, I thank my wife, Sarah, for her patience when I had none left, and for her unwavering belief in me. I thank our four wonderful children—Andrew, Elizabeth, Emma, and Michael—who stayed out of my office most of the time when they were supposed to and who quit dribbling basketballs in the garage whenever I demanded it for the sake of overcoming writer's block. I thank Ted and Nancy Sardinia for helping out with the kids and for talking us into taking some time out at the beach, which proved to be a surprisingly productive place to sneak in some work—and for Mel and Gladys Bartlett for offering us their place on the surf. Next time I'll leave behind a copy of this book for Mel, who coincidentally happens to be an avid Ohio State fan. (They really are *everywhere.*)

Of all the Ohio State fans I know, though, one looms larger than the rest. As best man at my wedding many years ago, Jim Vogel wowed the reception crowd with the best Woody Hayes imitation I have seen before or since—and he not only loves Buckeye football, but lives it. He and his wife, Shawna, gave me a base of operations in Ohio at times and

Jim facilitated several interviews while assisting in other ways even he may not realize. Without the accommodating Vogels, the book never would have been completed.

I will end with an anecdote. To help one comprehend the subtle beauty that sometimes accompanies the sledge-hammer that is Ohio State football, we take you to the elevator leading from ground level to the press box for a game at famed Ohio Stadium. Sometime not long after Woody Hayes's passing, his wife, Anne, still attended the home games. Before one game she was in an elevator at Ohio Stadium riding skyward along with several OSU coaches who were headed to their box perched high above the field. They wore grim game faces befitting the tension that looms before each kickoff. Suddenly, Anne Hayes broke into a cheer.

"Give me an *O!*" she shouted.

The somber and serious coaches looked hesitantly at each other.

Then, in unison, they gave her an *O.*

"Give me an *H!*" she shouted next.

And on it went, until the aging widow of Woody Hayes had coerced several very serious middle-aged men to spell out *Ohio* at the top of their lungs when they otherwise would have been poring over the day's game plan in their busy minds. It was time well spent. Then they filed out of the elevator, one by one, properly motivated to go make her and everyone else in the state of Ohio proud.

To Mom: Maybe now you'll finally read a football book.
To Dad: Thanks for raising me in Ohio and instilling in me a
love of sports and a respect for sportsmanship.
To Sarah, Andrew, Elizabeth, Emma, and Michael: I'm blessed
to have each and every one of you on my team.
And to the Vogels: What subject can we explore together next?

Contents

BUCKEYE MADNESS

1

Ghosts of Ohio State

JIM TRESSEL'S fiery eyes flashed as he scanned the young men dressed out in scarlet and gray Ohio State football gear that sat or stood, or even bounced on their toes, all around him. Some of the players could not sit or stand still; some were listening intently to his every word; some already had drifted off into their own private world of mental self-motivation. Kickoff against the Miami Hurricanes was only twenty minutes into their future. A national championship would be at stake.

In his heart of hearts, Tressel knew he already was looking at a championship college football team—a team that he had molded, prodded, and flat-out coached into this game for the ages. But first there was the matter of some unfinished business against an opponent that hadn't lost a game in more than two years, in front of millions who mostly didn't give the Buckeyes a snowball's chance in hell of winning. Tressel knew all of that, too, and knew how to get his players to feed off those facts like the hungry underdogs that they were.

"Men," he started out in a low voice, "tonight you em-

1

bark on the last portion of a journey that you started twelve months ago when we walked off the field after our last bowl game. Part of the journey involved some of our friends leaving us for various reasons to go their separate ways.

"But those of you who remain are a part of something special here at Ohio State University. You stayed for a reason."

Tressel paused for effect. Then he went on, his voice slowly rising.

"You stayed on because you cared about the school, what it stands for, your teammates, and yourselves. All of you recognize that you are part of something special here tonight. You recognize that you've come a long way from last January. I encourage you to savor it. Absorb this moment—and seize it! Embrace it and take it in the direction that *you* want it to go.

"There comes a point in each person's life when he or she asks himself or herself: How do I want to be remembered?"

Tressel had known for years how he would want to be remembered. He simply had kept redefining his legacy—upgrading it—at every available opportunity along the way. Critics would charge at times that he sometimes did so at the expense of others, sticking his head in a pile of sand he called morality. But Tressel always plodded ahead toward the goal, figuring that whatever methods he employed, the ends usually justified the means. This was the grandest of all opportunities he had been presented, one that really began roughly two years earlier when he was named the twenty-second head coach in Ohio State's glorious but sometimes tumultuous history.

Like the legendary Woody Hayes more than half a century before him, Tressel overcame tremendous odds to beat out better-known candidates to land the job in the first place.

Most thought the position would go to Glen Mason, the head coach at the University of Minnesota, who had played for Hayes in the early 1970s and later served as an assistant coach with the Buckeyes for eight years. Other more high-profile candidates had included Jon Gruden, then head coach of the Oakland Raiders in the National Football League; longtime Ohio State assistant Fred Pagac, who also had played for Hayes; and one of the greatest and most popular players in Ohio State history, Chris Spielman.

When Hayes became Ohio State head coach in 1951, he beat out Paul Brown, among other notables of the day, for the position. Brown had *won* a national championship as coach of the Buckeyes in 1940 before leaving the school to join the U.S. Navy, and was almost akin to a politician seeking reelection with the considerable dual backing of important alumni and respected former players. Hayes at the time was a relatively unknown candidate who had made his mark at smaller schools: first at tiny Denison and then at Miami— the university in quaint Oxford, Ohio, not the behemoth in Florida that later would stand in Tressel's path on the biggest night of his coaching career.

Like Hayes, Tressel gained the job by winning over a panel of Ohio State bigwigs. First Tressel wowed an eight-member advisory committee and then, in a one-on-one interview, he had greatly impressed school president William E. Kirwan. School officials would later say that what had convinced them the most about Tressel was his plan not only to make the Buckeyes winners on the field, but also to emphasize improved player behavior off the field and the pursuit of academic excellence as well. More than anything else, Tressel was thorough and prepared.

Plus Tressel had deep Ohio ties, perhaps the single most important quality any head coach needed to succeed at Ohio State University. He had played at Baldwin-Wallace College

3

in Berea, Ohio, where he was a quarterback for four years under his father, Lee, a firm coaching disciple of Woody Hayes. Jim Tressel did not become head coach at Division I-AA Youngstown State until he had served as an assistant coach at Akron, Miami of Ohio, and then on Earle Bruce's staff at Ohio State, where for three years he coached quarterbacks, receivers, and running backs. In 15 seasons at Youngstown State, he won 135 games, lost 57, and tied 2, winning four Division I-AA national titles in the process. His résumé was impressive enough that Jim Stillwagon, a former Buckeyes teammate of Mason's, had written to Kirwan recommending Tressel, and not Glen Mason, for the job. Stillwagon and others who recommended Tressel figured it didn't matter that he hadn't played for the Buckeyes.

"Woody Hayes wasn't a Buckeye when he came here. He didn't go to school here and he had never coached here," Stillwagon noted. "And he went on to become one of the greatest Buckeyes of all time."

Spielman, who wasn't called back after his initial interview with athletic director Andy Geiger and associate athletic director Archie Griffin, applauded the hiring of Tressel, recalling Tressel's tenure as an assistant coach while Spielman was chasing down opposing ball carriers for the Buckeyes.

"I remember him as a detail guy, a go-getter, and that's why I think he will do a good job," Spielman told the *Columbus Dispatch* at the time. "And I think it's important that everybody in the state get behind him and back him. I know I'm going to."

They were backing him tonight. This was the national stage. Though Tressel had been in six national title games at Youngstown State, winning four, he knew this was dramatically different. The world was watching this time. More important, so was the whole state of Ohio. Tressel knew the speech he was giving now was one of the most important of his life.

"The reality is that so few people have the chance that you have tonight," he told his players. "You have the chance to affect the answer to the question of how you want to be remembered. The moment is at hand. It is not about tomorrow. It is not about yesterday. It is not about what you did ten minutes ago. But part of your future and how you'll be remembered will be shaped *by you* over the next three and a half hours!"

By now Tressel was almost shouting when he hit the high notes, and his players were responding like ardent followers listening to their favorite preacher at a gospel revival meeting.

"Look around this room and look at the person next to you. How do you want that guy to remember you? How do you want him to remember the way you played in this game? How do you want your parents, family, and friends to remember your performance on this night? Will you be remembered as ordinary or extraordinary?

"Thirty years from now when you have your team reunion, you'll see many of these faces again and you'll shake hands. Wouldn't it be nice to grasp the hand of that teammate thirty years from now and look down and see a giant ring on his finger? You'll reminisce and you'll soak up the common bond that you have with your teammates that can never be broken."

Finally, after touching several key points, which included imploring the team to "play with heart and passion" and to "play like champions" who weren't afraid to win, Tressel was ready to wrap up the biggest pregame speech of his fifty-year life.

"Own the championship, men! Claim it! . . . Don't let anyone take this moment from you! Not the press! Not the fans! . . . And certainly not the Miami Hurricanes! Go out there tonight and show the world what Ohio State football is all about!

"We talk about the tradition that exists here! We talk about great men such as Hayes, Kern, Griffin, Pace, and Paul Brown. . . . You're not alone on that field, men! The ghosts of Ohio State will be with you!"

Tressel had always loved the ghosts at Ohio State. When he arrived on campus as an assistant coach years earlier, he wanted to learn as much as he could about the grand traditions that surrounded the program. There were so many of them. Because he hadn't attended Ohio State as a student-athlete, there was much to learn.

There was the tradition of placing the Buckeye Leaves on players' helmets, which had made the Ohio State helmets unique, and among the best recognized helmets in college football. It was a tradition started by Hayes in 1968 when he and Ernie Biggs, the longtime trainer, decided to change the look of the Ohio State uniforms. The new look included placing the names of players on the back of the jerseys and putting a wide Buckeye Stripe on the sleeves. The Buckeye Leaves were awarded on a weekly basis, given for outstanding plays.

There was the tradition of the Victory Bell. Located 150 feet high in the southeast tower of Ohio Stadium, the Victory Bell is rung after every Buckeyes victory by members of the Alpha Phi Omega fraternity, honoring a tradition that began after Ohio State beat California on October 2, 1954. It is said that on a calm day the bell, which weighs 2,420 pounds and cost $2,535 to install, can be heard five miles away.

There was the tradition of Buckeye Grove, where since 1934 a buckeye tree has been planted in honor of each Ohio State player who is named an All-American. Located in the southwest corner of Ohio Stadium after being moved when the Horseshoe was renovated in 2001, the trees usually are planted in a ceremony prior to the annual spring game. Buckeye Grove long ago had started to resemble a small forest. One hundred twenty-eight trees had been planted from 1934 through 2001, and four more would be planted the following spring in honor of four players on the 2002 team that was getting ready to play Miami for the national title—strong safety Mike Doss, punter Andy Groom, placekicker Mike Nugent, and linebacker Matt Wilhelm.

There was the tradition of the Captain's Breakfast. Also begun in 1934, this annual event held on homecoming weekend features all past captains being invited back for a breakfast where the newest captains are welcomed into their exclusive fraternity for all time.

There was the tradition of the Gold Pants, an almost silly-looking gold charm replica of a pair of football pants awarded to each member of the team and staff following wins over archrival Michigan. This also was begun in 1934 when Coach Francis Schmidt, in his first year on the job, responded to a question about the supposedly superior team from up north thusly: "They put their pants on one leg at a time just like everybody else." Schmidt's Buckeyes then proceeded to hold Michigan scoreless the next four times they played.

There was the tradition of the Senior Tackle. This one began in 1913 and for many years was held following the last practice prior to the regular season finale against Michigan. Seniors are invited to hit a tackling dummy, or more recently a blocking sled, one last time in a symbolic gesture signaling the impending conclusion of their college careers. Depending on the Buckeyes' bowl obligations, sometimes in recent years the ceremony has been held at the last home practice before the team departs for a bowl. It was never more emotional, however, than in 1987 when players urged Coach Earle

Bruce, who already knew he was being fired, to participate before departing for Bruce's final game in Ann Arbor, Michigan.

"He tried to kill the thing," Chris Spielman recalled of Bruce's assault on the blocking sled.

Then the Buckeyes tried to kill Michigan, as they did every year. Donning "EARLE" headbands, they upset the Wolverines 23–20 that year in Ann Arbor, carrying Bruce off the field afterward.

And of course, that was the greatest tradition of all: playing Michigan every year in the final game of the regular season. There was nothing quite like it, and Tressel had long ago come to understand that as a native of Ohio who for years had watched the game every year with his father and extended family. Amazingly, his predecessor at Ohio State, John Cooper, never fully understood the enormity of the rivalry—and therefore never fully understood why he would be fired after posting the dismal record of 2-10-1 against the Wolverines in his 13 seasons of wandering in the Ohio wilderness.

Tressel understood and embraced all of it. When he landed the head coach's job in Columbus, he invited scores of former players into his office to ask not what he could do for them necessarily, but what they could do for the Ohio State program. They were thrilled to be asked.

Tressel had always heard about the legendary 225-member Ohio State band—long ago dubbed "the Best Damn Band in the Land"—and their Skull Session that they held at St. John Arena prior to every Buckeyes home game. But he had never experienced it. So he arranged to have his staff and players go by and witness what essentially is the rowdiest pregame pep rally in college football. They all loved it. The Skull Session, which begins ninety minutes before kickoff, now is regularly attended by more than 10,000 fans. At its conclusion, the band marches out of St. John Arena and across Woody Hayes Drive to the big Horseshoe, Ohio Stadium, where they march in and perform "Script Ohio" and oftentimes have had someone famous, like a retired Woody Hayes or comedian Bob Hope, come out and "dot the i" in Ohio.

The band, of course, also played a part in the relatively new tradition of singing "Carmen Ohio" after victories. The bigger the victory, the more boisterous the performance. Tressel, who had begun this tradition after arriving as coach, soaked up these moments and fully participated—singing his lungs out.

Oh come let's sing Ohio's praise
And songs to Alma Mater raise
While our hearts rebounding thrill
With joy which death alone can still
Summer's heat or winter's cold
The seasons pass the years will roll
Time and change will surely show
How firm thy friendship . . . O-HI-O!

Tressel hoped to sing it again, more passionately than ever before, after beating the Miami Hurricanes in the Tostitos Fiesta Bowl on January 3, 2003.

Not everyone was all that excited to see the Buckeyes in the 2003 Fiesta Bowl, battling for a national championship. In fact, the nationwide consensus seemed to be that the Buckeyes didn't belong on the same field as Miami, the defending national champ that was riding a winning streak that had stretched to 34 games.

A headline in the *Washington Times* blared: "Siesta Bowl? Awesome Hurricanes could blow away Buckeyes early."

The accompanying article insisted that "the Buckeyes better start praying for a fluke." It quoted an anonymous NFL scout who gushed about a Miami defensive line that included "seven guys in their eight-man rotation that will play on Sunday." He didn't mean the following Sunday. He meant every Sunday in the NFL. Then the scout added: "Right now, I'd say Ohio State might have seven guys on the whole team who are future draft picks."

But Jim Tressel wasn't worried about who was going to be drafted into the NFL. Cooper, his predecessor, had made that mistake. Then the emphasis on the program seemed to be different, which Dave Foley, a team captain on the Buckeyes' undefeated 1968 national championship team, had duly noted upon Tressel's arrival. Foley had watched and smiled as Mike Doss, a strong safety with enormous talent and sure high pick in the NFL draft, had decided to forgo the pros for a year to try to come back and do something special as a senior with the Buckeyes. That had rarely happened in Cooper's era.

"I think that one of the keys to this great year [in 2002] was Michael Doss coming back for his senior year," Foley said. "Prior to that, it seemed like every great player Ohio State had in recent years would leave early for the NFL. It seemed like the recruiting pitch must have been, 'Hey, come to Ohio State. We're going to put you in the weight room. We're going to make you bigger and faster and stronger. We're going to give you national exposure. And we're going to get you into the pros.' Now I don't know for sure if that was the pitch or not. But to a former player looking on from the outside, it seemed like that was the pitch.

"The pitch now seems to be, 'You come to Ohio State and you've got the opportunity to play for the greatest college football program in the country. And we want you to graduate. And then after that, you can make your own bed because you've got the education and the football experience.' It seems like they've put things back in perspective, as far as Ohio State being the focus of the deal compared to just being an ends to the means for these guys getting to the pros.

"I think that's what Tressel has done. He's put the spirit back in college football. Obviously the fans in Columbus are going crazy. If you live in Ohio and you don't wear scarlet and gray now, you're an oddball. And it used to be that you could go around town even in Columbus and see a bunch of people in Michigan shirts. . . . And that's horrible, isn't it?"

But on this night, anyone wearing anything with Miami on it was the enemy. The Hurricanes came in as 11-point favorites to become the first team since Nebraska in 1994 and 1995 to repeat as national champions. The Buckeyes had won several close games, some of them in, well, quite ugly fashion throughout their undefeated season.

What Ohio State needed to do, Tressel told his team, was create some turnovers on defense. And that is precisely what it did in the first half, forcing five in all and converting two of them—a Mike Doss interception and a fumble forced by Kenny Peterson that was recovered by Darrion Scott—into first-half touchdown runs by quarterback Craig Krenzel and tailback Maurice Clarett for a 14–7 halftime lead.

The Buckeyes were clinging to a 17–14 lead and appeared ready to put the game away in regulation when Chris Gamble, who doubled as a wide receiver and a cornerback, apparently caught a pass for a first down. But officials ruled that he had been juggling the ball as he went out of bounds, and the Buckeyes were forced to punt. Miami's Roscoe Parrish returned the punt 50 yards to the Ohio State 26-yard line, setting up a 40-yard field goal by Miami placekicker Todd Sievers that tied the game as time expired.

Gamble later would argue that he caught the ball for the first down and therefore the Buckeyes should have been able to run out the clock, but that's not the controversial play everyone would be talking about at the end of the game.

"They said I juggled the ball going out of bounds, but there's no way. I made that catch. The replays showed it," Gamble insisted. "So if you look at it like that, it should never have even gone into overtime. No one talks about that. But if I get that call like I should have, we could have run the clock out. I had that ball right in my hands."

No one talked much about that later because the two overtimes that followed took what had been a rather average national championship game and turned it into one of the best of all time. Miami struck first in overtime, with quarterback Ken Dorsey flipping a seven-yard touchdown pass to terrific tight end Kellen Winslow, one of 11 passes he would catch on the night for 122 yards.

The Buckeyes didn't score quite so easily on the other end when it came their turn to take the ball at the 25-yard line. They had to make two fourth-down conversions, the first coming on fourth-and-14 when Krenzel hit wide receiver Michael Jenkins for a first down at the 12. Then, on fourth-and-three from the five, Miami's Glenn Sharpe was called for pass interference while covering Gamble in the end zone.

And that was the play everyone wanted to talk about afterward. At the least, though, it appeared that defensive holding should have been called—and that would have given the Buckeyes a first down near the goal line. As it was, the interference call set up a one-yard touchdown sneak by Krenzel on third down. After an illegal-procedure call on the Buckeyes added some more drama, placekicker Mike Nugent delivered the extra-point kick that sent that game to a second overtime.

This time, the Buckeyes had the ball first and drove

quickly to set up a five-yard touchdown run by Clarett, the enigmatic freshman who had often carried the team during the regular season and, some would argue, later tried to kill it. Even though Clarett had been held to a mere 47 yards rushing on 23 carries against the Hurricanes, he still scored two touchdowns and capped a remarkable freshman season by making one of the most memorable plays of the night. Midway through the third quarter, Miami's Sean Taylor killed a potential scoring drive by the Buckeyes by picking off a Krenzel pass in the end zone. But as Taylor zipped up the left sideline, Clarett raced up from behind on a great hustle play and pulled the football from Taylor's embrace at the Ohio State 28-yard line, stealing possession back for the Buckeyes and setting up a 44-yard field goal by placekicker Mike Nugent that gave them a 17–7 lead. His later touchdown in overtime was less spectacular but more important, and when Nugent added the extra-point kick it was 31–24 Ohio State.

When the Buckeyes' defense subsequently held on the other end, the final blow being delivered by linebacker Cie Grant to force a bad pass from Dorsey on fourth down from the one-yard line, it was time to cue up "Carmen Ohio." Buckeyes fans, who far outnumbered Miami fans, stormed the Sun Devil Stadium field to celebrate. Ohio State had won more games than any previous team in the school's history. It had gone 14-0 and won the national championship, no doubt stirring up cheers from the ghosts of Ohio State's storied past.

Jim Tressel was pretty certain how this team would be remembered.

2

Woody's World

WOODY HAYES sensed that he was about to come into something special. The year was 1968, and Hayes had a rare ability to sense when he was about to embark on a journey that would, in time, become part of history. He believed, in fact, that he had been placed on this earth fifty-five years earlier to help make some of the history that he so loved. As head football coach at Ohio State, he headed into the 1968 season with the instruments that he felt he needed to etch a mark in the record books that would never be forgotten.

Hayes had been born on Valentine's Day in 1913 in tiny Clifton, Ohio. Even the exact location of Wayne Woodrow Hayes's place of birth was no simple matter. His house, it turned out, straddled the Clark County and Greene County lines. He would joke in later years that whichever county claimed him often depended on how his Ohio State Buckeyes performed on a given Saturday afternoon.

His father was Wayne Benton Hayes, a dedicated teacher who instilled in his youngest son an insatiable thirst for knowledge. His mother was Effie Hayes, whom Woody would later describe as "the balance wheel, driving, competitive, puritanical, and the businessperson of the family."

"When she believed in something, all hell couldn't change her mind," Woody once said of his mother. The same would later be said of the son.

Wayne Benton Hayes was intelligent enough that after completing the eighth grade, he had taken the Boxwood Exam and passed it, allowing him to teach school in the state of Ohio before he was old enough to apply for a driver's license. He eventually attended as many as six different colleges before earning a degree from Wittenberg University in Springfield, Ohio. Finally armed with the certificate he needed to apply for better jobs, the elder Hayes, now thirty-eight years old and well used to the demands of balancing career and family, soon landed a position as superintendent of schools in Newcomerstown, Ohio. It was on the initial train ride to their new home in 1920 that Woody Hayes, at age six, passed through the city of Columbus for the first time.

Aptly named Newcomerstown seemed perfect for the newcomers from the other side of Ohio. Nestled alongside the Tuscarawas River, the town of about 3,500 was surrounded by rich farmland and just a few miles removed from an Amish community. The town itself was inhabited by just one industrial plant, the Clow Pipe and File works. The high school was made of red brick, and graduating classes contained no more than forty to fifty students. Just a couple of blocks away from where the Hayes family settled in, the Ohio Canal snaked its way through town. Though it was no longer used for commercial shipping of goods, it would soon become a source of endless boyhood pleasure for Woody, his brother, Isaac, and their friends. They would swim there in the summer and ice-skate there in the winter, and some would even fish there—but not young Woody. He never had the patience for it.

Woody's father would read six or more books at the same time and leave them lying half-open around the house. The father would study the books himself, leaving the lasting impression with Woody that no one is ever too old to learn something new. Other times the father would read aloud to Woody and his two siblings, older brother Isaac and older sister Mary. Then he would question his children about what they had just heard, or simply open up a discussion about the subject matter that could lead to long, involved, thought-provoking conversation. The books invariably would pertain to a variety of complex subjects—history and math, science and psychology, language and philosophy, politics or music—but never romance or mystery novels or anything that the elder Hayes deemed a waste of time. At Sunday dinners following church, more discussion of books and theater and music, but also family matters, sports, and current world events, would take place in the Hayes household. These dinners often lasted three hours or longer as the Hayes family engaged in lively debates.

Woody idolized his brother, Ike, who was two years older and became a high school football star. The Hayes brothers at one time developed a strong interest in the sport of boxing, and used to spar in the family living room even as their sister, who was eight years older than Woody and infinitely more interested in the fine arts, attempted to practice the piano. The brothers even staged bouts under assumed names to avoid facing the wrath of parents they knew would not approve. After they staged one exhibition at a local stag picnic, a spectator scolded them and asked if their father knew they were there.

Ike Hayes eyed the man and replied, "Well, does your wife know you're here?"

Woody chuckled years later when remembering the retort and his brother's quick wit, which he greatly admired. It taught him that words could be a devastating weapon as he moved through life—and it wasn't the only life lesson that he gleaned from his older brother.

Isaac Hayes didn't enroll in college right after high school, but several years later decided to attend Iowa State to pursue a degree in veterinary medicine. He also decided to play football again, and despite the years away from the game he eventually earned All-America honors as a 162-pound guard. The determination and persistence and hard work that Isaac displayed at every turn had an impact on his younger brother, who wanted to emulate his idol in virtually every way.

By then Mary, the older sister, was already making a name for herself. She went off to college, then on to a music conservatory in Ithaca, New York, where she decided to become an actress somewhat against the wishes of her father, who believed in more practical pursuits. He came around when she began landing roles on Broadway in productions that garnered great reviews and drew large crowds night after night. She eventually married and, together with her husband, ventured into the new and booming medium of radio, where they wrote for shows and quickly became one of the more respected writing teams in New York City.

But his older siblings and his parents weren't Woody's only role models as he grew up in Newcomerstown. The manager of the local baseball team was none other than the great Cy Young, who had won a record 511 games in the major leagues and for whom baseball's annual award for most outstanding pitcher would later be named. The old player-turned-coach took an immediate liking to the young Woody, letting the youngster do small chores around the ballpark where the Newcomerstown team played. In spare moments, Woody would sit fascinated as Cy told stories of his days in the major leagues, fueling in the young boy a great appreciation for sports and the traditions that accompanied them. Woody learned that Cy's real first name was Denton, and that he had earned his nickname as a youth when someone commented that the pitching prodigy "threw the ball with the speed of a cyclone."

Old Cy Young told salty stories of his days in the big leagues, Woody sitting on the edge of his seat at every word. Cy was no saint. He had retired to a farm near Newcomerstown following his storied career and was fond of throwing the types of get-togethers where Woody and Ike would take part in boxing exhibitions. In fact, Woody quickly became one of Cy's favorites to watch during rousing beer parties, where the local men came out in droves to experience brew that supposedly was superior in every way to the pale stuff peddled elsewhere during Prohibition.

The round-faced, chubby Woody was sixteen years old at the time. And when Cy Young asked him to get into the ring to battle against mostly other kids his age but occasionally against older, more experienced middleweights, the 160-pound Hayes was more than willing to jump at the chance to prove his toughness in front of one of his idols and more of his peers.

"He's got the best left hook in town," Young would tell others.

Hayes earned $5 every time he boxed. But he would have done it for free. He loved the competition. He enjoyed hitting people. And he especially liked the challenge of proving he was tough of mind and body to people like Cy Young—a mentor whom he figured mattered because of what Young already had accomplished in life.

Boxing wasn't the only source of revenue for young Woody. He also mowed lawns and delivered newspapers, although Mary later remembered him as "a terrible business-man at handling his accounts." Woody didn't mind the work, but he didn't like going around and trying to collect money from those who owed him for his labors.

"He was always neglecting to collect from his newspaper accounts, and our mother constantly had to remind him. I think if she hadn't, weeks would go by before Woody would ask people for the money," Mary once told Jerry Brondfield, author of *Woody Hayes and the 100-Yard War*.

Largely because of his early association with Cy Young, Hayes's first true athletics love affair was with baseball, not football. Woody wanted to become a major league pitcher just like Cy Young, but as his career advanced through high school and on to Denison University he soon began to realize that while he may have had the will and the mind for it, he lacked the talent. He played mostly outfield and pitched little over the years.

It was at Newcomerstown High School where Wayne Woodrow Hayes began falling for football. Unlike his affair with baseball, which was like a meteor, this was a slow romance that in time would grow into a deep infatuation that knew no bounds. As a sophomore, when the Hayes family obtained their first radio, Woody grabbed a large piece of cardboard and decided he was going to chart every play in the 1928 Rose Bowl. He started as a tackle for three years at Newcomerstown, serving as team captain his senior year as he earned a reputation as being stubborn, hard-nosed, and a tireless worker. He also was a reserve on the basketball team in addition to playing for the baseball team before graduating in 1931 and moving on to nearby Denison.

Woody majored in English and history at Denison, crediting Clyde Bartholow, his sixth- and seventh-grade teacher in the subjects, with helping fuel what would be lifelong interests. He waited tables at his Sigma Chi fraternity house, stoked furnaces, and performed various other odd jobs to meet his college expenses, and he continued to play football.

He earned three letters as a 200-pound tackle at Denison and later called himself "a good player, but not great." What he was, though, was intensely competitive and perhaps the hardest worker on the team. And even then, he hated to lose.

When he left Denison upon graduating in June of 1935 to go into the world and forge a professional life for himself, he wasn't thinking that he would become a legendary football coach. Hayes wanted instead to become a lawyer. But he had a Plan B. Hours after receiving his diploma at Denison, Hayes hitchhiked to a football coaching clinic in Toledo. Among the speakers there was Francis Schmidt, then the highly respected head coach at Ohio State. Shortly thereafter, in what he perceived as an effort to accumulate money for law school, Hayes accepted a job as a seventh-grade teacher and assistant football coach in Mingo Junction, Ohio, at a salary of $1,200 a year.

He applied for law school at Ohio State the following summer, only to discover that the College of Law at Ohio State did not accept new students in the summer quarter. So he began graduate work in education administration at the school, still thinking that he would become a law student. At worst, though, he figured he could work toward his graduate degree in education and perhaps follow in the footsteps of his father, whom he admired greatly.

Fate, and history, had a different path in store for the man who would become synonymous with Ohio State football.

In the fall of 1936, Hayes took another job at New Philadelphia High School in Ohio, where he served as a history teacher and assistant football coach. It was there that he mingled with one Paul Brown, at the time an Ohio State graduate student who was beginning to make a name for himself as head coach at Massillon High School. Hayes and Brown inevitably found themselves talking more about football than about education administration or any other subject. Hayes was beginning to embrace an affinity for football that he would never shake.

More importantly, it was while in this job that Woody met the future and influential Mrs. Woody Hayes. Her maiden name was Anne Gross, and they would be married in 1942, six years after being introduced by mutual friends. They later learned of hard evidence that it had been predetermined that they were placed on the planet for each other. Just as Hayes had charted football games he listened to on the radio throughout his teen years and even after he began to coach, Anne Gross often used to sit at home with her brother and chart plays to games that they listened to on the radio. The future Mr. and Mrs. Woody Hayes later figured out that they probably had both sat at home and charted every play to the 1928 Rose Bowl, and almost certainly several other major games of the era.

Eventually Woody succeeded John Brickels as the head football coach at New Philadelphia—but even as he courted the popular and vivacious Anne, there were other, more pressing world events on his mind. Ever the avid student of history, Hayes watched with great interest what was transpiring in Europe and in the Pacific as 1940 approached. Once Adolf Hitler invaded Poland, triggering World War II, Hayes quickly became convinced that the United States would eventually have to become involved in the conflict.

"The war against Hitler cannot be won without us. We've got to get in there and fight 'em," Hayes, then twenty-seven years old, told friends again and again. Hayes believed that as a young man it was his duty to serve his country in the time of need. So five months before Japan bombed Pearl

Harbor on December 7, 1941, Hayes enlisted in the United States Navy.

At first he was assigned to the Navy's training program, then headed by former heavyweight boxing champion Gene Tunney. Hayes felt an immediate connection, remembering when he and Isaac would pretend they were battling for the heavyweight championship. Later he was assigned to another training program headed by another well-known athlete of the day, former Navy football star and coach Tom Hamilton. Hayes was a natural fit, training others for duty after he had been trained himself. But he wanted more. Especially after the Pearl Harbor bombing, he was sure he could contribute more to the war effort if he could only get assigned to a ship at sea.

So he approached a yeoman who worked as sort of a secretary for his commanding officer.

"How can I get my orders signed so I can go out to sea on a ship?" Hayes asked, somewhat more sheepishly than was his usual custom even then.

"I shouldn't tell you this, but the commander usually reads the first three letters I give him every morning. But then he stops reading them because he's got so many he's supposed to rubber-stamp and sign. He just signs everything after that," the yeoman said.

"Are you telling me you can get my orders signed without him knowing it?" Hayes asked.

"If you write your own orders, I'll put it down among the other letters in the stack I give him—and I think he'll sign it without even realizing what he's doing. If you want to get to sea that bad, I'll do it."

The trick worked. Hayes didn't feel good about it, but he got what he wanted. A few days later, he ran into Commander Hamilton at the U.S. Navy base in Pensacola, Florida.

"Sir, I just wanted to thank you for all that you've done for me now that I'm heading out to sea," Hayes said.

"What the hell are you talking about?" Hamilton demanded.

When Hayes produced the orders, an angry Hamilton stormed off. He didn't want to lose Hayes, whom he considered a valuable trainer of other young men. He later told Hayes that he also was jealous, because he was waiting for his own orders to sea and hadn't yet secured them.

It would be years before the two men saw each other again, and even then, on their first encounter, an embarrassed Hayes avoided Hamilton when he saw him at the officers club in Pearl Harbor. They didn't discuss the incident until long after the war when Hayes, then head coach at Miami University in Oxford, Ohio, took his team to play at the University of Pittsburgh, where Hamilton was athletic director.

It didn't take Hayes long once he was at sea to prove that he had the mettle to excel on the high waters of the Atlantic and Pacific Oceans. He came aboard a PC1251, a submarine chaser, as chief executive officer, and within a year was promoted to commanding officer before the ship participated in the invasion of the Palau Islands in the Pacific. The same scenario repeated itself when he was reassigned to the destroyer escort *Rinehart*, which sailed in campaigns in both the Atlantic and the Pacific. While Hayes was sailing the oceans for the U.S. Navy, his wife gave birth to a son, Steven. The boy would grow up used to his father being away from the household much of the time, fighting other battles.

His father would be shaped, too, by his time fighting the Japanese in the Pacific theater. Though Hayes would go on to be considered a groundbreaker in the coaching community in terms of advancing the cause of the African-American athlete, he went through much of the rest of his life harboring a general prejudice against those of Japanese descent.

"Woody was a product of his time, that's all," a future Ohio State assistant coach who later became familiar with Hayes said many years later, long after Hayes had passed away in 1987. "Your father, my father, my grandfather is what Woody was. And it appeared that Woody had a real like for your typical Eastern European kid who had thirteen syllables in his name and it ended in 'ski.' The kind of kids you could hit in the head with a board and they would keep running at you and trying to take you down. He liked the hardworking kid."

By the spring of 1946, Woody Hayes wasn't sure what he was going to do next. With the *Rinehart* safely docked in Long Beach, California, and his tour with the Navy coming to an end, he was thinking about finally enrolling in law school or simply returning to his old job as head football coach at New Philadelphia High School. But as often would be the case in his life, fate stepped in to determine his next course of action. A letter from his old coach at Denison, Tom Rogers, finally caught up to him after chasing him all over the world as Hayes sailed with the *Rinehart*.

Rogers said that he was leaving Denison and the head coaching position would be open for the 1946 season. Would Woody be interested in making the leap from New Philadelphia High School to his college alma mater?

Hayes immediately warmed to the idea, but was he too late? The letter had been sent weeks earlier and had nearly caught up to him several times in the Pacific but kept missing him. Hayes quickly sent a telegram informing Rogers that, yes, he was not only interested but excited about the possibility—but first he had to sail the *Rinehart* through the Panama Canal and up the East Coast to the naval base in Norfolk, Virginia. He wouldn't be able to arrive in Granville, Ohio, to formally discuss the position face-to-face with anyone for several more weeks.

There weren't a whole lot of coaches looking to grab the Denison job at the time. Plus Rogers had strongly recommended Hayes to the athletic board and the university president. The school decided to wait until Hayes returned, and soon thereafter hired him after a brief round of interviews.

Now the die was cast. Woody Hayes was a college football coach. Nothing for him or those coached by him would ever be quite the same. Hayes did continue working toward his master's degree in education administration at Ohio State. As always, he carefully plotted out a Plan B in case Plan A faltered and he found he couldn't hack it as a college coach.

During his first year, it looked as if he might embark on a career in education administration sooner rather than later. The Denison players, several of whom were veterans just returning from active duty in one branch of the armed forces or another just as their coach was, didn't take an immediate liking to him. In fact, just the opposite.

One player walked into Hayes's office shortly after the new coach's appointment in September of 1946, fell into a chair, and propped his feet up on the astonished Hayes's desk.

"I was a regular last year on this team and intend to be again. What are your plans for me?" the player asked.

Hayes fumed, displaying for the first time in his new position the temper that would soon become famous.

"My first plan for you is for you to get your god-damned feet off my god-damned desk! Then you get your god-damned ass out to the practice field, where you can work your god-

25

damned tail off until we as a coaching staff decide when and where or even if we're gonna use you. Now get outta my god-damned office!" Hayes bellowed.

Other veterans of the war who were in their mid-twenties quickly took offense at Hayes's brusque attempts to teach them discipline. They were just coming out of a life where discipline was the watchword and where a little more than which team was going to win Saturday's game hung in the balance. They at first had trouble taking Hayes seriously, which only infuriated the new coach even more.

Hayes was convinced that he was right and they were wrong. There was only one way to coach a team, and that was to instill discipline day and night if necessary. There could be no exceptions. In this, he was at his stubborn best—and worst. If the team was practicing and didn't run the first play right, they would run it again. And again. And on and on until they did get it right, even if it was the only play they could practice until darkness enveloped the field. Hayes did not compromise with anyone that first season—and the team stumbled to a record of two wins against six losses.

Hayes then proved that he was going to have staying power as a coach. He admitted to his team, and even publicly, that his approach had been all wrong. He called his team together.

"Fellas, I made mistakes this year. But I learned from 'em and I won't repeat 'em next year. We have some real potential here. I really believe that. If you stick with me and come back again next year to give it another go, I think we could be a great team."

Privately, Hayes told many of the older veterans of the war that he was wrong to have handled them the way he did that first season. He admitted to others that it was his single greatest regret about his first college coaching season.

"I should have realized that they deserved more respect.

They were worn out from the war and all the stuff that came with it, and they didn't need me breathing fire down their necks all the time," he told coaching acquaintances.

At the same time, Hayes became more convinced than ever that the most disciplined and best-conditioned football team would always come out on top—even against teams with more talent who weren't as careful or as diligent in their approach or who weren't in top shape. In this, the former military men who were now his players needed some additional training. They may have been in tip-top shape to fight the war when they left basic training many months or years earlier, but that was a different type of shape than it took to play hard-nosed football—plus many had used their time off after leaving the service to relax and cut loose. They hadn't bothered to keep fit so they could excel at postwar football for Coach Woody Hayes at Denison University. Yet it took Hayes some time to realize the dynamics of all this. He finally reached the conclusion that he simply needed to find a way to explain to the men that getting in top football shape started with some basic conditioning that had little or nothing to do with football in the strict sense. But it was necessary to allow them to perform at their highest level later when the hitting began in the more physical, yet technical practices.

"If a man isn't in shape, he'll hold back because he doesn't want to get too tired," Hayes explained years later. "I found that breaking training was more a symptom than a cause, and that once these men got in shape these symptoms would disappear."

In his first Denison off-season, Hayes appointed a committee of five returning players whom he thought were loyal to his cause and could instill his beliefs in the rest of the team. He met with them often, picking their brains and making them feel vested in the common interest of doing great things as a team the following season. But there was a problem looming. Star halfback Eddie Rupp was planning to pass up spring drills to serve as captain of the golf team.

Hayes gathered himself and went over to see Rupp, an Army Air Force veteran, at Rupp's fraternity house on the Denison campus.

"Eddie, why are you thinking about skipping spring drills? That won't set a very good example for the rest of the guys. They consider you a leader," Hayes pleaded.

Rupp shook his head.

"I don't want to be a problem, Coach. But listen, I just got out of the Air Force. Then I come here to school and I play football and then basketball. I need a break from all the discipline I always hear you talk about. Golf is relaxing to me. I need that right now."

"Golf? Over football?" stammered Hayes, not quite comprehending how this could be.

"That's right, Coach. No spring football. I'll come back and play for you in the fall, but I need some time away from it."

Hayes thought for a moment. He could sense that Rupp was physically and mentally exhausted from the nonstop whirlwind that had become the young man's life. Then he proposed an idea, his first true compromise as a head college coach.

"The football team needs you, Eddie. I need you. So let's make a deal. If you come out for the first week of spring drills and give it your all, setting an example for the rest of the guys, I'll excuse you from the rest of the spring sessions and you can go play your relaxing game of golf or do whatever else it is that you want to do," Hayes said.

Rupp hesitated, thinking it over.

"Okay, Coach, I'll be with you. But only for that first week."

It was a watershed moment in Hayes's young coaching career. He had encountered a problem and calmly found an intelligent, simple way to deal with it after carefully hearing both sides of what turned out to be a complex issue. When Rupp ended the first week of spring drills by running for three long touchdowns in the team's first scrimmage, both player and coach felt vindicated. The team applauded Rupp heartily as he left the practice field that day for his well-deserved time off away from the game, knowing the story about what had transpired between him and the young, usually uncompromising coach. Hayes later declared it the most important building block in what became a 9-0 season for Denison, which in turn became an important stepping-stone in Hayes's suddenly hot new career as a college football coach.

While Hayes was off to war and then forging his first collegiate program at tiny Denison, the football world at Ohio State did not stand still. It already was a force. And then, as now, the perceived success or failure of the program in any given year hinged greatly on how the Buckeyes performed in the annual showdown against archrival Michigan. Oftentimes in Columbus, perception was all that mattered.

As Hayes was beginning his own fledging career as a coach at high schools in Mingo Junction and New Philadelphia in the late 1930s, Francis Schmidt was winning over the Ohio State faithful with a wide-open offense and, at first, a knack for racking up victories over Michigan. Schmidt was the first Ohio State coach to toy with the I-formation in the backfield, and was widely hailed as an offensive genius for his use of reverses, double reverses, and lateral plays out of all kinds of formations. He even had plays designed for two or more laterals, and taught his players not to hesitate if they thought they could complete the risky pitch back to a team-mate as they were about to be brought down by the opposing defense.

A bayonet instructor in the Army in World War I, Schmidt was a throwback in many ways and an innovator in others. He was loud and boastful, prone to toss out a string of swear words that made it seem a little humorous that he came to the Buckeyes from Texas Christian University. The most famous story to develop from his tenure as coach, which many have since insisted was absolutely true, involved a Schmidt visit to a local Columbus filling station to have his car's oil changed. Schmidt remained in his seat, furiously di-agramming Xs and Os, as the car was sent skyward on a jack so the mechanics could do their work. Sometime during the oil change Schmidt put his pencil and pad down, satisfied that he had come up with yet another great play. Nodding to himself with satisfaction as he gazed at the pad held in front of him, he simply opened his car door and stepped out, falling eight feet to the ground.

Schmidt challenged conventional Columbus wisdom, often for the betterment of the narrow-minded fans who fol-lowed his football team with a passion that sometimes clouded their sense of logic. Schmidt wondered aloud if it might be okay to call his boys "Bucks" instead of "Buckeyes" on occasion, offering the opinion that "the buck is a hell of a fine animal, you know." He also is the man credited with cre-ating one of the great sports clichés of all time, noting after four consecutive whippings of the Wolverines that "shucks, I guess y'all have discovered that they put their pants on one leg at a time just like everybody else."

From that moment forward, every Buckeye—or Buck—player or coach who defeated Michigan became the proud re-cipient of a tiny little charm replica of gold football pants.

Players past and present often begin reminiscing with the simple question: "How many pairs of Gold Pants do you have?" Usually they know the answer before asking it, and it's the ones who have the most who love to get the needle out and ask the others.

But Schmidt, offensive genius that he may have been, was not the best facilitator of staff talent. His staff felt as if they never knew what he was going to do next and that, while he may have been brilliant at designing plays and even coaching the boys to execute them, he was a poor organizer who heaped blame on others—players and assistant coaches alike—when something went wrong.

After beating Michigan four years in a row, Schmidt's Bucks soon began succumbing to the fine animals from the state up north. His teams lost three in a row as Michigan rolled behind the legendary Tom Harmon, putting the final nail in Schmidt's Ohio State coffin with a 40–0 rout in 1940. Sensing he was about to be fired, Schmidt quit—and so did five of his assistants, including one Sid Gillman, who would go on to make a name for himself at Miami of Ohio, the University of Cincinnati, and in professional football. When the newspaper photographers came around in search of documentation of Schmidt's departure, he waved them away.

"You guys have dozens of my pictures in your files. Just dig one of them out and use it. And while you're at it, underneath it just say: 'Rest in Peace.'"

Three years later, after coaching briefly at Idaho, Schmidt died of a heart attack. Some claimed that he never got over the fact that he had been run out of Columbus.

Schmidt's departure paved the way for Paul Brown to add to his coaching legend. Between 1935 and 1940, Brown won six consecutive state championships at Massillon High School, averaging more than 40 points per game while holding opponents to less than a field goal each time out. In 1940, the Massillon Tigers drew 171,000 fans to eight home games. The Ohio State program was looking for long-term stability and thought the high school hotshot would provide it, so Brown was hired for the annual salary of $7,000. So as Woody Hayes was about to head out to sea to help the United States win World War II, Brown was settling into his new job as head coach of the Buckeyes. By all accounts, Hayes applauded Brown's promotion and never thought that Brown wouldn't be a long-term success at an institution where the twenty-six-year-old Hayes could only dream of one day coaching.

The war changed everything for everybody, including Brown and the Buckeyes. After two fine seasons, including one that produced a national championship in 1942, Brown found himself coaching a mishmash of players—mostly freshmen and upperclassmen who had been rejected from various branches of the armed forces as being unfit for active duty. The best athletes, including most of the ones Brown had recruited to come to Ohio State, were off fighting the war all over the globe. And Brown soon decided to join them, although after joining the Navy he was assigned to coach a formidable Great Lakes Naval Training Station team in Chicago.

So much for longevity. Brown was gone after three years and was followed by three more coaches—the forgettable trio of Carroll Widdoes, Paul Bixler, and Wes Fesler. None won enough, or beat Michigan often enough, to hang on to the job for more than two or three seasons.

Meanwhile, Hayes had moved on from Denison to Miami of Ohio, where he replaced Gillman, another budding offensive genius who had experienced success as head coach of the Redskins after leaving Ohio State with Francis Schmidt. As at Denison, the new coach struggled in his first season at Miami and then won eight of nine games—including a huge upset of much larger Arizona State in the short-lived Salad Bowl in Phoenix.

In 1951 Hayes was thirty-eight years old. It had been ten years since the day he learned that Paul Brown had been named head coach at Ohio State, and he suddenly realized that his dream job might actually be there for the taking.

"But I wasn't certain that I was ready for it," he later admitted to reporters.

Nonetheless, Hayes offered his name for consideration and soon discovered that he was one of eight finalists for the job. Paul Brown was one of the others. So was Sid Gillman, the former Ohio State quarterback whom Hayes never forgave for taking several of Miami's best players with him when he left that school to go to the University of Cincinnati just prior to Hayes's arrival at Miami.

Brown, however, was the biggest name and seemed certain to get the job. After the war, Brown had gone on to coach the Cleveland Browns to tremendous success in professional football. He was earning a reported $40,000 a year to coach them. It wasn't even a sure bet that he would return to Columbus, surely for a lesser salary, if he were offered the job.

That didn't stop alumni and students and even a Columbus newspaper from embarking on a furious campaign to bring Paul Brown back to the campus he had left during the war. As Hayes made the two-hour drive to Columbus from Oxford for his initial job interview, the pro-Brown campaign was in full swing and no one outside of the Buckeyes' screening committee even knew who Woody Hayes was. In a reader's poll in the *Columbus Citizen*, Brown garnered 2,331 of a possible 2,811 votes. Hayes was little more than an afterthought, finishing behind the Ohio State freshman coach, movie dog Lassie, actress Lana Turner, and President Harry

Truman among others (including an inmate serving a life sentence in the nearby Ohio state penitentiary).

That all changed during Hayes's interview, when the coach impressed one committee member with specific comments on how he would handle a blocking scheme problem and impressed another with his homespun honesty. Still others on the committee considered another factor: of all the players who participated in the 1949 North-South Ohio High School All-Star Game, Hayes had lured twelve to come to play for him at Miami. Ohio State had managed to recruit only two. Gillman at Cincinnati had snared another two—and no other school had landed more than one.

Following the three-hour interview, Hayes was told it was time to go, that another candidate was waiting to be interviewed. Hayes stood and smiled at all around, adding: "Well, gentlemen, I guess the hay is in the barn."

Then he left. But he had left a lasting impression.

When Hayes returned to Miami, he wasn't so sure of that. A few days later he was playing handball with one of his favorite Redskin players, a senior tackle named Bo Schembechler. After swatting the ball around for several minutes, Hayes stopped and looked hard into the eyes of the young Schembechler.

"Bo, who do you think should get that job at Ohio State?" he asked.

"I think you ought to get that job, Woody," Schembechler replied.

Hayes squeezed the ball in his hands, almost as if he was going to rip it apart.

"You sure of that?"

"Yeah, I'm sure of that, Coach."

Hayes still wasn't convinced.

"Why?"

"Because," answered Schembechler, "I think you're the best man for the job."

Hayes grunted, a grin spreading across his chubby face. "You really think so, eh?"

"Yep. I really think so, Coach."

Schembechler was right. Despite continued public pressure to bring back Paul Brown, Hayes was chosen to become the nineteenth head coach of the Ohio State Buckeyes. He was the seventh coach in eleven years to try to bring long-term stability to the program. To outsiders, there was little convincing evidence that he would have any more success than his predecessors.

3

Setting the Stage

A S IN his first two college coaching positions at Denison and Miami of Ohio, Hayes arrived at Ohio State to discover that his players and coaches had grown comfortable in a calm and undemanding environment.

Previous head coach Wes Fesler was considered a good guy, a player's coach who was competitive and knowledgeable about the game, but lacked the fierce intensity that Hayes immediately brought to the fore. Hayes knew exactly what he wanted, according to former assistant coach Esco Sarkkinen, and knew only one way to demand it. Hayes wanted things done his way—and he wanted them done right now. Players and assistant coaches used to Fesler's more democratic, laid-back style at first rejected Hayes and his blunt approach.

"There were periods where there was nothing but silent shock from players and coaches," Sarkkinen, who served as an Ohio State assistant for a remarkable thirty-two years, later told *Columbus Dispatch* sports editor Paul Hornung.

One of Hayes's first goals was to surround himself with assistant coaches whom he considered not only talented and knowlegeable football experts, but also educators. He thought coaches, including himself, should be teachers who molded young men. The Ohio State staff consisted of the head coach and just six assistants. Two of Fesler's assistants had followed him to his new job at the University of Minnesota. That left Hayes with decisions to make on Sarkkinen and three others—Harry Strobel, who had been a candidate for the head coaching position himself; Gene Fekete, a standout fullback on the 1942 Ohio State squad coached by Paul Brown that captured the national championship; and Ernie Godfrey, who had been an assistant at the school for twenty-two years and had survived seven previous head coaches.

After speaking with each of the men, Hayes decided to keep all four. He later admitted that, despite all his bluster and the fact that it ended up working out well, he couldn't have fired any of them. "I couldn't have brought myself to do it," he said.

Then Hayes completed his first staff by hiring two Columbus-area high school coaches, Doyt Perry and Bill Hess. Neither had any major-college coaching experience. And in the fall of his first year, he hired Bo Schembechler, his former Miami captain, as a graduate assistant. All three would go on in time to become successful college head coaches—Perry at Bowling Green State University, where the stadium today bears his name; Hess at Ohio University; and Schembechler, of course, at Michigan.

The cohesiveness of the staff was testament to Hayes's ability to bring a diverse group of people together despite his more than occasional tantrum. In time, they came to know what to expect—which was often the unexpected. Hayes might go off over the slightest thing, or he might spend an entire afternoon talking about history or something else that seemingly had little to do with football.

His first year, however, he compromised little and learned much. The Buckeyes struggled to a record of four wins, three losses, and two ties—and Vic Janowicz, the returning Heisman Trophy winner, could not adapt to Hayes's T-formation offense after establishing himself the previous year as the best player in college football in Fesler's old single-wing formation. The players even locked Hayes out of the locker room prior to one game that first season, an indication that their relationship was hardly on solid ground. Though years later Hayes would admit that he had failed to utilize Janowicz's considerable talents, he didn't listen to suggestions of that sort at the time and blistered anyone who dared to oppose him.

At the end of his first season, Godfrey approached Hayes. This was before the time of athletic scholarships, and the players earned tuition and expense money by working part-time for local businesses and state-assisted departments such as governmental offices. One of Godfrey's duties as an assistant over the years was to take charge of the jobs program for the players, and he didn't like what he was hearing from the alumni who provided the jobs.

"Word is that the downtown jobs might be withdrawn," Godfrey told the coach.

"If I resign, will the players keep their jobs?" Hayes asked.

Godfrey said yes, that appeared to be the case.

"Goddammit, I'll mortgage my house and pay the players myself! To hell with those downtown folks!" Hayes roared.

Godfrey knew then he was dealing with an unusual man. He also now knew that the next time someone "downtown" had something to say to Woody Hayes, he'd better let that person say it himself. Or better yet, he had better tell that person not to bother, lest he get his head chewed off.

In 1952, the team improved and the downtown folks backed off a little. The final record of six wins against only three losses included a 27–7 thrashing of Michigan, Ohio State's first win in the series since 1944. That came on the heels of an upset of favored Illinois by the same score a week earlier, which led, according to Hayes, to what would become a rather famous exchange between him and an elderly woman who had followed the Buckeyes for years.

Hayes claimed that the woman came up to him after the Michigan game that year and asked, "What was the score of your Illinois game?"

"Well, ma'am, we won twenty-seven to seven," Hayes replied proudly.

"Oh, I see. And what was the score of your Michigan game?"

"We won that one by the score of twenty-seven to seven also," Hayes answered, beaming.

The woman snorted.

"You aren't making much of an improvement, are you?" she added as she turned to walk away.

He stood, staring after her. For once in his life, Woody Hayes was speechless.

Behind the scenes, Hayes made it clear very early that he wanted each of his players to receive an education. He wasn't interested in merely having his student-athletes do the minimum work required to stay eligible. Dave Foley, an offensive lineman who would captain his 1968 team, learned that during the recruiting process and again early in his Ohio State academic career.

Foley grew up in Cincinnati, 111 miles to the southwest of Columbus, which is in the middle of the state. But at the time of his recruitment, Ohio State wasn't yet considered the undisputed king of the region in football—at least not in the environment in which Foley grew up.

"We had lots of other major-college football in the area," Foley remembered years later. "There was the University of Cincinnati, Xavier, and Dayton. There was Miami. Then Kentucky was right own the road. You had Louisville right down the road the other way, and they were always on Xavier and UC's schedule.

"So as far as press and as far as promotion, Ohio State was on about the fifth page of the sports section as far as the Cincinnati newspapers went. They never got any pub down there."

This was despite the fact that Hayes by the early 1960s had built the Ohio State program into a national powerhouse, somewhat against the wishes of many of his superiors at the school, who felt the football program was getting more attention than it deserved. Hayes's 1954 team went 10-0, whipping Southern California 20–7 in the Rose Bowl. Although this technically cleared the way for the Buckeyes to be acknowledged as national champions and the team had done all it could by beating each of the opponents it faced throughout the year, the national championship lost some of its significance because UCLA, also unbeaten during its season, had not been allowed to face the Bucks in the Rose Bowl. The Bruins had gone to the Rose Bowl the previous year and there was a "no repeat" rule for the schools from the Pacific-10 and Big Ten conferences.

The next time the Buckeyes went to the Rose Bowl, in 1958, they already had been proclaimed national champions under the format of the day. Their 10–7 victory over Oregon only placed an exclamation point on the honor, capping a record that included nine wins against only one loss—the lone defeat coming at the hands of Texas Christian by four points in the season opener.

By the time Foley was being recruited to come to Ohio State, though, those memories had faded and Hayes was fighting a perception problem. His boys had won the Big Ten in 1961, too, only to be told by the Ohio State faculty that they had to stay at home. Fearful that the program in general and Hayes in particular were becoming too big and too influential, a board of faculty members voted after much debate not to spend the money to send the Big Ten champions to play in the Rose Bowl. Though they were voted national champions anyway by the Football Writers Association of America, based on their record of eight wins, no losses, and one tie (7–7 to Texas Christian, once again in the season opener), a fuming and exasperated Hayes had to spend the next several years trying to explain to potential recruits why it had happened and why he would make certain it never happened again.

Told that the vote of the faculty council had been twenty-eight against sending his team to the Rose Bowl, and twenty-five for it, Hayes admitted he didn't care for the twenty-eight who voted no, but pledged—at least in public, if not in private—not to hold too much of a grudge.

"I respect their integrity, if not their intelligence. We have to learn to accept defeat under pressure and that may help us now," Hayes added. "But it's difficult to explain to the boys when, after fifteen years, the Rose Bowl is jerked out from under them."

To one professor who later admonished Hayes for his methods and argued that the football program had become too much a focal point of the school, Hayes narrowed his gaze at the man.

"Just remember this: I could do your job and maybe even do it better. You know damn well that you couldn't do mine," Hayes said.

And finally, Hayes added this parting shot: "I wish everything brought as much credit and as much teamwork and loyalty and just outright fun to the university as football did."

The toughest part for Hayes was explaining the fiasco to recruits who were thinking of playing football for him in the future. Foley was one of those young candidates. At the beginning of his stroll down the recruiting trail, Foley did not believe it was possible to fall under the magical spell of any of his recruiters. He thought he was shrewd, but he underestimated the head coach of Ohio State.

"When I started off in the recruiting process, Ohio State was not on the top of the list by any means," Foley said. "I really knew very little about the Ohio State program, even into my senior year [at Cincinnati Roger Bacon High School] when I started to be recruited. It seemed like it was so far away from where I was that I never even paid much attention to it.

"Back then you weren't limited to two or three recruiting trips. So I probably went on nine or ten of them."

He went to Notre Dame, Michigan, and Michigan State. He visited Purdue, Illinois, and Kentucky. He got around to visiting Ohio State only because he was pursued by and visited virtually every Big Ten school. Hayes invited Foley to Columbus for the Michigan game at Ohio Stadium in 1964.

Coach Hayes was there along with his wife, Anne, to greet all the recruits as they arrived. Then they ushered them all over to St. John Arena, where, the coach explained, they would get to begin their Ohio State experience by listening to a dress rehearsal by the Best Damn Band in the Land. Called "the Skull Session" in reference to a former band director's decision to insist upon one final rehearsal to ensure members had memorized the music before taking the field for football games back in the early 1930s, the tradition had taken on a whole new life when it was moved to newly constructed St. John Arena in 1957. By the time Foley and his parents visited, thousands of fans attended what amounted to a combination of a band concert and a pregame pep rally. Hayes loved it, and always made a point to personally bring recruits by or make certain that someone else did.

At the end of the Skull Session, the band formed outside the St. John Arena entrance and marched across the street to an even larger audience at Ohio Stadium—where everyone works themselves into a frenzy as the band enters the stadium through the ramp that leads directly to the field and launches into a rousing rendition of the "Buckeye Battle Cry."

"Like all the recruits who were taken into St. John for the band show, I was impressed," Foley said. "I mean, inside that arena with a full band? They were playing the Ohio State fight song and all that, and people were going nuts. It was unbelievable. Inside that arena, it would knock your ears out.

"Then after they do their whole routine and started marching, we followed the band out. I had never been in the stadium. We had probably driven by it on the way into town—but the whole experience hadn't dawned on me. And then we walk into the place, and it's absolutely, completely packed. There wasn't an empty seat in the house. And, of course, it's Michigan."

Something else struck Foley that day.

"It was about zero degrees. There were these ice crystals floating in the air, but it wasn't snowing. The sun was out. But it was so cold that there were these ice crystals."

It was even colder up near the top of the stadium, where the wind was whipping through the stands.

"We were sitting in the top deck of the stadium," Foley said. "After the game was over, we were going to go down to the car. And there were people, honest to God, who physically couldn't stand up. They had gotten so cold that they had to bring in some people to help these old people stand up. I thought, 'Man, if these people are that crazy that they're going to sit through this thing and sit there so long in cold like this that they can't even stand up afterward, man, these are some crazy football fans.' There wasn't anybody who was going to leave. They were going to stay there until the end. It was the place to be. The whole day was a neat experience."

What Foley may not have realized at the time is that some of the fans no doubt were doubled over by another kind of pain. Michigan won that day 10–0, making the frostbite and all other physical ailments pale in comparison. There was nothing worse to Buckeye fans than losing to Michigan in Ohio Stadium. Foley made another point years later, emphasizing why the Hayes method of exposing recruits to all the glorious aspects of the Ohio State football tradition was so effective in luring talent to the school.

"The whole experience of being recruited and the exposure to college football that we knew was a completely different thing," Foley said in 2003. "Now you can watch almost any team you want on television. The Mid-American Conference has their own network and their own Game of the Week.

"I'm just saying that if you want to watch a game nowadays, you can find a way to watch almost any team on any given Saturday. I think that really has made the recruiting process a lot different. I think recruiting back then was more regionalized—especially for us in the Cincinnati area. We didn't have guys coming in to recruit us to go to Southern Cal. If you were from out west, somewhere west of the Rocky Mountains, you'd get recruited by Southern Cal. Just like in the Midwest, you were recruited by the Big Ten. You didn't have this deal where you were the top prospect in the nation, and you're going to be recruited to every school across the board."

Even after his eye-opening visit to Ohio State, Foley still wasn't certain he was going to become a Buckeye. That is, until the persuasive and enigmatic Hayes put on his closing act.

"One of the things that did close the deal, so to speak, was that after making all the recruiting trips that I did, his approach stood out," Foley said. "Almost every other school I went to, the coach or someone would say, 'Well, what do you want to do with the rest of your life?'"

"Well, when a kid is eighteen years old, that's a tough question for him to answer. It's real tough for him to say I want to be a doctor or I'm going to be a teacher or whatever. There very well may be kids that age who have those goals set, but I wasn't one of them."

So as the process went on for Foley, the questions from coaches at schools who wanted him to play football for them became tedious and predictable.

"Hey, I've got you set up to see a professor," one said.

"We've got it set up for you to go get a workout in while you're here," another said.

"Well, most of our guys are in communications or recreational therapy," a third added.

Foley started to think it was all a joke. Then Hayes called.

"Woody Hayes was different," Foley recalled. "He called me up and said, 'I realize you're coming up for your recruiting trip. I checked your high school transcript and you have exceptionally high scores in math. I think you ought to be an engineer.'"

At first Foley sort of chuckled to himself. Then he forgot all about it. He didn't even remember the conversation when he arrived in Columbus for his recruiting trip—but Hayes quickly reminded him.

"I've got this thing set up for you where you're going to visit with the dean of engineering," Hayes said.

"Hey, Coach, I don't know nothin' about engineering, you know? I don't know about this," Foley said.

Hayes ignored him. He started talking about how Foley would be a great engineer, and about how wonderful the Ohio State engineering program was. Then he told Foley that he was going to take him over to see the dean of engineering. They still hadn't talked anything about football.

"So Woody dropped me off at the office of the dean of engineering—and this guy launches into a whole routine about what great pride Woody had taken in guys that had gone there who had gone into fairly tough majors," Foley said. "He tells me that like three or four years before I was there, either the top dental student or the top medical student coming out of Ohio State were football players. Can you imagine that?"

And still, there was no talk yet of football. Foley found that refreshing and honest. At the very least, he knew he would get a good education. So Foley ended up going to Ohio State and majoring in engineering—but there is a footnote to the story.

"The other part of the story is that Woody wouldn't let a guy get out of something once he got in it," Foley said. "So I get into engineering, and my first year I get pretty good grades at first. But by about the third quarter, the spring quarter of my freshman year, I'm home with my buddies over a break and I'm like, 'This is killing me. I've got nineteen credit hours. I'm trying to play football. I'm trying to do this; I'm trying to do that. All my buddies are out having a good time. I'm transferring out of the school of engineering. I'm going into something else that's easier. I don't know what, but something else.'"

His buddies applauded his plan of action. His mother did not. When Foley went home, he made the announcement of his decision to pursue a new major at Ohio State.

"Hey, Mom, I've got this whole thing figured out," Foley said. "I'm killing myself. I've got to get out of this engineering thing."

"But what will Coach Hayes think?" Foley's mother wondered aloud.

"I don't really care. I've got to do it," Foley said.

The next day, Foley got in his car and made the ninety-minute drive from Cincinnati to Columbus. As soon as he arrived at his dormitory, some friends who lived in the same dorm frantically tracked him down.

"Woody Hayes was on the floor," they said, looking ominous. "And he wants to see you in his office at nine o'clock in the morning."

"Oh my God, what's going on?" Foley asked.

"Well, he heard you were thinking about transferring out of engineering. He said that he wants to talk to you personally."

The next morning, Hayes did almost all of the talking. Foley sat and listened.

"Your mother called me and said you're thinking of transferring out of engineering. You're not going to do that," he said.

Then he explained why he thought doing so would be such a mistake for Foley.

"You can always go later in life from engineering to something else you might want to do, because once you have that background they can never take it away from you," he said. "But if you start lower than what you have the potential to be, then you will never rise to the level that you can become."

Foley stayed in engineering.

"And to be real honest with you," he said many years later, "I wouldn't have hung in there if I had been anyplace else. But as it was, where I was at that point in my young life, I probably had no other way out other than shooting my mother and Woody Hayes both."

■

During his first three years at Ohio State, Hayes personally tutored student-athletes, receiving help only from Katie Hess, a former teacher who was the wife of assistant coach Bill Hess. But Hayes also demanded that each of his assistant coaches carefully monitor the progress of the players who manned the positions that were their areas of responsibility.

"If we bring a young man to Ohio State University and don't do everything possible to see that he gets an education, we're cheating him," Hayes would tell his assistant coaches.

In 1954, before his fourth season as coach, Hayes hired a professor to serve as part-time tutor to his players—and in 1957 he made the professor, Tom Daly, full-time academic counselor for the program. When players left the Ohio State program without a degree, Hayes would hound them to do whatever it took to return and earn what he thought was rightfully theirs. Not only that, but players who left without degrees and didn't return to get them haunted him because he believed he had failed in his most basic duty, which was to see that each and every player he recruited would leave armed with that piece of paper that was to be his entry pass into the real world.

Hayes worked incredibly long hours, and it seemed that it was all paying off in January of 1955 when he went to his first Rose Bowl and beat Southern Cal to earn the 1954 national championship. But his world was shaken a few weeks later when his older brother, Ike, died suddenly of a heart attack. No one else had seemed to revel in Woody's early coaching successes more than Ike, who had attended the 1955 Rose Bowl along with his family and spent countless hours reminiscing with his younger brother. Convinced that Isaac's premature death had been the direct result of his dedication to his job as the town veterinarian in Waterloo, Iowa, Woody vowed to begin working more reasonable hours.

"This is a lesson to me. I'm going to slow down," he told friends and family.

No one really believed him. In the end, Hayes didn't believe the vow himself. Within less than two months of his brother's death, though he was still grieving over the loss of the man who had meant so much to him, Woody was back at his Ohio State office, staring at film for hours at a time even though the rest of the building was empty and the opening kickoff of the 1955 season remained months away. Sixteen- and seventeen-hour workdays were common.

Examples of Hayes's doggedness abounded everywhere. If he wasn't watching film in his office or off visiting the homes of potential recruits in the off-season, he was following up on what many of his former players were doing. And if they had left Ohio State without their degree, God help them.

Dick Schafrath, who left Ohio State in 1958 without a degree, was playing with the Cleveland Browns in the National Football League when Hayes started hounding him. He finally agreed to return and eventually went on to become a state senator in Ohio. When two-sport standout Tom Perdue left Ohio State in 1962 to pursue a professional baseball career, he was only two quarters short of a degree. Three years later, when Perdue was playing for a Cincinnati Reds farm team in Hampton, Virginia, Hayes tracked him down.

"What are your plans for finishing school?" Hayes demanded.

"I can't afford it right now. Financially, I mean," Perdue insisted.

"Is that all? Is there anything else that would prevent you from earning your degree?"

Perdue said no. He had to admit that his baseball career had stalled and that getting a degree didn't seem like such a bad idea.

A few weeks later, Hayes called again and said that he had arranged a coaching job for Perdue.

Dan Poretta was a starting guard at Ohio State who left without a degree in 1964. He stopped by Hayes's office after playing four years in the Canadian Football League, ostensibly just to say hello. Of course that never happened with Hayes, and soon they were engaged in a wide-ranging conversation that eventually included the subject of Poretta's immediate future.

"I'm not sure what I'm going to do," Poretta admitted.

"I'll tell you what you're going to do. You're going over to the registrar's office right now to sign up for the classes you need to graduate," Hayes said. "Then you're going to be my assistant freshman coach this fall."

When a young running back named Earle Bruce suffered a knee injury and made the decision to leave school, Hayes got in his car and drove after him. He convinced the young man to stay in school, get his degree—and help him coach as a graduate assistant along the way. Maybe, just maybe, Hayes told Bruce, he would like the coaching gig and decide to stick around even after he graduated.

These were examples of Hayes's softer side, which he didn't like to advertise. Former trainer John Bozick once put it accurately when he said that Hayes "wanted you to think he was a real SOB, and he was disappointed when you realized he wasn't." But just as there were times when he wasn't and he did some wonderful things that made folks want to hug him, there were others when he blew his stack and embarrassed himself and those around him. Hayes simply didn't care what people thought about his explosions.

"They can call me anything—just as long as they don't call me a 'nice old man,'" Hayes said.

Players and assistant coaches grew to label Woody's rages "megatons." When he really went nuts over something, they called them "hundred-megatons." When these explosions occurred, the best advice was to stay silent and keep out of his way until it blew over. Early in Hayes's coaching tenure with the Buckeyes, one assistant coach made a severe mistake as the staff grew bleary-eyed from watching film for more than four hours straight one night.

"Woody, we haven't come up with what we're looking for yet and we're all exhausted. So why don't we break it up for tonight, get some rest, and come back to it in the morning?" the assistant sheepishly suggested.

Hayes rose from his chair like a gathering storm. His eyes began to bulge, his famously chubby cheeks rapidly reddening. Then he brought his arms up slowly, with his hands clenched in tight, shaking fists.

"Don't anybody *ever* tell me we've had enough!" he boomed.

Then Hayes wildly began beating himself silly with his own clenched fists. It was a hundred-megaton in full swing. Hayes didn't stop until he had given himself two black eyes, but he eventually calmed down enough that the staff watched film for another hour or so before going home. At the beginning of another sixteen-hour workday the next morning, despite the two very visible black eyes, Hayes acted as if nothing out of the ordinary had happened.

Over the years, Hayes would erupt during practices, games, or late-night film sessions at any moment. He smashed watches and his own steel-rimmed eyeglasses time and time again on the practice field, sometimes bloodying his hands or his face in the process. He used to tear up so many of his OSU caps in the early days that team managers stood by just in case they needed to run in and get him another on a moment's notice. That practice ended only when the team began purchasing hats that were impossible for Hayes to rip apart, even with his strong hands.

Hayes worked so hard and so many hours that he once answered his wife's complaint that they hadn't gone on a date in a while by promising to take her to dinner and a movie. Dinner was at the Jai Lai restaurant in Columbus, one of Hayes's favorite haunts. That was fine with Anne Hayes. But the movie turned out to be showing back at the office. Hayes said he was stopping there simply to make a couple of quick telephone calls—but deep down Anne knew better. The couple's night out involved watching Michigan State's offense and defense, over and over and over again until it was past one o'clock in the morning.

"Now, wasn't that a nice evening out—and a good film as well?" Woody asked his wife on the way home afterward.

"Yeah, and it was damn cheap, too!" Anne shot back.

Hayes didn't care much for the movies that were shown in actual theaters. But they did quickly become part of his meticulous preparation for Saturday battle. Believing the players needed rest and some mindless recreation the night before games, he had them watch a movie early every Friday evening before Saturday kickoff, appointing an assistant coach the special and important duty of selecting a suitable Hollywood feature for "the boys." Hayes was clear about what he meant by suitable: no sex, no comedy, as little violence as possible, and definitely no drugs or excessive use of alcohol. That ruled out most movies even of Hayes's early days, but usually the assistant coach in charge of the selection found that something like a John Wayne western was the type of macho movie that would fit Hayes's standards.

There was, then, the logistical problem of getting to the movie on the road. One time the night before a game at Michigan Sate, Hayes looked at the newspaper and said that he had found the week's movie. It was, as his assistant coaches could have guessed, another John Wayne epic. The problem was that Hayes failed to notice that the picture was showing at a drive-in nearly twenty miles from the team's hotel near East Lansing.

When confronted with this problem and told that the largest vehicle available was a thirty-six-passenger bus, Hayes grabbed the phone himself and called a local Oldsmobile dealer—who agreed to send several cars out to pick up the players. The team also rented the bus, which left for the drive-in after the rental cars and then, much to Hayes's dismay, was turned away at the theater gate. Lou McCullough, the assistant coach in charge of that particular night out at the movies, tried to get the young woman at the gate to sell him three individual tickets so he and two other assistants could run in and round up the players, but the woman initially refused—either because she was a Michigan State fan or because the coaches didn't have a car in which they could drive into the place.

Finally, McCullough and the others were permitted entrance. But they weren't sure what all the rental cars looked like, so they simply started yanking open the doors to any Oldsmobiles they came across.

"I yanked open one door, and a boy and a girl were making passionate love," McCullough said. "I excused myself and went on."

When they finally gathered up all the players and reported back to Hayes, the coach was furious that the careful routine had been botched so badly.

"You sonsofbitches have lost us tomorrow's game!" he bellowed. He didn't have to add that McCullough was no longer in charge of Friday movie night, but then rarely did anyone hold that job for more than a few months before Hayes insisted someone else could do it better. That usually meant Woody thought he could do it better. But sometimes when he took matters into his own hands in areas that weren't necessarily his field of expertise, there was sort of a mad professor quality to him that surfaced and details went awry.

One time the great Red Grange, the famed Galloping Ghost from Illinois when he played in the 1920s, spoke at a luncheon in Columbus during the football season. After the program, Hayes grabbed Grange and talked him into taking a later flight out of Columbus so he could give a little inspirational talk to the Buckeyes after practice that afternoon. Hayes, the lover of history, was ecstatic when Grange agreed to stay over and address the squad.

His joy soon turned to frustration when he arrived at the practice facility and excitedly began telling players who was coming by to visit later in the afternoon. They met his enthusiasm with a blank stare. They had no idea who Red Grange was.

"How can they not know who this guy was? He is one of the greatest college football players of all time," Hayes fumed to his assistant coaches.

Then Hayes had an idea.

"I'll give them a history lesson on the Galloping Ghost when I introduce him this afternoon," he said with a smile.

When the appointed time came for Grange to arrive on the practice field, however, Hayes looked all around and saw that he was indeed a ghost. Grange was a no-show. Hayes kept glancing at his watch, nervously pacing as he waited for the big moment and his boys plodded on through practice. As it turned out, Hayes's own obsession for security at practice sessions was the culprit. Hayes rarely allowed visitors to practice. The "No Visitors" sign was up when Grange arrived, and the gate to the field was locked. When Grange and his small traveling entourage tried to insist that Woody Hayes himself had invited them to come in, the campus policeman guarding the gate said that he had no personal knowledge of any such arrangement and he had his orders.

"You can't go in," he said.

"But Woody invited me to speak to the team," Grange said.

The campus policeman checked with an assistant trainer, who said he knew nothing about it. The assistant trainer obviously needed a history lesson on Red Grange's identity as well.

Grange eventually shrugged off the snub and left for the airport with his party.

When Hayes discovered that the great Red Grange had been turned away at the gate to the practice field, he was furious. Assistant coaches said that Hayes's response was beyond the typical hundred-megaton.

By the time the 1968 season rolled around, Hayes's idiosyncrasies as an individual and a coach were well documented. He was a history buff and an educator. He was a man who believed that everything he did, including his many self-implosions, worked ultimately toward the betterment of society as a whole because it was helping him discipline and develop young men who would be sent into the world to become doctors, lawyers, and politicians. Even if they went on to play professional football, he would see to it that they eventually earned their degrees and made something more of themselves than mere football players.

And as 1968 approached, a war he supported in Vietnam raged. Opposition to it mounted in Columbus as it did elsewhere throughout the country. But Woody focused on the 1968 Ohio State football season. It would turn out to be one of the most magical years in what many would come to consider the beginning of the modern era of big-time college football.

4

Perfection

THE 1968 Ohio State football season was the culmi-
nation of a work in progress that actually began the
previous fall with the arrival of perhaps the greatest
freshman recruiting class in the history of college football.
And they arrived just in time for Hayes and his staff, who
were in danger of being fired after a 1966 season that was
Hayes's first losing year since 1959, and only his second since
assuming the head coaching position in 1951.

The 1966 season had been a disaster in many ways. The
team started out with a win over Texas Christian, but then
proceeded to lose three straight games to Washington, Illinois, and Michigan State. A win over Wisconsin was followed
by yet another unforeseeable and unforgivable Big Ten loss
to Minnesota, leaving the Buckeyes with a record of two wins
and four defeats heading into the home stretch of the season.

All might have been forgotten, however, after the Bucks
beat Indiana and Iowa in their next two games to even their
record for the season heading into the annual season-ending
showdown with hated Michigan. A win over the Wolverines
would have produced at least a winning season and another

year's worth of satisfaction that they held the upper hand over the team from up north. Instead, Michigan ground out a 17–3 victory—worse yet, at Ohio Stadium. That gave the Wolverines two victories in three seasons in the series and left Buckeye fans wondering if it might be time for a change.

If there was any doubt about the intentions of Woody's growing number of dissenters, the evidence was displayed at the corner of Fifteenth and High Streets in the middle of campus. There, disgruntled students hung Wayne Woodrow Hayes in effigy and called openly for his dismissal.

Hayes, though, sensed correctly that the next recruiting class he had assembled was perhaps his best ever. It included a quarterback named Rex Kern and others such as middle guard Jim Stillwagon, one of the best defensive linemen of his time in the country; Jack Tatum, a running back who would be turned into a defensive back; safety Mike Sensibaugh, likewise a converted running back who not only also returned punts but would serve as the team's future punter; running backs Larry Zelina, Leo Hayden, and John Brockington, each of whom would play a role at different times in the backfield; guards Brian Donovan and Phil Strickland, who would provide key blocking; and wide receiver Bruce Jankowski and tight end Jan White, who would catch most of Kern's passes.

Virtually all of the new recruits were from Ohio. Hayes was back to picking up most of the best athletes in the state after a couple of years when some slipped away elsewhere. And Hayes was going out of state when he felt he needed to pursue a special talent. Brockington, for instance, was from Brooklyn, New York. Jan White was from Harrisburg, Pennsylvania, and Bruce Jankowski played his high school ball in Fairlawn, New Jersey.

They were hungry to prove themselves. But with only two games scheduled that year for the freshman squad, and with NCAA rules forbidding the use of freshmen in varsity games, they realized immediately where their proving grounds would be: on the Ohio State practice fields. Foley, by then a veteran who was entering his junior season in 1967, remembers the arrival of these freshmen with little fondness.

"Right away," said Foley, "the practices were heated up."

"They didn't have much respect for the seniors," defensive tackle Butch Smith, a junior in 1967, added of the incoming freshmen.

Foley and Smith were part of the frustrating 1966 season and knew that it was time for the Buckeyes to turn it on or turn to a new page in the program's already storied history.

Foley and most of his teammates believed they could turn it around. Shortly after the arrival of the new recruiting class in 1967, they and Hayes's assistant coaches were sure of it—if Hayes and the assistant coaches would be permitted to stick around. Earle Bruce, who coached defensive backs in '67 but moved to the offensive line the following year to make room for a young new assistant named Lou Holtz, was sick to his stomach thinking that perhaps he wouldn't be back to coach the players as they evolved from tantalizing freshmen into Super Sophs.

"Man, we were hoping we could survive as a staff," Bruce said. "When they told us we might get fired in 1967, we said, 'Oh, God, we won't have a shot with these guys.' We didn't know it was going to be in 1968, but we knew the potential was there for something great."

Dave Foley and the other upperclassmen thought that the hard scrimmages in practice against the freshmen paid off toward the end of the 1967 season. After opening the season with a loss at home to Arizona and a road win over Oregon, the Buckeyes were thoroughly embarrassed by Purdue, then ranked second in the nation, at Ohio Stadium. The final score was 41–6.

"We had a really horrible game against Purdue. That was when they had [running back] Leroy Keyes and [quarter-back] Mike Phipps and all those guys," Foley said. "They just killed us. It was brutal."

This was followed by a totally uninspiring 6–2 win at Northwestern and yet another loss at home to Illinois—the fourth consecutive loss on Ohio Stadium soil for the Buck-eyes, dating back to the previous year's debacle at the hands of Michigan. The calls for Hayes's scalp increased.

Then, an amazing transformation began to take place. Buoyed by the everyday wars in practices that fueled their overall improvement, the varsity reeled off three wins in a row—at Michigan State, then at home over Wisconsin and Iowa to set up the season finale against Michigan. It was to be at Michigan, though. And despite Michigan's subpar record of four wins against five losses coming in, winning in Ann Arbor was never an easy task for the Buckeyes or any visiting team.

All year long during practices, freshman Phil Strickland had been building a reputation as being tough-minded and mean-spirited as he blocked for the scout-team offense against the first-team defense. He cut the veterans no slack whatsoever, much to their dismay and to the pure delight of an amused coaching staff. During the week leading up to the Michigan game, Strickland challenged senior nose guard Vic Stottlemyer even more than usual during one practice. It got ugly when Strickland allegedly punched Stottlemyer in the groin, setting off a brawl that defensive tackle Butch Smith later said "caused probably the biggest fight in the history of the school."

Lou McCullough, the defensive coordinator, looked at fellow assistant coach Bill Mallory. They smiled at each other, waiting until it had escalated a bit more to break it up. Hayes, who was lurking nearby as always, also was caught with a smirk on his face as he surveyed the scene. The boys were ready to take out their anger and frustration on the boys from up north—plus something special already was building for next season. A few days later, the Buckeyes extended their winning streak to four games with a rousing 24–14 victory at Michigan, setting the stage for bigger and better spoils to come.

"All during the season we got better because we had to practice against those guys," Foley said of the Ohio State freshmen. "They just made us better. They were great athletes."

As winter gave way to spring in Columbus in 1968, Jim Stillwagon and many of the other newcomers were doing whatever they could to impress the coaches. Jack Tatum, an all-state running back in high school, was adjusting to his move to the defensive backfield. Jan White, a wide receiver in high school, was moved to tight end, where his blocking was more important than his pass receiving. Others were moved around as well, including coaches—as Bruce reluctantly gave way to Holtz in the defensive secondary and moved over to the other side of the ball to coach the guards and centers on the offensive line. Spring practice in 1968 was where it started, and for some players, even veterans, it was where it ended.

"The team was really made in spring ball," Foley said. "That was one of the most interesting times I've ever been through. There was so much experimentation. There was so much number one against number one, because there was so much trying to figure out where people were going to be— and all of a sudden, man, you were playing against some great athletes."

Hayes, meanwhile, set the tone the very first day of spring practice when he started talking about beating Purdue. The Boilermakers were coached by Jack Mollenkopf. After his team took a 35–0 halftime lead in the game the previous year against the Buckeyes, Mollenkopf retired to a seat on his team's bench and spent part of the second half with his hat pulled down over his eyes. Every time Hayes had tortured himself by watching film of the debacle, there was Mollenkopf in the background, appearing to take a nap.

The very thought of another coach being able to take it easy during a game against one of his teams infuriated Hayes. So before they hit the field for the first day of spring practice, Hayes reminded his players of what had happened against Purdue and about how Mollenkopf had insulted them—and the Ohio State program—at least in Hayes's eyes.

"Those guys at Purdue, we're going to beat those SOBs!" Hayes yelled. "And at the end, if we don't beat 'em on the field, I'm gonna get that old coach of theirs and I'll challenge him on the fifty-yard line and I'll beat the hell out of him!"

With that, Hayes grabbed a framed picture and hurled it across the room. It smashed into the wall, shattering the glass. The team, worked into a frenzy, jumped from the room as one and hurried out to the practice field. George Chaump, a new arrival to the coaching staff that spring, was mightily impressed.

"Holy Cow! This is the first day of spring practice? I thought we were playing for the national championship," he said.

The veteran players such as Foley had gone against the hungry freshmen earlier during the season, but now it was a little different. There seemed to be more on the line for everyone, as the older players scrambled to keep their jobs and the younger ones clawed to ensure that they would not be left behind when they at last became eligible the following fall.

Chaump and some of the other new arrivals on the staff had implored Hayes to add the I-formation to his offense, and only after some megaton eruptions, including one occasion when Hayes actually told Chaump to pack his bags and leave town because his views weren't welcome in Columbus, the old coach began to come around. He examined film of several other teams who had been running plays from the I-formation, including Oklahoma, Arkansas, and Southern California, and reluctantly concluded that perhaps he needed to add it to Ohio State's offensive repertoire. He still wanted to run certain plays his way, especially the one where the fullback ran off-tackle. Hayes called the play "Robust" because, he said, it meant "big and strong" and that's the way he wanted his boys to play football.

In the annual spring game, in March of 1968, the first-string held on for a 24–21 victory over the second string. Rex Kern quickly moved ahead of veterans Billy Long and Kevin Rusnak at quarterback because Long and Rusnak decided to skip spring ball and play baseball instead. Ron Maciejowski, another sophomore from Bedford, Ohio, impressed the coaching staff at the position while the veterans were away playing another sport. If nothing else, Kern and Maciejowski were given repetitions in practices that otherwise would have gone to Long and Rusnak—giving them more of a chance to improve and doubling the amount of time coaches would have to look at them on film.

What Hayes saw immediately from Kern was a unique ability to lead. He also saw a quarterback who could throw the ball accurately enough—and play intelligently enough—that Hayes was willing to entrust him to throw the ball more than most of his previous quarterbacks. And Hayes was the coach who once said of airing it out: "Only three things can happen on a forward pass, and two of them are bad."

Hayes was as straightforward in his approach to the

game as he was to the people who coached with him and played for him. He liked to run the football, yes. But if his offense could throw the ball efficiently enough to keep the ball in his team's possession, that was fine, too. He just didn't like to take chances because too many incompletions meant turning the ball over to the opposition on downs—and, God forbid, an interception meant giving it to them right now.

"Our offensive football is based upon the principle that we must first establish a sound running attack," he told anyone willing to listen. "A well-coached and well-manned running attack is the most consistent factor in football."

The plan was brilliant in its simplicity. For Hayes, a "consistent" offensive play was one that gained three yards or more.

"If each play gains at least three yards, it is almost a mathematical certainty that at least one of the three plays will gain considerably more than three yards, so that possession of the ball is the net result," Hayes added.

Yet after spring practices in 1968, Hayes began talking with his assistant coaches about devising ways to let Kern throw the ball at least a little more. It was an unusual and uncommon sign of trust from the crusty old coach, who saw the quarterback position—and not the running back, as some might have thought—as the key to everything he wanted to achieve with his offense.

"To eliminate mistakes, you have to pick the right quarterback," Hayes said. "The five big mistakes in football are the fumble, the interception, the penalty, the badly called play, and the blocked punt—and most of these originate with the quarterback. Find a mistake-proof quarterback and you have this game won."

The more Hayes watched Kern in the spring practices, the more he became convinced that he had found his mistake-free quarterback. As classes closed toward the end of June in 1968, however, Hayes and Kern received some horrible news. Kern, who had been experiencing lower back pain for some time, was diagnosed with a ruptured disc. Surgery would be required almost immediately—and not only Kern's 1968 season but his entire football career suddenly seemed in jeopardy.

"During this time," said Kern years later, "I didn't know—and nor did the coaches or doctors—if I would ever play football for Ohio State. . . . In those days, not many players who had back surgery ever returned to play."

Kern underwent the surgery in July, and a couple of teammates shortly thereafter brought down a leg extension machine to the barbershop owned by Kern's father in Lancaster. Soon Kern was using it to help speed up his rehabilitation—and to the amazement of everyone, including himself, he strapped on the pads and stepped back onto the Ohio State practice field by August 15.

The rest of the players, meanwhile, were jockeying for positions and playing time as the '68 season opener against Southern Methodist University approached. Kern was just beginning to look like he was getting the hang of mastering his position again when, suddenly, the hulking Stillwagon broke through the offensive line during a practice drill and absolutely leveled Kern—despite the fact that the recovering Kern was wearing the yellow jersey that signaled to all the defensive players that they were not to touch him.

"He really clobbered me," Kern said. "I thought my world was going to end."

Instead, it was Stillwagon's world that almost came apart—courtesy of a livid Hayes.

"Goddammit, what the hell are you doing?" Hayes yelled at Stillwagon. "Can't you see he's got the yellow jersey on? Don't you know what that means?"

"I was just trying to get to the guy with the ball, Coach. Isn't that what you're supposed to do on defense?"

"Goddammit, get this guy out of here!" Hayes screamed, waving to some security guards. "That's it! He's outta here! We're taking your scholarship away, son!"

Stillwagon, an intense person himself, muttered a few choice words in Hayes's direction as he was escorted off the field by the guards. His intention was to keep on moving until he was on another college campus. As he showered in the locker room, assistant coach Bill Mallory stopped in to try to settle him down.

"That's it. I'm outta here. I'm going to West Virginia to play. I'm not taking that bullshit off of nobody, Woody Hayes or not!" Stillwagon fumed.

"Jim, it's okay," Mallory said. "You did the right thing by getting out of there. Woody will cool off and everything will be fine, you'll see. He just goes off like that sometimes."

"I don't care. He might cool off, but I'm not going to cool off. I'm leaving," Stillwagon insisted.

Hayes hadn't necessarily wanted Stillwagon on his team to begin with, offering him the last scholarship he had available the previous year only after another player who had agreed to sign had changed his mind and decided to go elsewhere. But as he mulled over his overreaction and realized that Kern was fine, Hayes did indeed calm down and cool off. He approached Stillwagon and turned on the charm that always seemed to get Hayes off the hook when he experienced one of his hundred-megaton explosions.

"Look, I understand you didn't mean to hurt him or anything. But Rex is important to our team—and you're going to be, too. Why don't you stay? I didn't mean what I said when I said I was taking away your scholarship," Hayes told Stillwagon.

At first, the stubborn Stillwagon didn't budge. He was going to leave Ohio State to play at West Virginia. But then Hayes came with the closer.

"Son, think how disappointed your parents would be if you left our beautiful campus. You know you're going to get a quality education here, too. You don't want to disappoint your parents, do you? This is where they want you to play and to get that education."

Stillwagon finally relented and agreed to stick around. He ended up anchoring the Ohio State defense for the next three years.

On August 19, 1968, Hayes sent out a preseason letter to his players, as was his annual custom. But this one he began with an excerpt from an article he had read recently in *Sports Illustrated* that contained glowing references to the elegant passing game of Southern Methodist University, Ohio State's opening opponent. It read as follows, with Hayes highlighting the very first sentence:

SMU threw more passes per game (33) in 1967 than any other Dallas team—and completed more (18.9), too. This was a needle in the pigskin of the [NFL's Dallas] Cowboys. In fact, SMU completed more passes (57.2 percent) than any pro team except the Baltimore Colts (58 percent). The Cowboys' record: an average of 29.7 passes, 15 completed.

Over 300 TV spots, 700 radio pitches and numerous billboard ads will follow the theme "Excitement 1968." Mustang Coach Hayden Fry is even sounding like an adman in his enthusiasm for the campaign, which he calls emphasizing the four E's—exciting, explosive, entertaining and electrifying.

To this excerpt Hayes added his own interpretation of the situation facing his Buckeyes as the season opener approached. He left little doubt that he intended to emphasize his usual two Bs and two Ts—blocking and tackling, and blocking and tackling. Perform those two basic football functions with flawless consistency, and Hayes believed all else would fall into its proper place. Hayes told his players so in his own words in the rest of the preseason letter, adding of the SMU passing game: "There is one little catch to all this ballyhoo: they ain't gonna throw it if they don't have it."

He then implored his players to report to fall camp in shape, and added that he had no doubts that they would ultimately be in better shape than the SMU players by the season opener. Ever the practical thinker, Hayes then reminded the players "to bring your shoes back with you unless you want to practice barefooted." He also suggested that players bring along any extra footballs they had lying about "regardless of their condition . . . for we can use them as place kickers."

He signed the letter, "Your friend, Woody."

After the players returned to campus and resumed practicing, Hayes gradually began to feel that the Buckeyes would indeed handle what he considered the gimmick offense of the SMU Mustangs. They had five weeks to prepare for them, although much of that time was dedicated to getting ready for the Purdue game and not SMU. And the very night before the game, Hayes became rattled when junior linebacker Mike Radtke's wife went into labor. Worse yet, in Hayes's eyes, Radtke seemed rattled because the nurse at the hospital had given the news that it now appeared two babies and not just one would soon be arriving. Hayes called Radtke into his hotel room the night before the game and grabbed him by the shirt, as if to shake some sense into him about what Woody thought was most important at that moment in his life.

"Your wife better not screw up this game for us," Hayes told the player, glaring at him.

Radtke, still shaken by the fact that his family would soon be expanding by a set of twins, now wasn't sure what to think. But he went on to play an outstanding game, and Hayes awarded him a team ball for it.

The Southern Methodist passing attack put up some impressive numbers, with quarterback Chuck Hixson throwing an astonishing 69 times and completing 37 for 417 yards. But he also was intercepted five times, killing potential scoring drives every time at or inside the Ohio State 20-yard line.

Ohio State, on the other hand, piled up plenty of offense of its own, throwing for 227 yards and rushing for another 145. Kern, showing no ill effects from the recent back surgery or Stillwagon's slam to the ground during practice, passed for two touchdowns and ran for another. He completed eight of 14 passes for 139 yards, prompting Hayes to look at the stat sheet and smile as he pointed out, "We're becoming quite a passing team."

Hayes could smile because the game was a 35–14 victory for his Buckeyes. He had handed off much of the play-calling responsibility for the day to his new quarterback, who responded by displaying the moxie of a seasoned veteran. Kern even had the guts—some would say youthful stupidity—to wave off the punt team as it ran on with the Bucks facing a fourth-and-10 situation from the SMU 41-yard line in the first half.

Bill Long, the backup quarterback, couldn't believe what he was seeing. He was standing next to placekicker and backup center Jim Roman on the sideline when Kern waved off the punt team and Hayes started to fume, building toward what surely would have been a hundred-megaton explosion if Kern failed to get the first down.

"Well, that's it. Here we go. We're gonna go in next time we have the ball," Long told Roman.

The play seemed doomed from the start. Operating out

of a full-house backfield, Kern called a play designed for a delayed handoff to the fullback. But the fullback, Jim Otis, never got the ball because the SMU defense sniffed out the play and Kern initially seemed trapped eight yards behind the line of scrimmage. Sensing that his status as the team's new leader might be in jeopardy, Kern was determined not to fail. Staggering and twisting and turning to thwart three would-be tacklers, Kern scrambled 15 yards for the first down. Long stayed on the sidelines, and the Bucks' special season was off to a terrific start.

Just to be safe, though, Kern stayed as far away from Hayes as he could when he came off the field several plays later.

At the end of the preseason letter he sent his players in August, Hayes added a postscript reminding them that their own Big Ten conference had a quarterback who could throw the ball as effectively as SMU's Hixson. In yet another reference to Purdue, the team that Hayes seemed to want to beat above all others that season, perhaps even more than he wanted to dismantle Michigan, he wrote: "P.S. A guy with a No. 15 throws the ball pretty well too!"

That No. 15 was Mike Phipps, Purdue's All-America quarterback. But as well as Phipps threw it, he wasn't Purdue's best player. That was Leroy Keyes, a versatile two-way performer who starred at halfback and wide receiver on offense and at cornerback on defense. Keyes was considered the early front-runner for the Heisman Trophy in 1968, as the Boilermakers prepared to face the Buckeyes in the third game of the season.

Purdue was ranked number one in the nation. The Buckeyes, by virtue of their dismantling of SMU and the following week's 21–6 throttling of Oregon, also at Ohio Stadium, had moved up to the number five ranking. Hayes had been itching to face the Boilermakers again ever since the previous season's 41–6 thrashing, and now the showdown was at hand. In addition to unleashing nine sophomores in the starting lineup, Hayes intended to play five more who had been unable to play the previous season because of the NCAA rules forbidding freshmen from playing on the varsity. Hayes had another trick up his famous short sleeves, too—one he had mentioned in his preseason letter when he reminded his players that there would be times when they would run a no-huddle offense.

"Everybody thought of Woody Hayes as not being very aggressive or innovative—you know, three yards and a cloud of dust and all that stuff," Dave Foley said. "But the interesting thing was that if he had a single challenge facing him, he could normally overcome it. In this particular instance, he decided that the only way we were going to beat Purdue offensively was because their guys were too big and too slow and too this and too that.

"So believe it or not, back in the third game of the 1968 season, we went to this no-huddle offense. We had practiced this no-huddle offense, where they just call a name out, go to the line, and the ball is snapped. We had like ten or twelve plays scripted where there was a code name called out and then we would run that play."

As Hayes had predicted to his staff and his players, Purdue was surprised when Ohio State went to this offense on the first drive of the game. As the game wore on, his prediction about his boys being in better shape, about being more equipped to withstand the fast pace of the game, also proved to be true.

"The whole first drive, we get the ball and we never huddled," Foley said. "Now that's pretty progressive for the ol' coach who wasn't supposed to be innovative, don't you think? We came right to the ball and we snapped it and ran a play. Then we did it again. We had running plays scripted and we had passing plays scripted, the whole deal. I thought that was really fantastic.

"We went right down the field on that first drive. We didn't score, but all of a sudden those guys were on their heels a little bit and they thought, 'Hey, this might be a little bit of a game.'"

It was more than that. The Ohio State team that Purdue had destroyed one year earlier was not on the field this time. These newer Buckeyes were faster, more athletic, and played with an edge that quickly revealed their deep-held desire to avenge the previous year's defeat.

Lou Holtz, the new defensive backfield coach, had Jack Tatum shadow Keyes throughout the day to take away Purdue's most fearsome offensive threat. Prior to the game Holtz had told fellow assistant Hugh Hindman, who coached offensive tackles and ends (Bruce was in charge of the centers and guards), that he thought the Buckeyes would shut out high-scoring Purdue. At the time, Hindman laughed.

"I'll bet you a hundred dollars we don't shut 'em out," Hindman said.

"You're on. I'll bet you!" Holtz replied.

For good measure, Holtz also predicted that one of his defensive backs would return an interception for a touchdown. After holding Purdue scoreless in the first half—the first time in 28 games the Boilermakers had failed to score in the opening half—Holtz looked like a genius when safety Ted Provost stepped in front of a Phipps pass attempt in the flat, picked it off, and returned it 34 yards for an Ohio State touchdown. It broke a scoreless tie and eased some of Hayes's visible frustration over a first half in which the Buckeyes had more or less dominated but failed to score because of fumbles, untimely penalties, and three missed field goal attempts.

Late in the game, though, the outcome was still very much in doubt. The Buckeyes were clinging to a 6–0 lead when Kern was forced out of the game in the middle of a potential scoring drive because of an injured wrist. Billy Long, the popular starter the previous year, was now the not-so-popular backup. He had played some the previous week when Kern left because of a jaw injury—and had personally helped keep a game that should have been a rout close by throwing two interceptions. Foley, who had been named a team captain along with fellow senior Dirk Worden, a linebacker, welcomed Long in the huddle as the then record Ohio Stadium crowd of 84,834 went crazy in the background. The ball rested on the Purdue 14-yard line.

Foley was one of Long's close friends. They were fraternity brothers. But he wanted to make it clear what was at stake.

"I've got spit hanging out the side of my mouth, I'm sweating and all that stuff," Foley said. "And the first thing I say to him is, 'Long, goddammit, whatever you do, don't throw an interception!'

"So the first play is a pass play, and I don't know if I scared him into tucking the ball away and running, or if nobody was open and that's why he did it, but that was when he took off running and scored."

Long didn't score right away, though: met by two Purdue defenders at the goal line, he had to drag them across to clinch the victory.

"I had no idea we scored at first," Foley said. "I'm back there lying on the ground, and all of a sudden I heard a giant roar from the crowd. And so I jumped up and saw Billy Long lying in the end zone. He ran it right up the middle. I looked at him and thought, 'This is great, man. Way to listen to me, Billy!'"

The final score was 13–0. Suddenly, the Buckeyes were beginning to look like they just might be the best team in the nation.

The next two games were not without their own excitement. A 45–21 rout of Northwestern was followed by a near-miss against Illinois, when the Buckeyes blew a 24–0 halftime lead and found themselves tied 24–24 with less than five minutes remaining. This time, with Kern sidelined by yet another injury, having been forced out after a blow to the head, Hayes turned to another sophomore quarterback in Ron Maciejowski with the game on the line. Maciejowski led the Buckeyes on a game-winning drive for a 31–24 victory.

There were other sophomore heroes behind the scenes. Tatum had been held out of the game as a precaution after suffering a sprained ankle one week earlier against Northwestern. But when Illinois started picking apart the Ohio State secondary to mount their comeback, Hayes approached defensive coordinator Lou McCullough.

"Put Tatum in the game, Lou! We need him!" Hayes bellowed.

"I can't put him in, Coach. He's not taped up and he's got a twisted ankle. He can barely run," McCullough answered.

The Buckeyes were clinging to a one-touchdown lead at the moment. Hayes glared at McCullough, then Tatum, then turned and walked away. He came back a little while later after Illinois had scored a touchdown to tie the score.

This time, he headed straight for Tatum.

"Get taped," he told him. "You're going in the game."

Critics had a field day with the Buckeyes' close call at Illinois. After four consecutive home games, it was their first road test—and they nearly failed it. Hayes had probably relaxed a little too much himself with the big halftime lead. He spent most of his halftime speech rambling on about how Abraham Lincoln had once campaigned on the riverbanks near the stadium where the Buckeyes were now playing.

Stillwagon later remembered listening to Hayes's speech and feeling like he had a free pass to take the rest of the game off. That all changed a little later, but then afterward Hayes answered the critics by saying, "It was good for us to play a game like that."

There were more to follow. Michigan State, fresh off a win over high-ranked Notre Dame, roared back from a 19–7 deficit the following week and forced the Buckeyes to hold on for a 25–20 victory at Ohio Stadium. A 43–8 rout at Wisconsin was followed by another close call at Iowa, when the Hawkeyes rallied after falling behind 19–0 in the third quarter and made the final score closer than it should have been by scoring with nine seconds left to pull to within 33–27.

That made it eight wins in a row for the season and 12 straight dating back to the previous year. It also set up the biggest of the big games, even bigger than the earlier conquest of Purdue—although Hayes could neither see it nor admit it at the time of the Boilermakers' visit. Michigan was coming to Ohio Stadium to play for the Big Ten championship and a trip to the Rose Bowl (there was no faculty committee standing in the way of Hayes's Buckeyes this time). The Wolverines were ranked number four in the nation, the Buckeyes were ranked number two.

What transpired was stunning. Putting together by far their most complete game of the season, the Buckeyes, now starting a total of thirteen sophomores, ran up and down the field for a 50–14 victory. When fullback Jim Otis, who rushed for 143 yards on 34 carries, scored the last of his three touchdowns to make it 48–14, Hayes quickly signaled that he wanted his boys to go for a two-point conversion.

Later, when asked by reporters why he went for two, Hayes responded: "Because the sonsofbitches wouldn't let me go for three!"

Hayes was more diplomatic with other members of the media who questioned him afterward. But he could hardly keep his tongue in cheek when he added: "I don't feel comfortable these days without 50 points. Teams are so explosive on offense [now]. It's unbelievable how they can come back."

Otis later said that he goaded "the old man" into piling on the points against the archrivals. As they stood on the sideline and suddenly the Buckeyes faced a fourth-and-goal situation from the two-yard line on their final drive, Otis, who had long since been removed from the game, turned to Hayes and asked, "Do you want this TD?"

"Go on in," Hayes replied.

"What play do you want?" Otis asked.

"You call it," was Hayes's reply.

Once Otis scored, Hayes apparently could not resist the temptation to add two more to the final tally. For Bump Elliott, the embarrassing defeat spelled the end of his 10-year run as Michigan's head coach despite a final season record of eight wins against only two losses. Elliott's only Big Ten loss in 1968 was to the Buckeyes.

All that stood between the Buckeyes and the immortality of an unbeaten season and national championship after the rout of Michigan was Southern California in the Rose Bowl. But that was enough. The Trojans were led by sure Heisman Trophy winner O. J. Simpson, the best running back in the nation.

As a result of their dismantling of Michigan, Ohio State entered the game ranked number one in the country. But

Southern Cal was ranked right behind at number two, and they had more than just Simpson. They were large and athletic and talented, and they didn't have to fly across the country to a foreign land to play the game.

That was of great concern to Hayes. He didn't want his boys having too much fun once they arrived in sunny California. He began making sure they weren't going to be too comfortable by taking practices in Columbus indoors to the French Fieldhouse and literally turning up the heat. Hayes hauled in a bunch of portable heaters and had them blasting throughout the workouts, cranking the temperature in the building to more than 90 degrees while, outside, students scurried to their Ohio State classes amid snowflakes and cold, biting winds.

The players expected nothing less. Hayes was famous for taking care to have the team practice in whatever weather conditions he expected them to encounter on game day. It went back to the belief forged when he was running exercises years earlier in the Navy.

Just to make sure the players maintained their focus and didn't think they were headed to the West Coast for fun, Hayes had their ankles taped just before the plane touched down in California and told everyone to forget any fantasies they had of enjoying the sunny weather or seeing the sights. They were going straight to the practice field. When bowl promoters wanted to have players from both teams go against each other in the Lawry's Beef Bowl, an eating contest where they hoped to see who could pound down the most meat, Hayes angrily declined.

"They're trying to fatten us up," he told his players.

Once game day arrived in Pasadena, the Rose Bowl was packed with 102,063 fans and Hayes was ready to unleash his pent-up players for a little fun they would remember forever. It didn't start out the way he had planned, though, when

Simpson ripped through the Ohio State defense for an 80-yard touchdown run to give the Trojans a 10–0 lead early in the second quarter. At halftime, Hayes grabbed Holtz and demanded to know how Simpson could have taken a simple pitchout to his left, turned it up inside, and rambled all the way through Ohio State's secondary.

"Why did O.J. go eighty yards like that?" Hayes asked Holtz.

"Well," said Holtz, "that was all he needed. He could have gone ninety if he wanted. The only thing that could have stopped him was the Pacific Ocean."

By halftime, though, the Buckeyes had tied the score 10–10 on a one-yard touchdown run by Otis and a 25-yard field goal by placekicker Jim Roman with three seconds left in the second quarter. The Buckeyes sensed the game turning their way.

In the second half, Hayes ordered McCullough to put what he called "Mirror" into effect on defense. It essentially called for linebacker Mark Stier to defend Simpson man-to-man. Wherever the Juice flowed thereafter, Stier was right there to suck him up. Or knock him down. Or even knock the ball loose, which Stier did twice after the long run to set up Ohio State scores.

Simpson still ended up rushing for 171 yards and catching eight passes for another 85. But Kern was named the game's Most Valuable Player after completing nine of 15 passes for 101 yards and two touchdowns, while also rushing for another 35 yards in the 27–16 victory for the Buckeyes.

Afterward, Simpson visited the Ohio State locker room and told the Buckeyes: "You're the best ball team in the country, and don't let anybody tell you that you aren't. Congratulations."

Hayes wanted to give out so many game balls, he couldn't decide who to give them to. It had been a brutal

game. Fullback Larry Zelina left early after getting his ribs broken. Senior center John Muhlbach had what looked like a fractured ankle. The blocking of the offensive line had been great, with Otis racking up 101 yards and Leo Hayden, another of the Super Sophs, adding 90 on just 15 carries.

Hayes even thought to nominate Billy Long for a game ball, the senior quarterback who had lost his job the previous spring to the upstart Kern. Hayes pointed out that Long had been key in helping the Buckeyes win because he had played the role of Southern Cal quarterback Steve Sogge on the Ohio State scout team in the practices leading up to the Rose Bowl.

"It was everybody's victory. We all played a part. That's the way it was the entire season," said Foley, the senior captain. "We were a team in every sense of the word."

They were a team for the ages, one that would never be forgotten. And they were so young, they had the sure, confident look of a national championship dynasty.

5

End of One Era . . .
And Start of Another

A S T H E Buckeyes returned almost intact for the 1969 season, they were the nation's celebrity team. In attendance and cheering for them at the 1968 Rose Bowl triumph were the likes of President-elect Richard Nixon and comedian Bob Hope, a former Ohio resident. Coach Woody Hayes was close to both men, but particularly to Nixon. He had, in fact, honored one of Nixon's wishes shortly after winning the Rose Bowl by unabashedly displaying his support for what was becoming the increasingly unpopular Vietnam War. Within seventy-two hours of that great victory by his Buckeyes, Hayes was on a plane bound for Vietnam ostensibly to give troops there some of his famous pep talks.

Hayes had first met Nixon in 1957, and years later Nixon would recall the meeting.

"I wanted to talk about football. Woody wanted to talk about foreign policy. You know Woody—we talked about foreign policy," Nixon said.

Upon Hayes's return to the States, the coach's mood was bright. The Buckeyes seemed to possess more talent than any other team in the nation, and most of the talent was still

young. The possibilities for the immediate future seemed endless; the destiny of the team certain. No one seemed to question that more national championships were sure to follow, and sooner rather than later.

So when the Buckeyes began the 1969 season with eight consecutive victories, no one was surprised. This set up the usual season-ending showdown with Michigan, but this Michigan team was different. It was, for one thing, now coached by Hayes disciple Bo Schembechler. And though the Wolverines entered the day as 15-point underdogs, Schembechler had conceived a brilliant game plan born of the desperation of a young man who still feared displeasing his former boss. Beating Hayes would bring Hayes pain, to be sure; but bringing a team into such a big game unprepared to face him may have hurt Hayes even more.

The Buckeyes were ranked number one in the nation. They were seeking to extend a 22-game winning streak, seal up sole possession of a second straight Big Ten championship, and set up a successful defense of their national championship in the Rose Bowl. They had outscored their eight opponents that year by the astounding margin of 371–69. They began with a 62–0 rout of Texas Christian and went on to embarrass the likes of Washington (41–14), Michigan State (54–21), Minnesota (34–7), Illinois (41–0), Northwestern (35–6), Wisconsin (62–7), and Purdue (42–14) to set up the showdown against Michigan.

"We were so far ahead in the polls," said Hayes, "it wasn't even close."

But Bo's boys, though suitably impressed and respectful, weren't frightened. They refused to play scared. Schembechler tried to build his first and subsequent Michigan teams much in the same way that Hayes built his. It was all about the fundamentals of blocking and tackling and practicing until you got it right. It also was about getting the right kids, of course. It was no coincidence that Schembechler's first Michigan recruiting class included twenty-one players from the state of Ohio. Like Hayes, he thought that was where most of the best high school players were, and his raiding of fertile ground Hayes had only recently regained after the faculty had undercut his trip to the Rose Bowl back in 1961 was an omen of things to come.

What Schembechler loved about Hayes's teams more than anything else was their brutal simplicity. When Hayes ran one of his beloved run plays, and set the offensive line's blocking scheme just so, and then made his players run that play to perfection over and over again in practices, it was to Schembechler a thing of pure beauty.

"People don't recognize the subtle nuances of those plays that looked so simple," Schembechler later said of Hayes's scheme. "Take the off-tackle play. Truth of the matter is, probably more than any other coach, he refined everything included in that play to make it successful no matter what the defense did. The line splits had to be exact, and the blocking schemes just as exact. The ball handling looked the same, which is what the public sees. But the real innovation was up front."

Schembechler wanted to mold his first team and the ones thereafter along the same lines as the Ohio State teams of Hayes's era. He wanted them to be physical, yet precise. He wanted them to play smart and avoid dumb mistakes and penalties. He wanted them to look and play as if they were prepared—and he warned them that they simply could not afford to be intimidated by whatever the Buckeyes had done to the opposition in their previous 22 encounters.

"We can't lay an egg today. We have to come to win," Schembechler told his players and staff before the game.

They came to win and did precisely that in front of a record college football crowd of 103,588 at Michigan Stadium. With their own share of a Big Ten championship and a trip to the Rose Bowl on the line, twice-beaten Michigan took control in the first half and never relinquished it—intercepting Ohio State quarterbacks a total of six times (Kern, who threw four of them, eventually was replaced by Maciejowski, who threw two more). Barry Pierson, whose 60-yard punt return set up one Michigan touchdown, snared three of the interceptions.

The score was 24–12 Michigan by halftime and would not change, but it could have been much worse for the Buckeyes. While their offense crossed midfield only once in the second half, Michigan moved into possession for four field goal attempts—and placekicker Tim Killian missed them all. The vaunted Ohio State rushing attack managed the paltry total of 22 yards, while Michigan racked up 266 on the ground.

"They beat the greatest team that ever stepped on a college football field, the best team we ever put together," Hayes would tell *Columbus Dispatch* sports editor Paul Hornung years later when discussing the first Michigan team coached by Schembechler. "That team would have been national champions without a doubt. . . . But Bo beat us!"

Hayes blamed Kern's poor performance—in addition to throwing the four interceptions, Kern completed just six of 17 pass attempts for 88 yards—on a media photo shoot that had taken place the day before the game.

"Rex Kern was hurting," he told Hornung. "They wanted to take some pictures after we worked out on Friday, and he stood outside all sweaty and caught a chill. The next morning, his back was so stiff he couldn't get out of bed. I shouldn't have played him—because Maciejowski could have done a better job.

"But I'm not going to alibi. Bo had his team ready and they beat us. That was Bo's first year of coaching the team from up north."

It was, by all accounts, an upset of stunning proportions. It proved that Ohio State was not invincible, and that repeating as national champions that year or any year thereafter could not be ordained regardless of how a team stacked up on paper. It also marked the beginning of what would be referred to as the Ten Year War between Bo and Woody, raising the levels of intensity and expectations in what already was arguably college football's greatest rivalry to even more spectacular heights.

The ink was barely dry on newspapers chronicling Michigan's huge upset when forces in Columbus got to work to make things right in their world again. A Columbus carpet manufacturer figured it knew what it would take, so it produced a rug with the following woven in it:

1969: MICHIGAN 24, OHIO STATE 12
1970: . . . ?

Then the rug was mailed to Hayes, who did not need accompanying instructions to know what to do with it. When the players arrived for spring practice, the rug was positioned so the players would trample it on their way to the practice field each and every day. And there it remained not only for the rest of spring workouts, but through the fall, too.

By the time the 1970 rematch rolled around, it was a match-up of epic proportions even for Michigan–Ohio State. The Buckeyes again were ranked number one in the nation, but this time Michigan was ranked number two. Not only that, but for the first time in the seventy-three-year-old history of the series, both teams entered the season finale with undefeated, untied, unblemished records.

Some players had made the game into a mission. Center Tom DeLeone, for instance, had been so embarrassed by his play against Michigan the previous year that he cut out a picture of Henry Hill, Michigan's nose guard, and taped it to his dorm room mirror at eye level. He kept it there for a year, fueling his desire to even the score every time he combed his hair.

Hayes was at his best, and worst, in the two weeks of practices leading up to the game. He told his players unabashedly that it would be the game of their lives. He whipped them and coerced them and, yes, even physically prodded them to get themselves into the best state of mind possible for a contest that had been on *his* mind since the end of their meeting twelve months earlier.

He kept close watch on his players away from the field as well. One night after practice DeLeone was sitting in his dorm room with two girls who had dropped by for a visit and had brought along some beer, which DeLeone was helping them consume. All of a sudden there was a commotion outside the door.

"Woody's on the floor!" a friend shouted.

DeLeone scrambled to shove the beers under his bed, but he could do nothing to hide the girls on such short notice. Moments later, the door swung open and there was Hayes with a huge box of pizza in his arms. He glared at DeLeone, then turned his attention to the girls.

"Ladies, we have a big game this week. So you should probably leave now," he told them.

Then he glared again at DeLeone—and without offering so much as a single slice of pizza, he flicked out the lights and added, "Get to bed."

DeLeone got to bed, even though it wasn't much past 8:30.

As the game got closer, the practices became even more

intense. On the Thursday before the game, the offense was running through plays on the field and marching down the field against the scout team defense when Hayes noticed two reserves who were yukking it up on the sidelines, not paying attention to what was happening on the field. As he stormed over to them, their teammates knew a Woody megaton explosion was about to rain down on them.

Hayes threw his play cards in the air and started ripping his shirt off. Then he tore his latest watch off his wrist and smashed it into tiny pieces, and finally he fell to the ground in front of assistant coach Earle Bruce and started writhing around, crying like a baby.

"Earle! Help me, Earle!" Hayes sobbed. "They won't play for me! They won't play for me! My God, it's Michigan week and they won't play for me!"

The players stared at him. They hadn't seen a hundred-megaton quite like this, and they certainly had never heard Hayes use what they jokingly called "the M word." Hayes always had called them "the team from up north" and other less friendly terms.

DeLeone and right tackle John Hicks started to cry, too. They turned to Kern, the unquestioned team leader, and pleaded with him.

"Come on, Rex, get us ready!" they shouted. "We'll play for him! We'll play for him!"

Soon the entire team joined in. Contrived or not, Hayes had never staged a more effective megaton. It helped work his team into a frenzy, and kickoff was still two days away.

The coach saved perhaps his best psychological trick for last. He gathered the players together just before kickoff and said that he wanted to read them a one-line telegram that someone had sent to him anonymously. Since Hayes normally would have nothing to do with anything sent anonymously, there is some debate about whether the telegram was legitimate or simply a one-liner Hayes had thought of himself. Regardless, the point got across. It read: "THIS ONE LITERALLY IS FOR A LIFETIME."

Upon reading it, the Buckeyes worked themselves into such a frenzy that when they ran onto the field, their intensity startled many in the then record Ohio Stadium crowd of 87,331. Up in the press box, Paul Zimmerman, at the time of the *New York Post* and later *Sports Illustrated*, viewing the Ohio State players jumping up and down and pummeling each other in their pregame team huddle near midfield, turned to a colleague and remarked: "Those guys just aren't sane. I wouldn't want to be a Michigan football player today."

Middle guard Jim Stillwagon, by then the senior leader of the defense, was perhaps the most insane that day. He sacked Michigan quarterback Don Moorhead twice on crucial plays in the second half and helped the defense limit the usually powerful Michigan running game to 37 yards. Moorhead was a fine quarterback, one of the best in his school's history. But after establishing career school records for passes completed and yardage, he completed only 12 of 26 for 118 yards in arguably the biggest game of his career.

In nine previous games, Michigan had averaged 31 points. They would get only nine on this day. Michigan's Lance Scheffler took the opening kickoff at the Wolverines' 25-yard line, took a vicious hit from three different Buckeyes converging at high speed from different angles, and fumbled the ball. The Bucks recovered, setting up a field goal and, more importantly, quickly establishing the tone for the day.

The Buckeyes went on to win 20–9 behind the hard running of Leo Hayden and John Brockington, and the deft ball handling and timely passing of Kern. Like Stillwagon, none of these heroes of the day was a Super Soph any longer. They were seniors, and they played like them.

Kern converted one fourth-and-two situation at the

Michigan 29-yard line in the first half, then fired a 26-yard touchdown pass to Bruce Jankowski three plays later. In the second half, defensive back Tim Anderson of the Buckeyes blocked an extra point attempt by the Wolverines that would have tied the game 10–10, and later linebacker Stan White set up Ohio State's final touchdown by intercepting a Moorhead pass and returning it to the Michigan nine-yard line. From there, Kern faked as if he were going to run himself and pitched the ball on an option sweep to Hayden, who scored the final points of the day.

DeLeone was a junior that day, and he exacted his revenge on Michigan's Henry Hill, knocking him out of the game in the third quarter. It couldn't have pleased Hayes more.

"We've waited a year for this!" Hayes shouted to his players afterward, hugging each and every one with whom he came in contact.

As he continued to talk with his players, trainer John Bozick interrupted him with some unusual news.

"Woody, the President is on the phone for you," Bozick said.

Hayes did not like being interrupted. He stared at Bozick.

"Which President?" he wanted to know.

"President Nixon. The President of the United States," Bozick replied.

"Well, tell him he's going to have to wait," Hayes snapped. "I'm talking to my team right now."

Hayes wasn't kidding. The President of the United States and his heartfelt offer of congratulations could wait. Then, in more hushed, reverent tones a few moments later, a tearful Hayes quietly told reporters, "This is the greatest victory of my career. It was the most emotional game my kids have ever played, and, goddammit, I'm so proud of 'em."

Alas, another national championship was not to be. In the ensuing Rose Bowl, the Buckeyes ran up against college football's hottest quarterback, Stanford's Jim Plunkett. The Cardinals had not won a Rose Bowl since 1941 and came in as 10-point underdogs. But Plunkett and Company overcame a 14–10 halftime deficit, scored two fourth-quarter touchdowns—and handed Ohio State only its second loss in the 31 games the Super Sophomores had played.

Plunkett completed 20 of 30 passes for 265 yards and was named the game's Most Valuable Player in the 27–12 upset. He also was awarded the Heisman Trophy as college football's outstanding player that season. Kern did not go out the way he wanted: completing just four of 13 passes with one interception. But his record of 27-2 as Ohio State's starting quarterback would stand as one of the greatest in college football history.

Kern stood out among the recruiting class that arrived in fall of 1967, but he certainly did not stand alone when it came to possessing exceptional talent and the ability to milk every bit of it from his often pain-wracked body. Stillwagon finished his career as winner of both the Outland Trophy and the first Lombardi Award, signifying his status as the best lineman of any kind of all of college football in his final season. All in all, the senior class that departed in 1970 featured six All-Americans and nine All-Big Ten selections.

While the departure of Kern, Stillwagon, and others marked the end of one Ohio State era, another was soon to follow. The three games the Super Sophs had played against Michigan also helped shape the future of that rivalry, and of the two programs involved.

Until Hayes's arrival as coach, Michigan had dominated

the series. The rivalry was hardly a rivalry at first. It began in 1897 with a 34–0 victory for the Wolverines in Ann Arbor, and Ohio State would not win its first game in the series until 1919—putting the Buckeyes in a huge hole from which they have not yet recovered. By the time Hayes took over and lost at Michigan in his first season as coach, the all-time series record stood at 32-12 in Michigan's favor, throwing out four ties over the years.

Over the next 17 seasons, Hayes accomplished what it had taken his predecessors nearly half a century to do. He defeated Michigan 12 more times, culminating this run with the 50–14 victory in Columbus in 1968. But that victory came at a price, costing Bump Elliott his job as Michigan's head coach and thrusting Bo Schembechler into the unlikely role as his mentor's number one nemesis.

During the final two years for Kern, Stillwagon, and others from Ohio State's Super Soph class of 1967, Schembechler's teams served notice that it was time to escalate the emotional level of what already had been one of college football's hottest rivalries. Beginning with the Wolverines' upset win in 1969, the Michigan game suddenly seemed to mean more than ever.

In eight of the next 10 years, the traditional Ohio State–Michigan season finale settled the Big Ten championship. Six times the result would mean the two schools shared the title, and they would go to the Rose Bowl five times each in the span that marked the Woody versus Bo era, the Ten Year War.

To fully understand the depth of the rivalry, there is the story of assistant coach Ed Ferkany, who accompanied Hayes on a recruiting trip to Flint, Michigan, in February of 1972. As their automobile sped homeward on a gray night that foretold a coming snowstorm, Ferkany began to grow nervous. Columbus was three hours away, but the gas gauge was dipping below a quarter-tank. Hayes sat silently next to him, for once too tired to talk about football, history, politics, or whatever else might have been on his mind.

"Woody, it looks like we'd better get some gas at the next station we see," Ferkany said.

Hayes said nothing. Then he emitted a low grunt, almost a growl.

"Nah. Keep going."

Snowflakes began to dance on the windshield. They drove on, passing one gas station, then another and another. The needle on the gas gauge inched closer to E.

"Um, Woody, there's another gas station up ahead. I really think we ought to pull in and fill up," Ferkany suggested quietly.

Hayes turned his head slowly toward Ferkany, who was in his first month on the job and, despite repeated words of caution from colleagues who had experienced their share of megatons, wasn't sure what was coming next.

"Goddammit, I said *no!* We *do not* pull in and fill up. And I'll tell you exactly *why* we don't. It's because I don't buy one goddamn drop of gas in Michigan! We'll coast and *push* this goddamn car to the Ohio line before I give this state a nickel of my money!"

Ferkany kept driving. When relating the story a couple of years later to writer Jerry Brondfield, Ferkany estimated that they coasted across the Ohio line and made it to the first filling station pump "by about the length of a first down." The episode illustrated Hayes's feelings toward the team by then coached by one of his favorite former players, who was at that very same moment recruiting players by the bushelful right from under Hayes's nose in Ohio. Recruiting had become the war within the war, and Hayes wasn't always winning.

That was evident on November 20, 1971, when the Buckeyes visited Ann Arbor for the first time in four years without Kern and his teammates wearing the scarlet and gray. Ohio State already had lost three times that season—or one more time than they had in the previous three seasons combined when Kern was running the offense and Stillwagon was anchoring the defense. The Bucks had, in fact, arrived on Michigan soil having just dropped back-to-back games at home to Michigan State and Northwestern to fall to the unthinkable position of third place in the Big Ten standings.

Hayes, as even the most casual of observers might have guessed, was not in a good mood. Six starters had been lost for the season to injuries to further hinder a year that would have been difficult enough compensating for all the senior losses. Still, Hayes somehow had convinced his players that they could pull off the upset and salvage their season. And as the game entered the fourth quarter, the Buckeyes led the Wolverines, who were ranked number three in the nation, by the score of 7–3.

Billy Taylor, Michigan's All-America tailback, broke free for a 22-yard touchdown run after taking a pitchout, giving the home team a 10–7 lead. But the Buckeyes weren't finished. On the ensuing possession, they began moving the ball and were mounting a drive with about 90 seconds remaining when quarterback Don Lamka fired a long pass intended for wide receiver Dick Wakefield at the Michigan 32-yard line. But as Wakefield leapt high for the pass, Michigan defender Tom Darden rammed into him at full speed, knocking Wakefield to the ground and intercepting the football.

Hayes and his coaches called for pass interference, but no flag was thrown. Hayes simply could not believe it. He could not accept it, either.

He charged onto the field to confront the officials, which resulted only in his being assessed a 15-yard penalty for unsportsmanlike conduct. Several assistant coaches tried in vain to drag him back to the sideline, but Hayes wasn't yet finished with his tirade. He shed them like a blitzing line-backer would shed a would-be blocker and headed for the next thing he saw: the wide, colored-cloth sideline marker. He yanked it from the ground and proceeded to tear it into shreds, which he then threw angrily onto the field as the nearest official watched, mouth agape. Finally, the official threw a flag—signaling another 15-yard penalty on Hayes and the Buckeyes.

In the press box upstairs sat Wayne Duke, who was at-tending his first Ohio State–Michigan game as the new Big Ten commissioner. He lowered his head as if he could not watch any longer.

Newspapers from Michigan and Ohio launched editori-als denouncing Hayes's outburst. The *Cleveland Plain Dealer* implored Hayes to apologize for "his immature behavior" and went on to add: "First it was ludicrous, then revolting. It's one thing to be a fierce competitor—quite another to be a horse's rear end, which he was at Ann Arbor." Even the Ohio State student newspaper, *The Lantern*, chastised the coach: "Woody Hayes is given to lengthy discourses on the charac-ter, leadership, and sportsmanship developed by football, but certainly showed a dearth of those qualities himself."

Some angry alumni called for Hayes's dismissal as coach, saying he had embarrassed them and the university with his combustible personality for the last time. But most of the Ohio State faithful stood behind him, even when he re-fused to apologize for the incident.

"I did it for my players," he insisted. "I owed it to them and I would have been derelict in my duty to them if I had done less."

Don Canham, Michigan's athletic director, was not among those who called for Hayes's dismissal—and neither was Joe Falls, the award-winning columnist from the *Detroit Free Press*.

"I'll buy all the sideline markers Woody Hayes wants to tear up. Ohio State without Hayes would draw at least thirty thousand fewer people," Canham told reporters.

And in his column, Falls quieted at least some of the Michigan faithful calling for Hayes's head by reminding them of a few hard, undeniable truths:

> W. W. Hayes is not about to apologize for anything, and if he did, it would be the greatest upset intercollegiate football has ever known. . . . Woody Hayes is the only coach extant who draws more attention than the cheerleaders. More people follow him through their binoculars than follow all the pompom girls, majorettes, and cheerleaders in the land. And this is a fat, dumpy, gray-haired, bespectacled old codger who wears a silly-looking baseball cap as he prowls up and down the sidelines. . . .
> He is one of a kind. In my opinion the most colorful coach in the game today. I've hated him for years. . . . So chastise him if you will. Berate him. Even hate him. But the sad day will be when he's no longer the coach of the Ohio State football team.

So Hayes lost that game without apology. But when it came to firing subsequent salvos against "that team from up north" in the early 1970s, Hayes was about to unleash the greatest weapon he ever employed. Even he didn't realize it at first as he mourned the departure of Kern and the others while suffering the frustrating loss at Ann Arbor in 1971—but it already was in the works, and it would indeed be something very special, something the likes of which college football had never seen.

6

Archie Arrives

I T W A S only natural for the program to experience a bit of a letdown following the glorious years of Rex Kern and Company. But it did not last long because of the arrival of Archie Griffin, who nearly went elsewhere after starring in football, track, and wrestling at Eastmoor High School in Columbus. Named Back of the Year in Ohio following his senior season, Griffin was leaning toward attending the Naval Academy at first. Northwestern and, ironically, Michigan were other schools he was considering along with the Buckeyes as he was finishing up high school.

Northwestern's 14–10 upset of the Buckeyes in Columbus in 1971 influenced Griffin's opinion of the Wildcats.

"Northwestern was another school I was considering very seriously, because I liked the fact that it was good academically, and also because of the fact that they were playing pretty good football at that time," Griffin said. "They had finished second in the Big Ten in 1971, ahead of Ohio State. They actually had beaten Ohio State at Ohio Stadium, which wasn't easily accomplished. They were playing outstanding football at the time."

Michigan was in the picture because Griffin had formed relationships during the recruiting process with Bo Schembechler and one of his assistants, Chuck Stobart. He liked them both immensely.

"But Ohio State was in the picture, too, with it being right around the corner from where I grew up," Griffin said.

Griffin came from a close-knit family that included older brothers Larry and Daryle, who already were playing college ball. Larry Griffin was playing at the University of Louisville in Kentucky and Daryle Griffin was at Kent State University, which was closer to Cleveland than Columbus.

"The fact that my older brothers were playing out of town and my parents would have the opportunity to pretty much just come around the corner and watch me play if I went to Ohio State was appealing," Griffin said.

Then there were the sales pitches being given by Rudy Hubbard, the backfield coach at Ohio State, as well as Woody Hayes. Griffin had first met Hayes under what at first glance appeared to be terrible circumstances the previous year, early in the recruiting process. The Buckeyes, ranked number six in the nation at the time, had just lost to 10th-ranked Colorado at home. Not counting the previous year's season-ending loss to Stanford in the Rose Bowl, it was the first time since November of 1964 that the Buckeyes had entered a game ranked and lost to any team besides Michigan. Yet Griffin came away with positive first impressions of the volatile Hayes.

"What I remember about him is that I went to that big Colorado game as a recruit, and when we were in the locker room after the game I was amazed that he knew who everyone was and what many had done individually in their high school games on Friday night. It was very impressive to watch him in that room with all the recruits," Griffin said.

Griffin also was surprised and impressed that Hayes

was so gracious and calm, given the coach's reputation for going off after disappointing losses. Hayes seemed like a charming gentleman in complete control of himself and his emotions, and he made each recruit, including Griffin, feel as if they were the most special player ever to be recruited by him. For a coach who often was accused, and rightly so, of losing self-control, it was as if the bitter home loss to Colorado was in the distant past instead of having just occurred.

"I don't know for sure if he knew what everyone's stats were on Friday night. But he sure knew mine and several others. And I would imagine that there was a good group of forty or fifty guys in that room," Griffin said.

Yet Griffin still had a scheduled visit to Northwestern to make. As his father, James, was driving him to the airport, he turned to his son in the passenger's seat.

"We'd love to be able to see you play every week," he said simply.

His father said nothing more, but Griffin got the message.

Still, Griffin wasn't certain yet when he went to dinner with Hayes at a popular steakhouse on Main Street in Columbus. He soon would be. It was the occasion that Hayes had chosen to apply his famous full-court press, and it worked as well as it ever had.

"He always said he would have been a great salesman—because eventually he would get you to where you were saying, 'Yes, yes, yes!' He would start asking you questions where you would naturally answer yes. And before I knew what I was saying, I was saying, 'Yes, Coach, I'm coming to Ohio State University.'

"And I certainly meant it. I thought it would be the best place for me and for my family, because it would make it so much easier on them. I knew for sure it would make my dad happy."

It made Hayes happy, too, although no one could have predicted what the successful recruitment of Griffin eventually would come to mean for the program and the man running the program. Meanwhile, it just so happened that one of the men recruiting Griffin for Navy was Ed Ferkany. But somewhere toward the very end of the process, Hayes hired Ferkany to be his new offensive line coach. Griffin had no knowledge of this. So shortly after telling Hayes he was committing to Ohio State and calling Ferkany to give him the bad news that he wouldn't be coming to Navy, Griffin looked out the window of his house one day after hearing car doors slam and was stunned to see both Rudy Hubbard and Ed Ferkany marching up his driveway.

"Shoot, I told Coach Ferkany that I'm going to Ohio State. I wonder why he's still coming. I hope these guys don't get into it in my driveway," Griffin mumbled to himself.

The two men knocked on the door. Griffin hesitated before answering. Then he discovered that as serious as Coach Hayes seemed to be most of the time, the coaches from Ohio State had a sense of humor.

"They were playing a joke on me because I didn't know Coach Ferk had been hired by Ohio State as an assistant," Griffin said. "They came up to the house and knocked on the door and let me sweat a little bit, and then they let me know that Coach Ferk was on our staff at Ohio State. They were just messing with me a little bit."

The joke would soon be on the rest of the Big Ten.

Griffin arrived on the Ohio State campus at precisely the right moment in college football history. For the first time, the NCAA had ruled that freshmen could play for their varsity teams. Hayes grumbled about the change in the rule, griping to the assistant coaches that most freshmen weren't ready to do much of anything but commit costly mistakes. In the back of their minds, though, many of them wondered what the rule change could have meant to the recruits who came in five years earlier and had to wait until their second year on campus to be dubbed Super Sophomores.

None of this crossed Griffin's mind. He was mostly just glad to be on the team early that first year.

He began his career inauspiciously, fumbling the very first time he was asked to carry the football late in the 1972 season opener against Iowa. Griffin wasn't sure when he would be permitted to attempt carrying it again.

"I was in for one play against Iowa. One play. And I fumbled," he said. "I took my eye off the ball. I was excited, man, just having the opportunity to get in the game. It was the last couple of minutes of the game and all, but I was excited to get in."

When he ran off the field, Griffin deliberately avoided going anywhere around Hayes—even though the Buckeyes had the game well in hand and went on to win 21–0.

"He didn't say anything to me, but I didn't give him the chance to say anything on the sideline," Griffin said of Hayes. "As a matter of fact, I went as far away from him as I possibly could."

Next up for the fifth-ranked Buckeyes on the schedule that year was a home game against unranked but also unbeaten North Carolina. Rudy Hubbard, the running backs coach, wanted to give Griffin another chance. Hayes wasn't so sure. The old coach didn't like the new rule permitting freshmen to play anyway, and Griffin had proven his point that the youngsters generally weren't ready to play right away. Griffin felt certain that his fleeting chance to earn a varsity letter as a true freshman—his first year at the university—was over.

"After that fumble, I didn't think I would get the chance to carry the ball for the varsity again that year—because I continued to work on the scout squad the following week," Griffin said. "And when you worked on the scout squad, it was a battle because you were running against the first-team defense. It was hard to gain any yards at all because we had a great defense."

Behind the scenes, Hubbard was working Hayes to give Griffin another shot, against North Carolina.

"Rudy really pounded the table to get me in there," Griffin said. "Coach Hayes always said, 'If you believe in something, you have to pound the table.' So Rudy really pounded the table hard on my behalf."

Toward the end of the week, Hayes finally relented. He agreed to give Griffin another chance, but made no promises beyond that.

The game began badly for the Buckeyes, who seemed uninspired despite having a week off after the Iowa game to rest and prepare for the visiting Tar Heels. The Bucks' first possession ended in a punt, and the second time they had the ball they were stopped again. This time, though, Gary Lago's punt was blocked by North Carolina's Jerry DeRatt and was recovered on the goal line by Gene Brown for a Tar Heels touchdown.

On the sideline, a furious Hayes paced. Next time the Buckeyes' offense headed out to the field, he motioned for Hubbard.

"Get Griffin in there!" he ordered.

Hubbard nodded, and motioned to the shocked Griffin to take the field.

"I had no idea I would get into that North Carolina football game," he marveled years later. "It truly was a surprise to me, especially going into that first quarter."

The first three times he touched the ball, he gained a total of 18 yards—and held on to the football. Although Ohio

State eventually was forced to punt again, the standing-room-only home crowd of 86,180 stirred to life.

Griffin was merely getting warmed up—in the game and for the next four seasons. He carried the ball 13 more times in the first half and piled up 111 yards in all. He also caught a key third-down pass and turned it into a 17-yard gain to set up a second-quarter touchdown as the Buckeyes surged ahead 9–7.

By the second half, he was the focal point of the offense. He sparked three long, time-consuming touchdown drives, capping one with the first touchdown run of his collegiate career. It was an impressive journey to the end zone from nine yards out. First he darted for the left sideline, where he tightroped the out-of-bounds line before juking out a defender right at the goal line. The nine-yard touchdown run gave the Buckeyes a 23–7 lead in the fourth quarter, when the only suspense left was whether the freshman tailback from nearby Eastmoor High was going to break the all-time OSU single-game rushing record.

That fell with relative ease, as Griffin ended up with 239 yards rushing on 27 carries. The previous school record had stood for nearly three decades; Ollie Cline had set it by running for 229 yards against Pitt back in 1945.

"I was in a daze the whole time," Griffin said, looking back. "All I can really remember is that my number was being called and I was running with the ball. Some of the people on the line were telling me that my eyes were as big as saucers the entire time.

"You have those days when you feel that you're on—and you just hope they keep giving you the ball because you're in rhythm and you feel like you've got it going. That was how I felt that day."

After the game, Hayes apparently became an enthusiastic convert to the new NCAA freshman eligibility rule.

"I have never known whether I was for or against the freshman rule until now, but Archie tends to make up my mind," Hayes declared. "Archie has convinced me it's okay."

Hayes spoke at length about Griffin to reporters after the game. But he seemed to be almost trying to figure out for himself what exactly he had on his hands in this special back.

"Archie spoke for himself today," Hayes said. "What is it that makes players that good? I don't know."

It could have something to do with superior coaching at the high school level, Hayes theorized. He then offered his opinion that the new freshman eligibility rule would revolutionize college football.

"They give you a bigger squad to work with and show a great deal of where the fine coaching really is—in high schools," Hayes said of adding freshmen to the varsity. "Take Archie, for instance. All you have to do is hand him the ball and he does it. He has power for his 185 pounds, he has speed, and he has a definite sense of timing."

At 5-foot-9, and probably more like 180 pounds than the 185 Hayes mentioned, Griffin was small even by the standards of his day. But he had the uncanny ability to sidestep or even run through would-be tacklers, and the speed to kick it into another gear once he was in the open field. But even after Griffin's great coming-out party against North Carolina, Hayes wasn't quite ready to turn the offense over to a freshman. Plus the stubborn Hayes was reluctant to change his playbook too much in the middle of a season, and his offense at the time was designed to hand the ball off to the fullback, not a tailback like the undersized Griffin, no matter how much of a devilish combination of speed and power he displayed.

For the rest of the 1972 season, Hayes continued to run the ball more with a committee of several veteran fullbacks than with Griffin. Over the last nine games, Griffin carried the ball a total of 131 more times and caught just five more passes—touching the ball about 12 times per game. He still gained 867 yards, averaging 5.4 yards per rush attempt.

"I didn't carry the ball a great deal, to tell you the truth," Griffin said. "It was still a fullback-oriented offense, and the fullback carried the ball most of the time."

That was about to change.

The Buckeyes capped Griffin's freshman season with a trip to the Rose Bowl after stunning previously unbeaten Michigan 14–11 in an epic edition of the rivalry game at Ohio Stadium. As usual, Hayes pulled some motivational tricks to help get his team ready. Former standout Jim Stillwagon was playing in the Canadian Football League at the time when he received an urgent phone call from his old coach.

"I need you to come to Columbus and do something special for me the week of the Michigan game," Hayes said.

"Sure. I'll do it," Stillwagon replied.

When he arrived on cue the week before the game, Hayes pulled him into his office and told him what he wanted him to do.

"You have to tell them what it's like to play in the big game. You have to tell them what it means," Hayes pleaded.

Stillwagon nodded. But when he began to do what he thought Hayes wanted following practice later that afternoon, Hayes exploded.

"Yeah, yeah, you're doing great, Jim. But tell 'em how it really fuckin' was!"

Then Hayes reached back and punched Stillwagon right in the stomach, as hard as he could.

"Tell 'em it's like a war!"

This was punctuated by another punch to Stillwagon's gut.

"You gotta beat those sonsofbitches!"

WHAM! Another punch.

"Tell 'em! Tell 'em how it really is, Jim!"

WHAM!

By now Stillwagon was doubled over in pain.

"I'm getting the snot beat out of me," he told reporter Bruce Hooley of the *Cleveland Plain Dealer* years later. "It's like he's hitting a heavy bag. And I'm thinking to myself, 'How did I get into this?'"

Later, though, player after player came up to Stillwagon and told him what a great speech he had delivered. They said it motivated them to beat the snot out of Michigan. As usual, the ends justified the means in Hayes's mind—and Still-wagon soon got over the pain to watch Ohio State pound out its narrow victory.

Needing only a tie to secure a trip to preserve an un-beaten season, Michigan coach Bo Schembechler refused to kick the field goal that would have done so. He stubbornly went for a touchdown and the win in the fourth quarter, and quarterback Dennis Franklin, who earlier had fumbled away the football at the Buckeye one-yard line at the end of the first half on yet another fourth-and-goal try, was turned away by the Buckeyes' defense on fourth-and-goal from one foot away. Schembechler was defiant afterward with reporters who questioned his strategy to forgo the seemingly sure fourth-quarter field goal, the tie, and the trip to Pasadena that would have went along with it.

"I never even considered it," he snapped. "I didn't want a tie. We wanted to win."

The Buckeyes won even though they were outgained 344 yards to 192, with the Wolverines controlling the line of scrim-mage and the clock by running 83 plays to just 44 for the home team. Only three of the Buckeyes' 44 plays were passes. The two goal line stands by the defense were the difference.

"Our defense was just tenacious that day. I'll never forget that," Griffin said.

Even after the second goal line stand in the fourth quarter, Michigan got the ball back and mounted one more drive into Buckeye territory. But with seconds left, several hundred fans swarmed out of the Ohio Stadium stands to launch an assault on the south goal posts. Hayes sprinted to the end zone to help police restore order, but was unsuccessful in doing so before the goal posts fell. Initially, Hayes was distraught, fearing the worst.

"I was afraid the officials might let Michigan try a field goal at the other end of the field; then they would have had the wind at their backs and they might have tied us," he explained later.

He need not have worried. Someone pointed out that the Ohio State athletic department kept an emergency set of goal posts underneath the stands—and assured him that they would have taken the time to have them installed before ever permitting the team from up north to gain an advantage by kicking a field goal with the wind at their backs when they didn't deserve it.

"Damn, if I had known that, I could've saved myself a pulled [calf] muscle," Hayes responded with a grimace.

Although the Buckeyes went on to lose to top-ranked Southern California 42–17 in the Rose Bowl in January, the stage was set for a series of some of the greatest games ever played in the Ohio State–Michigan series. Only the next time, and for the next three years, Griffin was destined to play a more prominent role for the Buckeyes.

The very next season, for instance, Griffin no longer had to worry about the fullbacks getting most of the carries. He was the centerpiece of an Ohio State offense that steamrolled opponents from the outset. And the defense was dominating. The season opener was a 56–7 rout of Minnesota, followed by a series of lopsided victories that included three shutouts in a row, over Northwestern (60–0), Illinois (30–0), and Michigan State (35–0). The win over Michigan State was especially sweet because the Spartans were the only Big Ten team to have beaten the Buckeyes the previous year in a strange game at East Lansing, which by then had become yet another city in the place up north that Hayes despised.

For one thing, Hayes didn't really care for Duffy Daugherty, the colorful Michigan State coach. Daugherty was many things Hayes was not. He often employed a fly-by-the-seat-of-your-pants approach that flew in the face of Hayes's belief that all great things were accomplished only through hard work and relentless, meticulous preparation. Plus Hayes believed that Daugherty lied and cheated whenever Daugherty thought he could get away with it—in recruiting, by influencing officials, whatever. Some of this would later be proven true; much of it was little more than the Hayes paranoia.

When the teams met in East Lansing on November 11, 1972, Hayes was determined to avenge a 17–10 loss to the Spartans the previous season in Columbus. But Daugherty had a secret weapon waiting for him. Earlier in the season, Michigan State had lost a couple of games because of poor field goal kicking. Daugherty didn't want to risk that happening again against Ohio State.

"Good God, there's got to be somebody on this campus who can kick field goals for us. I mean, we've got 50,000 students here. There's got to be a kicker among them somewhere," Daugherty complained to his assistant coaches.

A few days later, one of Daugherty's assistants produced Dirk Kryt, a chain-smoking exchange student from the Netherlands with a soccer background who had never before played and barely heard of American football. When they took him out to his first practice and asked him to kick off, he looked at the kick-coverage team facing him and walked to the opposite side of the football, turning his back to the team that was waiting to receive the kick—and attempted instead to kick the ball under the goal post behind him.

"That's how you do it in soccer," Kryt told Daugherty as the head coach rushed out to explain the game to his newfound kicker.

Kryt's first active duty came against Ohio State. When it was time for him to attempt his first field goal, Daugherty found him on the end of the bench, smoking a cigarette with his legs crossed "like a girl," as a teammate would later say. But Kryt went in and kicked the field goal. Another time, Daugherty found him flirting with girls in the stands behind the Michigan State bench. But again, he went in and got the job done.

When the day was done, Kryt had kicked a school-record four field goals in a 19–12 Michigan State victory. Hayes was the one smoking on the opposite sideline because he couldn't figure out who the new kid was, or where he had come from—or how he had been declared eligible to play against the Buckeyes on such short notice. Hayes also supposedly had spotted Kryt smoking cigarettes on the Michigan State sideline and was furious about it.

Meanwhile, Daugherty's response to Kryt's smoking habit was much more nonchalant.

"Coach, what about this kid smoking in the locker room and down on the bench and everything?" reporters asked. "Won't that break the training rules down for everybody?"

"No, because none of the other guys can kick," Daugherty responded.

By the time of the 1973 Ohio State–Michigan game, Archie Griffin was established as the best running back in America.

And he was only a sophomore. The Buckeyes also were undefeated, having swamped their first nine opponents by the combined total of 361 points to a mere 33. Only one opponent had scored more than seven points, and that was Iowa—which lost to the Buckeyes 55–13.

More often than not, the player clearing the way for the real estate claimed by Griffin was senior tackle John Hicks. He was dominant in a way that few Ohio State linemen had been before or would be in the years to follow.

"John and the other guys on the offensive line who blocked for me really were the key to us having such great offenses," Griffin insisted. "And that year, John definitely was the key to our offensive line. He was the leader of everything up front for us. He was very fiery and emotional, and he definitely was very confident. He was the guy who fired the rest of us up."

Sometimes Hicks seemed a little too confident to Griffin. Hicks was so confident of his ability to physically dominate the player lined up across from him that he would tip his hand about which way a running play was going to come.

"I'd come up to the line, look at my guy and say, 'Hey, we're coming at you with this one.' That used to drive Archie nuts," Hicks told author Bruce Hooley years later in the book *Ohio State's Unforgettables.*

"John, don't tell them what we're doing! Don't tell them where I'm going to be running! You're going to get me killed!" Griffin would plead.

Hicks would just smile.

"The way I looked at it, I didn't care if they knew or not—because even if they knew, they weren't going to stop us," he told Hooley.

He almost always was right.

Hayes was by now sixty years old. His health, never the greatest as he battled diabetes and other related problems, was starting to drag on his frenetic, workaholic lifestyle. But he approached the 1973 showdown with what seemed to be his usual vigor, knowing full well what was on the line: the Big Ten conference championship and the coveted trip to the Rose Bowl. Furthermore, the number-one-ranked Buckeyes would set themselves up for a shot at another national championship with a victory.

Like the Buckeyes, the Wolverines entered the contest undefeated and feeling dominant. They had not lost a game in Michigan Stadium in nearly four years. A record crowd of 105,223 would be waiting in Ann Arbor to do what it could to help keep that streak alive.

As the week progressed leading up to the big game, Hayes harbored a secret. His quarterback, the popular Cornelius Greene, had a thumb injury that was worse than anyone outside the Buckeyes' inner circle imagined.

"His thumb is swollen twice its normal size. What in the hell are we going to do?" one of the assistant coaches asked Hayes.

"I have a plan," Hayes insisted.

On Wednesday, Greene tried to throw some passes in practice. It was too painful. He sat out the rest of the week's workouts altogether, lest he risk making the injury worse simply by taking a snap the wrong way.

When the game began, Hayes's plan quickly became clear. Greene played, but he wasn't going to do much besides take the snap and hand the ball off, mostly to Griffin. Archie took the ball and ran it 30 times, gaining 165 yards. When Griffin didn't run it, someone else such as burly fullback Pete Johnson did. Greene didn't attempt a single pass until the final minute, when the Buckeyes tried futilely to break a 10–10 tie.

"We just couldn't risk him throwing with that thumb so swollen," Hayes later explained.

Fred Pagac, who played tight end for the Buckeyes from 1971–73 and later would become a longtime assistant coach, remembered that it was perhaps the most physical game he had ever played in.

"The Michigan games were always very physical. But that one was particularly brutal," Pagac said. "We just pounded on each other for three hours. We got out in front in the first half, but then they came back in the second. We couldn't hold them off completely and they were able to tie it."

The tie left both teams with 7-0-1 records in the Big Ten. But Michigan was 10-0-1 overall to 9-0-1 for the Buckeyes. The conference's athletic directors would vote to decide who would go to Pasadena. Although Ohio State associate athletic director Ed Weaver said that the vote already had been taken shortly after the game, Big Ten commissioner Wayne Duke said that no announcement would be made until the following afternoon from Chicago.

In Ann Arbor, Schembechler was certain it would be his team. In Columbus, Hayes quietly admitted that he had prepared his players emotionally for the fact that they probably would not be chosen. Hayes had been despondent since the outcome of the game, mumbling in the postgame interview in a voice so low that reporters could barely understand him.

"I guess you'd say we won the first half and they won the second. I can't consider a tie satisfactory," Hayes said.

In the other locker room, Schembechler seemed more content with the outcome after registering his fourth Big Ten championship (three were shared with other teams) in his five years as coach of the Wolverines.

"My guys have character. They fought and came back. I'm extremely proud of them," he said. "We didn't settle for a tie. We did everything we could to win."

Then he added that he believed his team deserved to go to the Rose Bowl.

Hayes remained quiet when he was asked if his team deserved to go.

"I have no opinion on the Rose Bowl," he muttered almost inaudibly. "I have nothing to say about it. If we're selected, we'll go."

Linebacker Randy Gradishar, who a year earlier had been instrumental in leading the Buckeyes' goal line stands in the 14–11 victory over Michigan, remembered staying over in Michigan with friends after the 10–10 tie. Hayes, perhaps too stunned to tell the outgoing senior otherwise, had given him permission to stay overnight in the state from up north.

"We were numb. We didn't know how to feel. You know how to react to a loss or to a win, but a tie? What did that mean?" Gradishar said.

Hayes had always been outspoken about other schools and what he perceived to be the deficiencies in the way their programs were run. He had made many enemies within the conference.

"I'm not very popular with those other athletic directors. I've never tried to be," he told family and coaching associates. "They're bound to vote for Michigan. They stand very strong within the conference politically. I'm already writing my concession speech."

But shortly before noon the following day, Hayes received a confidential phone message from Duke in Chicago, where the commissioner was preparing to tell the world: Ohio State was the choice of the athletic directors to represent the Big Ten in the Rose Bowl. Hayes smiled, and called his wife, Anne, almost immediately after hanging up. Then he said he couldn't say anything until the official announcement came down from Chicago, but he hummed a few bars of "California Here I Come" before abruptly hanging up.

When the announcement was made, Schembechler felt like Hayes must have in 1961 when that Rose Bowl was jerked out from under him at the last minute. Schembechler called the decision "tragic," and suddenly he was the one despondent.

Gradishar was driving back to Columbus from Michigan when he heard the news over the radio. "At that point," he said, "I just went nuts."

Awaiting the Buckeyes in Pasadena on New Year's Day 1974 was a rematch with Southern California, the team that had whipped them 42–17 in the previous year's Rose Bowl. The Big Ten, in fact, had lost the previous four Rose Bowls and there was talk that the conference was slipping, that it wasn't as good as the Pacific-10.

Hayes had a surprise in store for the Trojans, who thought for certain that virtually all the Buckeyes would do was hand the ball off to Archie Griffin and Pete Johnson. Instead, the supposedly inflexible Hayes spent much of the time leading up to the game working on the Ohio State passing game instead of the running game. Greene's thumb was healed, although Southern Cal had no way of knowing that. Hayes wanted to be prepared to pick and choose his spots, and then the plan was going to be to throw the ball.

Greene ended up setting up two touchdowns with his passing before scoring the go-ahead touchdown late in the third quarter to break open what had been a close game. He ended up completing six of eight passes overall for 129 yards. Griffin registered his 11th consecutive 100-yard rushing game by rambling for 149 yards on 22 carries, including the final touchdown of the day on a dazzling 47-yard run late in the fourth quarter as the Buckeyes rolled to a 42–21 victory.

Hayes was as euphoric afterward as he had been despondent five weeks earlier following the tie with Michigan.

"We've never been this good in a Rose Bowl game," he told reporters. "Any team that wins by three touchdowns over Southern Cal has to be pretty good."

In the opposing locker room, losing coach John McKay admitted that the Buckeyes were the best team he had faced all season. He also admitted that he had been caught off guard by Greene's timely passing. That was all Hayes needed to hear.

"We worked fifteen days on our passing and it paid great dividends," exclaimed Hayes, failing to point out that there had been a whopping thirty-seven days between the tie in Ann Arbor and the Rose Bowl victory. That meant the Buckeyes still devoted less than half their practice time to improving the passing game, even when it was deemed a priority.

Hayes then was asked if the Buckeyes, by virtue of their convincing victory and the fact that they were undefeated if not untied, deserved consideration as national champions. His eyes beamed at the thought of it. He had believed any chance for that slipped away with the frustrating tie to the team from up north, but maybe, just maybe, there still was a chance.

"Well," he began with his familiar lisp, "you know I'm a little biased. But based on what happened here today, yes, I'd certainly say we're number one."

Hicks said that the Buckeyes had been waiting for the chance to beat Southern California since the previous year's drubbing, which is what had made the tie at Michigan seem so disappointing—because the players, like Hayes, had thought it would cost them their chance at Rose Bowl revenge. For seniors like Hicks and Gradishar, not getting back to Pasadena for a shot at Southern Cal would have been devastating.

"That [1973 Rose Bowl] was the worst whipping any of us ever took during our careers," said Hicks, "and we promised Woody we would do something about it. We dedicated that year to doing that for him."

The Buckeyes had spent the eight weeks leading up to the Michigan game ranked number one. But the tie had dropped them to third in Associated Press football writers poll. This time, Ohio State would not get the break Hayes thought it deserved when it came to voting by third parties. Despite OSU's convincing win over Southern California in the Rose Bowl, Notre Dame was voted the national champion in the final AP poll; Ohio State was voted second. In the United Press International coaches poll, Ohio State finished third behind Alabama and Oklahoma. Notre Dame was fourth.

So the national championship eluded Hayes once again. In the Heisman Trophy voting, three Buckeyes finished in the top six—with Hicks finishing second behind winner John Cappelletti from Penn State. Griffin finished fifth; linebacker Gradishar, a two-time All-American, was sixth. It could be argued that this was Hayes's best team to date, but with the blemish of the tie with Michigan on the record, it wouldn't be so recorded in the history books.

7

Recruiting Tales . . . And Missed Opportunities

AS THE Buckeyes licked their wounds from another missed national championship opportunity in 1973, one player being recruited out of Coach Gerry Faust's high school powerhouse at Cincinnati Moeller High School was linebacker Mark Lang. Faust, who later would gain more notoriety as a failed college coach at Notre Dame and Akron, ran a tight high school program and tried to funnel as many kids as he could to the Fighting Irish, then coached by the legendary Ara Parseghian. Faust would not permit any college recruiters to talk to his players until their senior season was completed.

"If Gerry heard of it, he would have blackballed that recruiter," Lang said.

What the players at Moeller didn't always realize until after their senior seasons was that Faust intercepted as much of their recruiting mail as possible, too. Then he would throw it in boxes labeled by school and/or the players' names, not to be touched by anyone until the recruited player's senior year was over. It was the way he, and other high school coaches of the era, made certain his high school seniors focused on their final season without the distraction of trying to figure out where they were going to play next in college. Lang, for instance, had little idea that he was such a highly sought-after recruit until the day after Moeller lost in the Ohio high school state championship finals in 1973.

"That next day, the seniors had a meeting [with Faust] and the team manager started walking in with these boxes with all of the different recruiters from the schools that were interested in us," Lang said. "I had about four boxes full. It was kind of a surprise. In fact, I found it to be rather amazing."

Another Moeller standout, an offensive lineman named Harry Woebkenberg, who eventually would sign with Notre Dame, was delivered five boxes full of letters. As they all began to sift through the letters, it was only the beginning of what would be a frenetic recruiting process.

"They dumped those boxes on you there, and then you immediately started getting deluged with phone calls," Lang said.

Notre Dame called, of course. And for Lang, at least, so did Northwestern, Pittsburgh, Michigan, and Alabama. Local schools such as the University of Cincinnati and Miami of Ohio took a shot, too. As did, naturally, Ohio State. Most of the kids coached by Faust at the time wanted to attend Notre Dame, which, like Moeller, was a Catholic institution.

Lang was going along with the flow and thought he probably would go to Notre Dame, too. When he visited the university in South Bend, Indiana, he stopped in to see Parseghian. The coach asked Lang to have a seat. Then Parseghian leaned forward, a serious look on his face as he prepared to launch the first question of his interview.

Lang swallowed hard. He was a little nervous. The man sitting across from him was a college football coaching legend. Next to the Father, the Son, and the Holy Ghost, Notre

Dame's coach was the one thing his high school coach admired most. But Lang was not prepared for what came next out of Parseghian's mouth.

"What size shoe does your dad wear?" the coach asked.

"I'm sorry. What did you say?"

"I asked what size shoe does your dad wear?"

"Um, I'm not sure. I think it's a size 13."

"I see. And what size shoe does your mother wear?"

Lang swallowed again. His mind raced. What did this man want with his parents' shoe sizes? Was this some kind of joke?

"Um, I have no idea what size shoe my mother wears," he finally stammered.

Parseghian stared hard into Lang's eyes. Then he reached behind him and pulled out a piece of paper.

"I don't have to go off campus recruiting," Parseghian said. "I don't do it. Notre Dame is the most prestigious school in the country and I only want kids who want to come here. I don't need to go recruit. Do you understand?"

Lang nodded, and Parseghian continued.

"Now I have a scholarship here in hand to offer you, and you would be a fool not to take it."

Lang was confused at first, then a little angry. He quickly decided that he didn't like giving out his parents' shoe sizes, and he didn't like getting muscled into making such an important decision so quickly.

"Sir, with all due respect, I just started my visits and I would like to visit some other schools before I make my decision," Lang replied.

"He fluffed me off and left me at that point," Lang said. "It just kind of turned me off. . . . The only thing I could ever think of with the shoe stuff is that back then I was wrestling at 188 [pounds]. I played football at about 200, and I was a linebacker. But when I would wrestle I would get all the way down to 185—and the only thing I could think of was that he was wondering if I was going to grow more. I think my own shoe size at the time was an 11, by the way."

Shortly thereafter, Lang made his official visit to Ohio State. He was being recruited hard by assistant coach Ralph Staub, who also was heavily interested in landing tight end Greg Storer out of Moeller and considered the two high school buddies a package deal. The two took their visit to Columbus together, and Storer was assigned to stay with Rich Galbos, a receiver who had just finished up his senior season. Lang's roommates were Randy Gradishar, who was as fun-loving off the field as he was intense on it, and Rick Middleton, another linebacker who, like Gradishar, had only his senior season ahead of him. Staub, a devout Catholic, casually mentioned to Lang that he had two daughters about Lang's age.

"We'll be going to ten o'clock Mass Sunday morning. Would you like to come along with us?" Staub asked Lang.

"Fine, I'll be ready," Lang replied, not giving it much thought.

That Saturday night, Gradishar and the others decided to throw a party. Lang was warned that Gradishar liked to play practical jokes. At one point during the party, Gradishar emerged from the kitchen with some fresh-baked brownies. Lang ate a couple and thought they tasted pretty good. It wasn't until later that he learned Gradishar had plied the brownies with crushed Rolaids tablets, which when mixed with ample amounts of beer could cause fairly severe stomach cramping.

Lang partied on through anyway, eventually making his way to High Street with Gradishar and finally returning to Galbos's place sometime around two in the morning to find the party still going, but nearly over. Lang just wanted to go to sleep.

"Just crash on the couch over there," Gradishar said to Lang, pointing.

Lang staggered over, tumbled onto the couch, and was dead asleep before he knew it.

The next thing he knew, it was morning and Staub was standing over him. The coach was clearly perturbed.

"Mark, I'm out in my car. You have five minutes to get ready for Mass," he said.

Lang started to scramble up to apologize for oversleeping. But with his first movement, he knew something was wrong. Empty beer cans were piled all around him, even on top of him. There were dozens of them, maybe even hundreds. As Staub angrily turned for the door and Lang tried to get to his feet, the empty cans scattered.

"When I went to sleep, they piled about a hundred beer cans on my body," Lang said. "So when I get up, the beer cans go flying. I just thought I was going to be butchered. I went out to the car feeling about two inches tall. Oh man, [Staub] had a look to kill. So that was the start of my Ohio State career."

Staub apparently overlooked the beer can incident when he reported to Hayes about Lang. Not long after, Lang came home from Moeller one night after a long day of school and wrestling practice. As he walked down his parents' winding driveway, he was surprised to see a vehicle he did not recognize.

"I come walking down there one night about 6:30 and I see this old white El Camino parked in the driveway. I walked by it and I see this old beat-up AstroTurf in the back and I'm thinking, 'Who the hell is this?'" Lang said.

"I went in and there Woody was. He had been there since about three o'clock. My dad was a history nut. So was Woody, of course. They had read some of the same books and they had been in the living room just talking, and there

Woody was telling history stories. I sat down and mostly Woody talked about the war [World War II]. And he did it until about eleven o'clock.

"You name it, he went from one thing to another. I was fascinated and my dad was fascinated. He reminded me of my grandfather. I didn't know anything in terms of his cussing. He came across as the most polite man I had ever met in my life. So that kind of won me over. I liked the way he reacted with my dad and I liked my visit, so I chose Ohio State."

Perception met reality for Lang when he walked into his first Ohio State football meeting at the Scarlet and Gray Golf Course on the Columbus campus.

"Woody would say some funny things that would throw you off guard," Lang said. "Coming into my first day of practice, I'm thinking of Woody as a nice, old, grandfather-style man."

That changed as Hayes started ranting about what was going on over at Notre Dame, where several Fighting Irish players were in the news for allegedly being involved in a rape. Hayes didn't want any of his players making the eleven o'clock news for such nonsense. He was addressing the entire Ohio State team, but made it a special point to make certain the incoming freshmen were hanging on his every word.

"Boys, you have two heads—one up here and one down there," he said, pointing at his skull and then at his genitals. "The minute you let that one below start being your conscience, goddammit you will fuck anything and you will be a loser for the rest of your life. I had this one player in the '60s, and he was so low he would fuck a snake. You can't be like that and be successful in football or life. Think with the head you have up top; not with the one you have below."

Lang couldn't believe his ears. Was this the same gentle fellow who had visited his home and talked history for hours with his father?

"He's cussing and using 'fuck' every other word," Lang said. "Our eyes were about as wide as they could be. And inside we're laughing, just hearing him cuss. That was the start of our four years with Woody."

By the third week of the 1974 season, Archie Griffin's junior year, the Buckeyes were ranked number one in the nation again. All seemed right in Woody's world. His players were focused and beating the hell out of every team they played. By November, they were 8-0 and had beaten their opponents by the average score of 45–9.

Hayes relished the thought of pounding their next opponent—unranked Michigan State. The game would be played in East Lansing, but Hayes did not think that would be a major problem. This Ohio State team was too good. Plus Hayes knew how to work the team to a fever pitch. He spent much of the week privately telling his players and assistant coaches that he had no intention of losing to "those goddamn cheaters" from Michigan State.

By this time, Hayes had good reason to believe what he had long suspected of the Spartans' program. When Gerry Faust's vaunted Moeller High School team had lost in the Ohio state championship final during Mark Lang's senior season there, the team that won, Youngstown Cardinal Mooney, was powered by an explosive running back named Ted Bell. Every college coach in the country wanted to have Bell running the ball for him the next season, and the recruiting battle for him was intense. Southern California, for instance, had famous alumnus O. J. Simpson charter a private jet and personally escort Bell to Los Angeles for a recruiting visit. Somehow, though, Bell ended up at Michigan State.

To Hayes, it was no great mystery. He figured the Spartans, now coached by Denny Stoltz, had cheated. Aaron Brown, who would become a three-year starter at middle guard for Hayes's defense, had been recruited by the Spartans at the same time they were wooing Bell. Brown chose Ohio State, but he had stories to tell, which he relayed to Hayes.

Brown told Hayes that Michigan State had offered him illegal recruiting inducements under the table. He further informed him that he was certain what had led Bell to spurn so many other schools was that Michigan State had offered him an automobile, cash, and other illegal gifts. It was enough to convince Hayes that he finally had the evidence to land hated Michigan State in hot water with the NCAA, so he blew the whistle on them.

All of this was swirling in the background when the teams met on November 9, 1974, in East Lansing. Hayes was determined to have his boys take care of business and stay on track for what he believed would be a solid run at another national championship.

The game, however, did not go according to Woody's plan. As time ran down, the Buckeyes trailed 16–13 but were driving toward what they thought was going to be a game-winning touchdown. With just over 20 seconds remaining, they ran a play that got them down near the Michigan State goal line.

"I recall that play vividly to this day," Griffin said. "We had twenty-some seconds left and we had run a play. And our center couldn't get up because the Michigan State players wouldn't get off him. I couldn't blame them. They were trying to stall the game by lying on our center, so he couldn't get up and get off the next snap."

What happened next, though, was hard for Griffin or Hayes or any of the Buckeye faithful to imagine.

"We thought the officials would call delay of game or at least stop the clock—because we didn't have any timeouts left," Griffin said. "And so we tried to run a play, and we thought we got the play off. There was a fumble on the play and Brian Baschnagel picked the ball up for us and ran into the end zone.

"The referee called a touchdown, we thought we had won the football game, and we went to the locker room."

Some time passed—Griffin thought it was forty-five minutes, others thought a little less—but eventually Big Ten commissioner Wayne Duke appeared at the visitors locker room door and asked to speak with Hayes.

"You didn't get the play off, Woody. The clock had expired. Michigan State won the game," Duke told the incredulous Hayes.

Hayes couldn't believe what he was hearing. He immediately exploded.

"We did not lose this goddamn football game! You're taking it from us! We did not lose!" Hayes shouted.

Duke left before it could get any worse, but Hayes continued to rant and rave, swearing and cursing the very existence of Michigan State University.

"Goddammit, I'm tired of these goddamn cheaters! They cheated me before in recruiting and now they've cheated me again!" he shouted to his players. "I'm tired of this cheating. Goddammit, we're going to go into their locker room and have a fight! I'm tired of this cheating! We're going to go kick their asses—right now!"

As fate would have it, only a narrow hallway separated the two locker rooms. A riot was about to take place—one that surely would cost even Woody Hayes his job. Defensive tackle Nick Buonamici, one of the true characters in Ohio State football history, stood at the locker room door ready to burst across the hallway for his coach.

"You're right, Coach! Let's go get 'em! Let's kick their asses!" cried Buonamici.

Lang and some of the other bigger offensive and defensive players pushed up from behind, ready to go. Hayes was at the front of the mob and flung open the door, fully intending to rush across the hallway and burst into the Michigan State locker room to physically vent his hatred on this underhanded foe.

As the door opened, Hayes cast his eyes on a longtime Michigan State employee.

"The guy had been so excited about the upset win that he was running around, screaming," Lang recalled. "And right as Woody opened the door for us to come out, the guy winds up having a heart attack. He grasped at his chest, collapses—and people were all around him trying to do something.

"Woody sees it and shuts the door."

Then Hayes turned to his agitated players.

"Guys, we're going home," he told them quietly.

Hayes somber mood did not last long. As the team bus carrying Hayes attempted to pull out of the stadium parking lot a little while later, some celebrating Michigan State fans blocked the path.

"Run 'em over! Run those sonsofbitches over!" Hayes shouted to the bus driver when they wouldn't immediately get out of the way.

No one thought he was joking.

Despite the excruciating loss at Michigan State, the Buckeyes were ranked number four in the nation two weeks later, heading into the usual season finale against Michigan—and the game against the third-ranked Wolverines was set for Columbus. In a game later described by *Columbus Dispatch* sports editor Hornung as "more unusual than outstanding," the Buckeyes held on for a 12–10 win. Placekicker Tom

Klaban's four field goals accounted for all of Ohio State's scoring, marking the first time in 81 games a Hayes-coached team had won without scoring a touchdown.

"We didn't care. It was still a win, and it was still Michigan," Griffin said.

It also meant another trip to the Rose Bowl, where Hayes figured a victory over fifth-ranked Southern California might mean Ohio State, now back up to number three in the nation, might have a shot at the national championship after all. Alas, it was not to be—this time the Trojans pulled out an 18–17 victory, leaving the Bucks with a record of 10-2.

In a small measure of consolation, Griffin was voted the Heisman Trophy, signifying that he was the best college football player in the nation. He was only a junior, but admitted later that he had had his eyes on the coveted trophy since finishing fifth in the Heisman voting a year earlier.

"In the back of my mind, I thought I had a chance to win the Heisman as a junior, mainly because the four guys who finished ahead of me the year before had graduated," Griffin said.

Rushing for 1,695 yards—breaking his own Big Ten conference and Ohio State school records for a single season—had more to do with it than who was left in the race. Griffin also broke Steve Owens's NCAA record of 17 consecutive games with at least 100 yards rushing. When the Heisman voting was tallied, Griffin was the winner by more than 1,100 votes over running back Anthony Davis of Southern California. Hayes beamed with pride at Griffin's selection. Each year, the player and coach had grown closer in their personal relationship, to the point where Griffin considered the coach a second father and Hayes considered the running back another son.

"He's a better young man than he is a football player," said Hayes, "and he's the best football player I've ever seen."

Hayes desperately wanted another shot at a national championship—not only for himself and the program, but especially for Griffin. He was getting older, his health worsening. He privately hinted to friends that he was looking forward to coaching Griffin's final season—but that he wasn't sure how much longer beyond that he was willing to coach. In the summer of 1974, as he was preparing to embark on that final season with Griffin, Hayes suffered a mild heart attack.

As he recovered in University Hospital in Columbus, among those inquiring about his health was entertainer Bob Hope, who was visiting the city to play in Jack Nicklaus's pro-am golf tournament. Hope arrived at the hospital unannounced to visit Hayes, talking for more than an hour before Hope had to head to Port Columbus airport to catch a flight. Among other subjects, they talked of Vietnam and their shared interest in making trips there to boost the morale of the U.S. troops. Hope told Hayes that he had once met General George Patton, Hayes's hero; Hayes mentioned that he had met Patton's son during one of the latter's tours of Vietnam.

Soon enough Hayes felt ready enough to go back to work. Doctors were concerned, but in the end convinced him to make only one minor concession: on those cold winter days when the wind was whipping the snow through the air, could the coach please refrain from wearing his trademark white short-sleeve shirts? Hayes agreed to try to remember to wear a coat on such afternoons, but he did little to cut back on his work schedule.

Meanwhile, Griffin was feeling pressure to become the first player to ever win back-to-back Heisman Trophies—and the season hadn't yet begun.

"I used to think about it all the time," Griffin said. "But that put too much pressure on me, when I thought about it like that.

"Coach Hayes used to always say this saying: 'You're either getting better or you're getting worse. You're never at the same level.' It was warped thinking on my part, but I thought that for me to get a little bit better, I needed to win it again. And that was a little too much pressure. I didn't need to be thinking that way."

Griffin found peace one evening while reading the Bible.

"I read a verse in the book of Psalms, the 37th chapter, the fourth verse, where it said: 'Delight yourself in the Lord and He will give you the desires of your heart.' And when I read that verse, it was like somebody lifted a big weight off my shoulders," Griffin said.

"That allowed me to take control over things that I had control over—because I had no control over how people were going to vote for the Heisman Trophy. All I could do was go out and practice as hard as I could practice, and be prepared as well as I could mentally and physically for the games.

"In actuality, what the verse told me was that my job was to find joy serving God—and that if I did that, He would do one of two things: He would take that desire away of me wanting to win that second Heisman Trophy, or He'd give it to me as a gift."

With the burden of trying too hard to repeat as Heisman Trophy winner lifted at least in Griffin's own mind, the running back's senior season went off as if it were scripted. Hayes was behind the only real hitch in Griffin's double Heisman hopes. He had assembled a team seemingly so much better than the rest of the Big Ten schools that Griffin rarely played much more than a half. And in goal line situations, Hayes liked to order the ball handed off to Pete Johnson, his big, physical fullback. The cut in playing time and lack of touchdown opportunities helped keep Griffin healthy and fresh; but in a more statistic-conscious Heisman era when teams weren't playing every week on television, it also kept him from matching his rushing totals from a year earlier.

Griffin, however, was at peace with himself. Soothed by the Bible verse that continued to surge through his brain, he helped the Buckeyes run over every opponent they faced—beginning with a 21–0 shutout against 11th-ranked Michigan State back at East Lansing in the very first game of the year. That was followed by a hard-fought 17–9 victory over number seven Penn State and a 32–7 triumph over North Carolina, setting up what many thought could be a Rose Bowl preview in an early October game at UCLA, which was ranked 13th in the nation at the time.

The Buckeyes, who began the season ranked number three, made it look all too easy—and their 41–20 triumph on the road vaulted them into the top ranking nationally. They would remain there the rest of the regular season, rolling over most Big Ten opponents by ridiculous scores. By midseason, Griffin ran past the NCAA career rushing record of 4,715 yards, held by Cornell's Ed Marinaro, and the Buckeyes as a team were running past everyone. Iowa went down 49–0, followed by Wisconsin (56–0) and Purdue (35–6). Indiana hung around for a while before losing 24–14, but that contest was followed by routs of Illinois (40–3) and Minnesota (38–6), leaving only the season finale against Michigan.

As usual, it wouldn't be easy overcoming Michigan. The game was to be played in Ann Arbor, where Michigan had won 41 games over six years. Hayes hadn't won there since 1967, and held a slim 3-2-1 edge in the series since Bo Schembechler had become coach. Furthermore, the Wolverines were having a dynamite season of their own, entering the contest ranked fourth in the nation.

For nearly three quarters, Michigan dominated the game while building a 14–7 lead. Hayes thought the game looked bleak. Even Griffin couldn't get the ground game going, and in the end would have his NCAA record streak of consecutive 100-yard rushing games snapped at 31 as he was limited to a mere 46 yards.

So with a little over four minutes left in the game, the Buckeyes turned to the pass—a sure sign of their desperation. Quarterback Cornelius Greene crafted an 11-play, 80-yard drive, completing a 17-yard pass to wingback Brian Baschnagel and two passes in a row to Lenney Willis for gains of 14 and 18 yards. Greene also handed off to Griffin for an 11-yard scamper that probably was Griffin's best run of the day, and scrambled another time for a 12-yard gain of his own. All that was left was to hand the ball off to Johnson, who registered the second of his three touchdowns by bulling in from the half-foot line on fourth-and-goal. Knowing he needed only a tie to clinch a Rose Bowl berth, Hayes ordered the extra point kicked to produce a 14–14 tie—although he later denied playing for the tie even though he admitted never even considering a two-point conversion attempt.

"There was still time to get the ball back, and we figured we could move it into position for a field goal," he explained.

Actually, they did better than that. When sophomore defensive back Ray Griffin, Archie's younger brother, intercepted a pass thrown by Michigan quarterback Rick Leach and returned it to the Michigan three-yard line, all Hayes had to do was direct Greene to hand the ball off to Johnson again for the fullback's third touchdown of the day and 23rd of the season. With 2:19 left, the defense had only to hold and the 21–14 victory was Ohio State's.

"Our greatest comeback victory," Hayes gushed afterward.

Griffin said it epitomized every Michigan game he ever played in.

"You talk about close and tough and hard fought, all of those games were just that," Griffin said. "And I think the reason behind it was that the personalities of the players involved in the games, and certainly the coaches, Bo and Woody, were so similar and so familiar with each other. They both knew each other very well. And they were both fierce competitors who would do everything in their power to win those football games.

"That game my senior year sticks out in my mind. That was very, very special because it was at Michigan and it broke that long streak they had going where they hadn't lost a game at home in years. To come back the way we did and score two touchdowns in the last four minutes to win that football game, well, that was really something. To beat them at their place under all those circumstances was truly outstanding."

The win set up the Rose Bowl rematch from earlier in the season that had been expected against UCLA. One more victory and Hayes would have the national championship he had sought since capturing his last one seven years earlier. Privately, Hayes hinted to assistant coaches that he might retire if, as expected, the Buckeyes waltzed over the foe they had pummeled by three touchdowns earlier in the year. Even some of the players picked up on it.

But as usual, Hayes was concerned. He thought his team was overconfident. He always worried about them going to California and soaking up too much sunshine and fun prior to the Rose Bowl, but this time he may have let a little overconfidence seep into his own mind, too. The Buckeyes were loose and confident, perhaps a little too much of both.

They not only had Griffin, who already had over 1,000 yards rushing, but also Johnson, who would finish with 1,029 yards and a school and Big Ten record 26 rushing touchdowns. The 6-foot-1, 247-pound Johnson, whose primary duty was to block for Griffin, averaged 4.6 yards per carry and made a first down on 34 of the 44 times he carried on third down, a remarkable individual conversion rate. They had the seasoned Greene at quarterback and a dominant defense that had already proven it could stuff the Bruins' high-flying offense.

"We had destroyed them in the regular season," Lang said. "It was 41–20 and they scored two or three touchdowns in the last quarter when all of the subs were in. It was being rumored by the assistant coaches that Woody was going to announce his resignation and go out with Archie as national champ. All the assistant coaches were talking about it.

"So we go to play them and the first half just wasn't going our way. We were just looking like crap. Well, the problem was we were out partying every night because everybody assumed we were going to win this easily, hands down."

At halftime, with the Buckeyes trailing, a dejected Hayes entered the locker room and started to address the team. But then he stopped. To some players, he seemed a little overly emotional.

"I will never forget it," Lang said. "Normally he would have had a rah-rah speech."

Instead, Hayes quietly stammered, "Guys, there is something I want to tell you."

Then he stopped. Everyone waited for what was going to come next. But after a pause, Hayes seemed to change his mind about what he was going to say.

"No, dammit, let's wait until this game is over. We have to go out there and kick their ass first!" he shouted.

This time, it wasn't to be. UCLA, then ranked number 11 in the country and the overwhelming underdogs, ended up pulling off a 23–10 upset over the number one Buckeyes. There was no national championship; no triumphant ride into the sunset for Hayes alongside the departing Griffin.

"I'm convinced that if we would have beaten UCLA in Archie's senior year, that would have been Woody's last game," Lang said. "It was like he was going to say he was getting ready to quit when he came in to talk to us at halftime, but he pulled off of it. Nothing happened and we ended up losing the game.

"That was the only time I really saw Woody unravel. On the plane ride home, he didn't say anything. We had experienced some other losses, but this time he didn't say anything. For the next two weeks, you couldn't find the man. That was the only time I really saw him shook up."

Griffin said that he doesn't share the perception that Hayes held back a retirement speech at halftime of the Rose Bowl game, but in general he agrees with Lang's assessment of Hayes.

"I really believe that he would have retired if we had won that game," Griffin said. "I really believe he would have done that. . . . It would have been a fitting end for him."

As a small consolation, Griffin ended up winning his second Heisman Trophy. Despite having lesser numbers than during his junior season, he still rushed for 1,450 yards. Johnson scored most of the touchdowns—proving once again Hayes's undying allegiance to a big, bruising fullback and his Robust T goal line formation—but Griffin did rush for four. In the end, it was enough to allow Griffin to beat out two other very capable running backs: California's Chuck Muncie and Southern California's Ricky Bell.

"A lot of people thought that would cost me the Heisman, giving the ball to Pete Johnson so much at the goal line," said Griffin, who finished his career with an NCAA record 5,589 rushing yards. "But the number of touchdowns I scored never bothered me. I always just felt everyone had a role at Ohio State, and you played whatever role Coach Hayes put you in to the best of your abilities. . . . So I didn't think that would hurt me as much as some other people. I didn't think that [the lack of yards and touchdowns] would hurt me as much as I just didn't believe they would give the

Heisman to the same person twice. They had never done that."

To this day, Griffin is the only player to capture it twice.

Hayes, meanwhile, had received two dozen roses and a congratulatory note from President Nixon after beating Michigan. Hayes took the roses over to University Hospital and gave one to each patient he met until he ran out. One was an older man who offered a recruiting tip to Hayes, suggesting he send someone out to Ironton to scout an obscure offensive lineman.

Upon his return to his office, Hayes called in the assistant coach whose recruiting area encompassed Ironton.

"Have you checked this kid out?" he asked.

"Yeah. I've seen him play. He's not bad. He played with a lot of heart. But I don't think he's good enough to play for us."

"Well, go check him out again. Take a closer look. I think there might be something there."

The player in question, Kenny Fritz, would become an All-American guard for the Buckeyes. But much would happen before then.

8

The Punch Line

MARK LANG never got to block for Archie Griffin. A linebacker in high school, Lang moved to backup nose tackle for his freshman and sophomore years.

Griffin was gone from Ohio State as of 1976, beginning his career in the National Football League just down the road from Columbus with the Cincinnati Bengals. There also was some fallout on the coaching staff from what happened at the end of the previous season. Certain Hayes was going to retire and figuring he would get the head coaching job, Ralph Staub was surprised when Woody stuck around. Staub decided to take the head coaching position at the University of Cincinnati instead, much to Hayes's dismay.

Lang and some other veterans were shuffled to new positions, with Lang going from the defensive line to the offensive line. Switching an athlete from one position to another, even from offense to defense or vice versa, was a common practice for the Buckeyes under Hayes, who recruited the best athletes he could find and didn't mind if several of his recruits had played the same position in high school. Yesterday's star prep running back became tomorrow's star collegiate defensive back more than once—and in the meantime, successful recruitment of the best running backs in the state would keep them from going somewhere else to play. If they weren't playing right away at Cincinnati, Bowling Green, Miami of Ohio, or one of the other Big Ten schools, the potential for them causing damage to the Ohio State program was eliminated.

This was a practice that would cease in later years when the NCAA started limiting scholarships. Then a player who might have been the second or third running back at Ohio State, or perhaps converted to another position where he could start, ended up going to the Mid-American Conference schools or previously second-tier Big Ten schools, where they were assured of starting right away. That wasn't a concern for Hayes as he neared the end of his run, or anytime before that.

By his senior season in 1976, Lang and the rest of the seniors knew Hayes's practice routine—and how to deliberately disrupt it just to see Hayes drop a megaton self-implosion for their amusement.

"Every day, the first play Woody would run was a Fifty-two. All it was was a tailback dive where the guard and center would double the nose tackle and the fullback would isolate on the linebacker, and it would open up a hole for the tailback to run through," Lang said. "That was his bread-and-butter play. If you didn't get at least three or four yards, he would just go bonkers.

"So the sad thing is that the defense knew every day exactly what was coming. So if they wanted to be a pain in the butt, they would overstack it and the back wouldn't get his usual three or four or five yards. Well, one day we ran the play and the defense decided to mess with us and we only got like two or three yards. Woody went nuts."

Hayes charged into the offensive huddle in a rage and literally began throwing punches.

"We get back to the huddle and he starts with me," Lang said. "He punches me in the stomach and goes around and, one by one, punches everyone in the huddle. But he stops on Greg Storer and didn't punch Greg."

All the while, Hayes was muttering to himself.

"Goddamn, goddamn, goddamn. How can we be this goddamn bad?" Hayes stammered with his customary lisp.

Lang tried to stop himself from laughing, but found the whole scene too humorous. He started to crack a smile.

"Just then he looks up at me. I'm half laughing," Lang said.

Hayes peered incredulously at the smiling lips beneath the facemask.

"Goddammit, Lang. What is so goddamn funny?" he demanded.

"Coach, you never punched Greg Storer. You left him out," Lang said.

Storer, Lang's teammate since their days together at Cincinnati Moeller High School, couldn't believe his ears. His eyes widened, locking with Lang's.

Hayes stood in front of Lang, staring. Then he walked over to Storer and punched the tight end in the stomach with every ounce of energy he could muster, doubling Storer over. As Storer fought to catch his breath, Hayes turned back to everyone else in the huddle.

"Okay, can we go hit them on the other side of the line now?"

Most of the Ohio State offensive linemen of the era shared a dirty secret.

"Back then the reason I could get away with being so

small was you could chop-block, which was hitting below the knee," Lang said. "And that is how we did a lot of our blocking."

It drew scrutiny and some unwanted national attention when, in 1976, a national magazine wrote how rampant chop-blocking in college and professional football was ending the careers of many players. The Ohio State program was among those singled out for condoning the technique. Lee Corso was the head coach at Indiana at the time, and after one game an angry Corso confronted Alex Gibbs, OSU's offensive line coach, about the blocking scheme that had taken two Indiana players out of the contest. Lang was the starting center at the time, with Bill Lukers at right guard and Jim Savoca at left guard. The starting tackles were Chris Ward on the left side and Lou Pietrini on the right.

"We had put out four players to that point, either broke their legs or did knee damage," Lang admitted.

The magazine article alleging Ohio State's abuses came out just before the Michigan game in 1976. Reporters assailed Hayes, asking him about it. The coach refused to answer their questions, but the accusations bothered him. He wasn't so much against doing whatever it took to win, to a degree, but he didn't like the idea that the program's reputation could be tarnished by these unsavory accusations. He also was bothered by the thought that some of his players could be ending the careers of other players, even if they didn't have the good sense to play for the Buckeyes instead of against them. Hayes called his offensive linemen together and told them to be more careful in the way they were executing their blocks.

Gibbs, however, later made it clear to his linemen what he expected them to do.

"If you allow your guy to make a play because you don't

chop-block," said Gibbs, "then you won't be playing. . . . If you're not cutting somebody, you'd better be cutting the referee."*

As usual, all things reached a fever pitch before the Michigan game in 1976. Another trip to the Rose Bowl was at stake, as the team, even sans Griffin, had proven formidable enough to shake off an early one-point loss to Missouri and a 10–10 tie with fourth-ranked UCLA to win all of its Big Ten contests. Michigan did the same, and the November 20 showdown for the Rose Bowl bid would be played in Columbus.

The Monday prior to the game, Hayes and the boys gathered for the usual team meeting. Only this was to kick off preparation for Michigan week, and therefore it was even more intense than usual. Hayes had told all the players to be there and be on time, and that there could be no exceptions.

"If you're late," he warned, "you won't play in the game."

As the meeting was about to begin, Hayes asked defensive coordinator George Hill if everyone was in attendance.

"Um, everyone but Nick Buonamici, Coach," Hill answered.

Buonamici was the high-strung, intense kid from a poor family in the Bronx who "never worked out and wasn't a good athlete—but when it came to game day he was the meanest SOB you ever met," according to Lang.

Hayes started pacing at the news that Buonamici, one of his starting defensive tackles, wasn't there.

"We'll wait a couple more minutes," he told Hill.

About five minutes went by, and Hayes's face was getting redder by the minute. A megaton self-implosion was about to occur.

"Goddammit, he's off the team! George, when he gets here tell him I don't want to see him ever again! He's off the team!"

---

*The chop-block was ruled illegal in college football two years later.

Then Hayes, standing beside a small podium, tried to compose himself and began the team meeting with yet another history lesson as it related to football and life, at least in Hayes's mind. About ten minutes into his carefully calculated monologue designed to begin the psychological buildup for the Michigan game, Buonamici sauntered into the meeting room. Most of the players were dressed in shorts. The room was hot. But Buonamici, they noticed, was wearing a pair of red Buckeye sweatpants.

Hayes exploded again at the mere sight of him.

"Goddammit, Nick, you're off the team! Get the hell out of here!" Hayes shouted.

Buonamici stopped, and looked hurt.

"But Coach, I did it for you," he stammered.

"What the hell do you mean? What did you do for me?"

"Goddammit, I did it for you, Coach. I swear I did."

The emotional Buonamici looked almost as if tears were welling up in his eyes.

"What the hell are you talking about, Nick?" Hayes demanded.

With this, Buonamici jumped up onto a table next to the podium that Hayes was standing behind. He pulled up his sweatpants and revealed a giant tattoo so freshly applied to his calf that it was still bleeding. It depicted a large vulture with an Ohio State emblem on top of several skeleton heads of Michigan players, presumably picking apart their dead bones.

Hayes loved it. Now he was the one with tears welling up in his eyes.

"Goddammit, this is great! We're going to kick their ass!" he screamed.

Needless to say, Buonamici was back on the team. But it didn't do much good. The eighth-ranked Buckeyes lost 22–0 to fourth-ranked Michigan and had to settle for an Orange

Bowl date with Colorado, which they won 27–10 to finish the first post-Griffin season with a respectable but disappointing 9-2-1 record.

Now another dynamic was beginning to work against Hayes and Ohio State when it came to the recruiting game. Word was leaking out about Hayes's health, and about the possibility of his retirement. It began to show when the Buckeyes tried to recruit some of the top talent in Ohio, oftentimes going head-to-head with Michigan. One such recruit in 1977 was Mike Trgovac, who would go on to gain fame as an All-Big Ten player and a second-team All-American before coaching at the college and, later, NFL levels.

As a kid growing up in Youngstown, there was no doubt about where Trgovac dreamed of playing his college football. The second oldest of four brothers, Mike had the size the other Trgovacs lacked. His mother used to joke that he ate not only his portions at the dinner table, but those of his brothers as well. When it came to football, he had a passion for the game and for the way Woody Hayes's Ohio State Buckeyes played it.

"I was a huge Ohio State fan. Huge. I hated Michigan," said Trgovac, who later became defensive coordinator for the NFL's Carolina Panthers in Super Bowl XXXVIII. "Some of the fondest memories I have of my dad are from in the fall, when we'd be working outside in the yard, raking leaves or something, and listening to the Ohio State games on the radio. You didn't have all the games on TV at the time. And the big thing then was whether or not Archie Griffin was going to get a hundred [yards rushing]. He went through that whole streak of gaining a hundred yards. We would sit there and say, 'He's gonna get it! He's gonna get it!' And me and my dad would talk about that and whatever else was happening in the game while we worked outside in the yard."

The Trgovacs had another family tradition that revolved around Columbus. Each year, Ed Trgovac would take Mike and his two younger brothers down to the Ohio State campus to attend the state high school wrestling tournament. One year, when Trgovac was a high school freshman, the boys got free of their father for a brief mischievous moment.

"We broke into the Horseshoe, broke into Ohio State Stadium, and it was turf at that time. There was a piece of turf over one of the drains, and I ripped it off," Trgovac said. "Me and my brothers snuck in there and my little brother— God, he had to be in about sixth grade—we stuffed the turf under his shirt, figuring that if anybody saw us they wouldn't expect the little one to be carrying the turf. . . .

"I just remember getting outside the stadium and all of us running our asses off so we wouldn't get caught. Tommy had that turf stuck down inside his shirt and it was all wet, because it was February and it had been snowing and raining and stuff. We came out and we just ran; we ran back to the hotel. . . .

"I remember my poor little brother, he was running with that thing under his shirt and he was just soaking wet. He was almost crying. And my other brother, Johnny, who was a year younger than me, we were both older than him and running faster than him. He was trying to catch up with that turf under his belly."

Trgovac kept that prized piece of turf long after his loyalty to Ohio State began dissipating. He eventually hid it underneath a loose ceiling tile in his bedroom back in Youngstown, occasionally pulling it out to look at it and dream of one day playing on the field from which it had been heisted.

"I was a huge Ohio State fan until my senior year in

high school," Trgovac said. "I never thought I would go to Michigan until I went to a game there. And that's where I met Bo [Schembechler]. I saw the Minnesota game. I believe Tony Dungy was their quarterback, for Minnesota. I just fell in love for the place there and got a great feel for Bo.

"Still, you come back to Ohio and your emotions die down. That was my first trip that I took to watch a game. What happened is that my senior year in high school, I went to the Ohio State–Michigan game."

It was the game when Rick Leach, then a junior quarterback for Michigan, shredded the Buckeyes 22–0 despite Nick Buonamici's tattoo.

"I remember [Ohio State] got me tickets up in the stands, but I wanted to get down in there," Trgovac said. "So I was walking the sidelines and I ended up watching from the Michigan sidelines. I sort of ended up migrating over there. Obviously they won the game, so they were a lot happier than the Ohio State guys. And it was played at Ohio State.

"That was the first time I really felt, 'Hey, I might end up going to Michigan.'"

As a senior at Austintown Fitch High School near Youngstown in 1977, he was recruited hard by both schools and several others. His perception of the Buckeyes was that Hayes probably wouldn't be around for his full college career, and that tipped the scales in the favor of Michigan.

"First of all, the guy who recruited me [for Michigan] was Tom Reed. He did a real good job on me. And then when I met Bo, he was really a lot like my father," Trgovac said. "And at that time, when I got recruited by Ohio State, it was a little bit shaky there. Woody was coming down to the end. I didn't feel the same sense of loyalty to the program that I did when I went to Michigan. You could just feel that it was kind of coming down to the end there [for Woody], and I've always been the kind of guy who was around a steady home, a

steady environment. My high school was a steady program. I didn't like shake-ups and changes a whole lot."

Not that Hayes didn't try to convince the Ohio kid, who was named the state's Defensive Lineman of the Year following his senior season at Austintown Fitch, to come to Ohio State. Hayes tried. He even put on the double-full-court press, bringing his wife, Anne, with him to help convince the parents that Columbus was the place Trgovac ought to be.

"The hardest thing was when he brought me down to my basement, by myself. He's Woody Hayes and you're an Ohio boy. He was hitting me pretty hard, so that was the hardest thing," Trgovac said.

"My mother wanted me to go to Ohio State. She told me she was going to make me a little afghan blanket of whatever school I ended up going to. She actually bought some scarlet and gray yarn and put it on the kitchen table. She was ready to start that afghan. I told her 'You might not want to buy that yarn just yet,'" Trgovac said.

"I kind of knew where I was going, but it was one of those deals where I was actually afraid to say it—because I knew it was going to be hard on some people I knew. I knew some people in Ohio were going to give me shit."

Trgovac remembers precisely what Hayes told him once they were by themselves in the basement.

"You know, you're an Ohio kid. You need to be going to Ohio State. We'd love to have you, and you know you'd get a quality education," Hayes told him.

Trgovac mostly stayed silent. Then Hayes told him that he knew he was considering going to Michigan.

"I'm going to tell you something right now. You go to that school up north and you'll regret it. An Ohio kid going to that school up north trying to come back to Ohio after he's done playing isn't going to find a job anywhere. No one will want to hire you because anyone who goes to that school to

play his college football when Ohio State wants him is disloyal," Hayes said.

It took everything Trgovac had to stop himself from saying he would come to Ohio State. But in his heart, he did not believe Hayes was going to be around much longer. Plus he had hit it off with Schembechler, Reed, and the rest of the Michigan folks. They seemed to have a brighter immediate future.

"It was funny because that year [1977] in the Big 33 Ohio [vs. Pennsylvania] All-Star game, which was played up in Canton, I got the defensive MVP and B. J. Dickey got the offensive MVP. Dickey was going to Michigan also. That had to kill Woody. He was PISSSSED off! In fact, one of their coaches told my high school coach, 'Don't ever ask us for another favor again!'

"You look back on it and it did look real bad for them. Two Michigan kids getting the MVPs of the Ohio all-star game."

This was a perception Hayes was finding himself having to fight with annoying frequency. He was beginning to lose out to Schembechler on top Ohio prospects more than ever.

Signs that Hayes was slipping became more frequent the following season. There was a 29–28 loss to Oklahoma in front of 88,113 at Ohio Stadium. The Sooners scored a touchdown and a field goal in the final one minute, 29 seconds to pull out the victory. It wasn't an upset; the Buckeyes entered the game ranked fourth in the country, the Sooners third. But even after scoring their late touchdown, the Sooners trailed 28–26 upon getting stuffed on a two-point conversion attempt. The Buckeyes prepared for the onside kick that was to come next, but Oklahoma placekicker Uwe von Schamann

squibbed it just right and Oklahoma recovered. A few plays later, von Schamann shocked the home crowd by kicking a 41-yard field goal for the win.

There was another 14–6 loss to Michigan with the Big Ten championship and a Rose Bowl trip hanging in the balance. The game was in Ann Arbor, and Mike Trgovac very nearly played a key role in the outcome, much to his horror.

"What happened in the game was they were driving on us and they ran an option play and they fumbled the ball and we recovered it. I was a freshman and I jumped off-sides, almost, but I got back on that play," Trgovac said. "I can still see the TV replay of that, showing me as I walk off the field to the sidelines after that play. I'm holding my head and looking for a flag. I'm thinking, 'My whole career could be ruined.' And it could have been.

"They fumbled the ball there, but if I would have been called for off-sides they could have kicked a field goal there or gone in to score a touchdown. My stomach was just in knots. Luckily they didn't throw the flag, or my whole career could have been different."

Instead, it was another loss to Michigan for Hayes. In what would prove to be his final appearance in Michigan Stadium, Hayes went out in typical style. On the play described by Trgovac, the Buckeyes were driving with about four minutes to go in the game, hoping a touchdown and two-point conversion would tie the score. But after reaching the Michigan 10-yard line, quarterback Rod Gerald took a hit in the backfield and lost the fumble to the Wolverines at the 18-yard line. The chance for a tie was lost along with the fumble, and Hayes exploded in typical fashion on the sideline.

After ripping off his headphones and slamming them into the turf in disgust, the enraged Hayes turned to find a cameraman from ABC-TV, Mike Freedman, closely filming his every move. Hayes was furious, and later described the scene for Hornung of the *Columbus Dispatch*.

"We were going down the field with a chance to score in a great game for a great championship, and we lost the ball and a chance to score a touchdown. I was sick about it—and as I turned around, right there in my face was this damn television camera. I took a swing at it."

The roundhouse missed, but Big Ten and Ohio State officials were not amused. Although Big Ten commissioner Wayne Duke conceded that Freedman had violated the NCAA-approved TV camera restraining line of eight to 10 yards—some observers placed Freedman as close as to within two yards of Hayes when the incident occurred—he let Hayes know that kind of behavior would no longer be tolerated. He slapped the coach with a one-year probation. Ohio State president Harold Enarson issued a statement backing Duke's position.

"The cruel fact is that a coach is subjected to great provocation. However, this does not justify assault on another person. Coach Hayes understands that," Enarson said.

The loss sent the Buckeyes packing to the Sugar Bowl, where Hayes was to meet another fading legend face-to-face in Alabama's Paul "Bear" Bryant. But it didn't go the way Woody wanted.

The offense struggled against the Crimson Tide and the Buckeyes fell behind 13–0. But the defense, which would, in fact, force a total of 10 Alabama fumbles, was playing great. Following a turnover, the Buckeyes drove inside the Alabama five-yard line just before the half. They had one timeout remaining when Hayes called for a running play that went nowhere. The clock kept running. Bewildered players looked for a signal to call a timeout, but none came.

"Instead of calling a timeout where we could have thrown the ball like twice, he didn't do anything and we ended up not scoring. We didn't kick a field goal or any-thing," Lang said. "He came in and he was so flustered with the assistant coaches at halftime that we ended up getting blown out 35–6. I mean, I've never felt so flustered or screwed in a game all my life. We weren't playing too bad in the first half, but then we fell apart after that goal line fiasco. Maybe that was the start of him losing it a little, too."

Lang by then had witnessed yet another side of Hayes. He was sitting at his locker one day when the coach came up to him.

"Mark, I have a tradition where I take a senior with me down to the Children's Hospital to visit with some folks and sign autographs. I want you to come with me," Hayes said.

"That's great, Coach. I'd love to go," Lang replied.

So they went to the hospital together.

"Mark, I want you to meet a little girl. This is my fa-vorite person. I always talk to her," Hayes said upon their ar-rival.

"Great, Coach. I'd love to meet her and talk with her, too."

Hayes grabbed Lang's arm, tears in his eyes.

"I'm not sure you understand, Mark. This girl, she was burned as a baby and she was burned over 99 percent of her body. She's seven years old now, but she's had something like over a hundred operations. You've probably never seen any-thing like what you're about to see, but I want you to talk to her just like she's a normal person—because inside, that's just what she is."

Lang walked inside the room and saw that the girl was lying face down. She had to lie on her stomach.

"Go on, son. Get down under there and talk to her."

Lang crawled under the bed and, lying flat on his back,

looked up at the girl. There was a television mounted under the bed as well, and there was a hole cut in the bed so the little girl could breathe and communicate and watch TV to pass the time. As Hayes had predicted, she was thrilled to have some company.

"So I was down there, talking to her. This girl was acting like nothing was wrong at all. She was happy to see someone who would spend a little time with her. I'm almost crying at that point. I'm looking at her life—and that was enough to bring me to the brink of tears," Lang said.

But he tried to do as Hayes had instructed, engaging her in casual conversation.

"Woody visits me all the time," she said. "He brings me candy and all kinds of stuff. He's great."

After about fifteen minutes or so, a nurse came into the room and interrupted, saying that Lang could find Woody in the intensive care unit where children were sent to recover after having open heart surgery and other more serious procedures. Lang made his way down the hall and gently pushed open the door to the room where the nurse had indicated Hayes would be. Even if she hadn't given him a hint, he could hear Hayes's unmistakable voice through the door.

Hayes was talking to a couple, obviously the parents of a boy who now lay before them in a hospital bed, staples running nearly from his chin all the way past his navel as he began the early stages of recovery from open heart surgery. The mother of the boy was sobbing.

"My boy is lying there, and I don't know how we're going to pay for this. My husband just lost his job. I just don't know how we're going to make ends meet and get through this," she said.

Hayes put his arm around the woman. As he pulled away he reached into the inside pocket of the sport coat he was wearing and extracted an envelope.

"What's your name?" he asked the husband.

The husband told him. Hayes pulled his uncashed pay-check for the sum of roughly $2,800 from the envelope and promptly signed it over to the man.

"Use this to get caught up on bills and get back on your feet. And it's a gift, not a loan. Don't think about paying me back," Hayes said.

"Oh, and the bill for your son's operation, don't worry about that, either. I will get that taken care of. I know a few people around here."

Finally, Hayes told the man to go see a friend about possibly getting a new job.

"Tell 'em I sent you," Hayes said.

Only then, as he turned to leave the room, did Hayes notice that Lang had been observing the entire scene. Hospital officials later confirmed that Hayes regularly had been performing such good deeds behind the scenes for years, never seeking nor wanting publicity for it.

But Hayes was slowing down. Years of the frenetic work pace, coupled with his mounting health problems related mostly to his ongoing battle with diabetes, were taking a toll mentally and physically as he prepared for the 1978 season. When the season did not begin well, his frustration mounted. The Buckeyes opened the season ranked sixth in the nation, but lost to number five Penn State 19–0 in the opener—at Ohio Stadium no less and with a highly touted freshman, Art Schlichter, suddenly throwing the ball all over the place in a radical departure from Hayes's past teams. Two games later, they barely beat Baylor 34–28, and that was followed by a 35–35 tie with Southern Methodist. Both games were in Columbus, and neither opponent was ranked. Then came a

27–16 loss at unranked Purdue, and the Buckeyes held a 2-2-1 record that represented their worst start under Hayes since opening 2-3 in 1967, the year before the Super Sophomore recruiting class hit the playing field.

Although the Bucks then won five in a row to set up the usual Big Ten showdown against Michigan, they came into that contest a huge underdog. At least they were ranked 16th, having clawed back into the top 20 rankings after falling out altogether for the first time since 1967 following the loss at Purdue. Michigan entered the season finale ranked sixth, and proved the superior team by winning 14–3 in Columbus, where the Buckeyes no longer seemed invincible.

That left the Buckeyes with a record of 7-3-1. They accepted an invitation to play in the Gator Bowl on December 29. It didn't seem right from the start. The Buckeyes played in the big bowl games on January 1 or January 2; they didn't play in these second-tier bowl games. The opponent was heavily favored Clemson, ranked sixth in the nation. The Buckeyes were hanging on at number 20 in the Associated Press poll.

Yet Clemson hadn't won a bowl game in nineteen years. And the Tigers were being coached by thirty-year-old Danny Ford, who was making his head coaching debut because Charley Pell, the former coach, already had announced that he was moving on to the University of Florida.

From the start the game did not go the way the Buckeyes wanted. Twice in the fourth quarter they were stopped on fourth-and-one plays—once at the Clemson two-yard line and another time at the Clemson 21. By the middle of the third quarter, Clemson was in control, leading 17–9. The Buckeyes scored to cut it to 17–15, though, and were driving late in the game when, with one minute, 59 seconds remaining, Schlichter threw a pass that was intercepted by Clemson middle guard Charlie Bauman at the Tigers' 18-yard line near the Ohio State bench. Bauman was tackled by Schlichter and the two fell out of bounds almost at Hayes's feet.

When he jumped up, Bauman appeared to direct a few words toward Hayes and the Ohio State bench. Hayes reacted instantly, perhaps even before any words were uttered. Regardless, the coach delivered a quick punch with his right fist just under Bauman's chin, followed quickly by two other glancing blows. Tempers on both sides flared then and players poured out onto the field as officials and at least some of the coaches tried to restrain players from going after one another.

But Hayes wasn't one of the peacemakers. He was spinning out of control. After hitting Bauman, Hayes turned on two of his own players who tried to restrain him, punching one player squarely in the facemask. Then he had to be restrained from going after the officials by assistant coach George Hill, when Hayes started to go onto the field to protest his 15-yard unsportsmanlike conduct penalty. Hayes continued jawing at the officials until they rewarded his bizarre behavior with yet another 15-yard unsportsmanlike conduct penalty.

All of this transpired before a national television audience, and in that instant everyone but Hayes himself seemed to realize that the long, glorious, often tumultuous run of Wayne Woodrow Hayes at Ohio State University was over. Athletic director Hugh Hindman, who had played for Hayes for one year at Miami of Ohio and had served as an assistant coach under him for seven years, was left with little choice. He headed straight for the locker room and offered Hayes the chance to resign as head coach. Stubborn as always, Hayes refused.

"I'm not going to resign. It would be too easy for you. You better go ahead and fire me," Hayes told Hindman.

So Hindman fired him. He called it "an extremely difficult decision" but in reality it wasn't anything of the sort.

University president Harold Enarson said he supported Hindman's decision and attempted to put it in proper perspective.

"I, along with many people, feel great sadness for a coach with such an illustrious record for a quarter of a century to leave the business in this tragic fashion. There's not a university or athletic conference in the country that would permit a coach to physically assault a college athlete," Enarson said.

Yet, in truth, Hayes had been doing it for years—in his own practices. Why should anyone have been all that surprised that Hayes slugged an opposing player in a moment of frustration when he had been doing it routinely to his own guys?

Hayes, who as a young man had so impressed baseball legend Cy Young with his sharp punching in the boxing ring, no doubt was left disappointed by the fact that he didn't even connect with the last roundhouse of his career. Clemson's Bauman pointed out that fact, while trying to be somewhat sympathetic toward the old coach.

"He was such a competitive man. I don't know; if I had been in his shoes, maybe I would have done the same thing," he said. "It didn't hurt. I didn't even feel it."

9

Earle Takes Over

A S HAYES retreated to seclusion behind the drawn shades of his Columbus home at 1711 Cardiff Road immediately following the Clemson incident, the stunned Ohio State football community suddenly was faced with a question it hadn't had to answer in twenty-eight years: who would be the next head coach of the Buckeyes? The university moved swiftly to hire Earle Bruce, the former Hayes assistant who had since gone on to become a successful head coach at Tampa and Iowa State. For at least a brief time, though, the focus remained more on Hayes than anything else. Former players Archie Griffin and Daryl Sanders were the first to go over to see the old coach at his home.

"I don't really remember talking a whole, whole lot. We were just there," Griffin said. "And he talked about a lot of his experiences and memories and whatnot. But you know, we were not there to talk about anything in particular—not even football. We were just there for him. If he wanted to talk, then we were there to let him talk.

"But we were happy that he let us in because he was going through a lot at that time—and we just wanted to let him know that we were there for him. We said, 'Coach, you've always been there for us. Now we're here for you. If you want to talk, talk to us about anything. And if there is anything else we can do to help you, just let us know. We certainly want to do that.'"

Mike Trgovac had been watching the Ohio State–Clemson game on television from his hotel room in Pasadena, where Michigan was preparing to play in the Rose Bowl.

"I had sprained my ankle in the Ohio State game. . . . So we go to the Rose Bowl and I'm trying to get ready to play. They put a cast on me to try and get the swelling down and I go to the Rose Bowl and I tweaked it that day in practice. Well, they have the Big Ten dinner. So they all leave for the Big Ten dinner, and I stay at the hotel and lay in bed with my foot elevated. Well, Woody punches that kid from Clemson and I say, 'Oh my God, he's done.' So Bo [Schembechler] doesn't know anything about it. So when I heard the buses come back from the dinner, I went down and told Bo what happened and we didn't see him again for a long time. I don't know if he left that night or what. But he was gone for a while—because he really had a love for Woody.

"They were rivals, but he had a genuine respect for Woody. What we heard was that he was making some calls and he was making sure Woody was okay and everything."

Schembechler later confirmed that he broke down emotionally when he heard of Hayes's firing. In a subsequent interview with author Paul Hornung, Schembechler said he figured he knew exactly what had happened at the Gator Bowl, even though he was 3,000 miles away and saw only videotape of the incident.

"I wasn't there, but I'm convinced this is what happened: he had had a long, trying season, we'd beaten him, he was in the throes of his final game, he was tired, he neglected his medicine, and his blood sugar was out of whack."

Maybe so, but these sounded like weak excuses from a close friend. Regardless of the circumstances, Hayes had lost control. Schembechler recalled a conversation he had with Hayes shortly after hearing of the incident.

"All I was trying to do was wrestle the ball from [Bauman's] hands," Hayes insisted to Bo.

"Have you seen the film or the television replay?" Schembechler asked.

"No. I don't intend to."

"Well, that's not what you were doing."

In his own mind, Hayes justified what he had done by coming to that conclusion. He told others that Bauman had "waggled" the ball in his face, and still others that Bauman had taunted him verbally. He remained defiant and unapologetic.

Two weeks later, Schembechler met with Hayes at the Bowling Green home of mutual friend and former Ohio State assistant Doyt Perry. Bo implored Hayes to apologize for what he had done in the Gator Bowl. Hayes flatly refused.

"Goddammit, I'm not going to. Should I apologize for all the good things I've done?"

Schembechler pretty much gave up trying to get Hayes to apologize at that point. But one thing was certain. Ohio State–Michigan games wouldn't be quite the same without Woody prowling the sideline any longer. Trgovac noticed it right away, the very next time they played in Bruce's first season.

"The Ohio State–Michigan rivalry lost something when it was no longer Woody and Bo," he said. "That rivalry got to be Woody versus Bo. It was almost like you were playing for Bo and they were playing for Woody, and not the schools. You wanted to win for your coach; you knew how much it meant to them."

■

Hayes didn't emerge in public for nearly three weeks after the Gator Bowl. Then he spoke at a Chamber of Commerce luncheon, drawing a standing-room-only crowd estimated at 1,200 at the Neil House ballroom in Columbus. Hayes spoke about many things, but made one thing perfectly clear: this was Earle Bruce's football program now.

"Earle is the Ohio State football coach," Hayes told the crowd. "I'm not going to horn in on him in any way. It's his show now."

The two were friends, and more than that. Bruce had arrived on the Ohio State campus more than a quarter of a century earlier, hoping to play for Hayes. But when an injury cut short Bruce's playing career, Bruce packed up and started to head for home. Hayes literally jumped in his car and went after him, talking Bruce into sticking around to earn an Ohio State education and promising him a job on his staff as a student assistant. Later, after he graduated and coached successfully at Salem, Sandusky, and Massillon high schools, Bruce came on board as a full-time assistant in 1966. He ultimately worked his way up to where he was in charge of the Friday night movies—the one job no assistant wanted, but Hayes deemed a privilege to have.

Bruce held the movie job for a while, but he, too, was fired by Hayes when he made a mistake before a game at Minnesota in 1969. Unaware of the film's content, Bruce saw that *Easy Rider*, the controversial and cutting-edge flick about motorcyclists that included plenty of sex, drugs, and violence, was the early showing and would permit the boys to be back at the hotel and in bed before ten o'clock. So he thought it would be fine.

Hayes didn't watch the movie with the team. He preferred to go back to his room following Friday night dinner to read a book. Usually the book had something to do with history. But when the team returned to the hotel after watching *Easy Rider*, several of the players were snickering. One of the assistant coaches, Dave McClain, who would go on to become a very successful head coach at Wisconsin, let it slip to Hayes that the movie's content had been highly questionable.

"It was the worst movie I've ever seen, Woody," he charged.

The Buckeyes won that 1969 encounter at Minnesota, thumping the Golden Gophers 34–7. But Hayes didn't think the boys looked sharp enough. They had been averaging close to 50 points a game and, in his opinion, made way too many mistakes, especially on offense.

"What's the matter with us?" he asked his staff the following Monday.

Then he repeated one of his favorite pet sayings.

"You never stay the same in this game. You're either getting better or you're getting worse. So if you're not working hard enough to get better, you're getting worse. And by God, we're getting worse! There's got to be a reason for it!" Hayes bellowed.

Then it was as if a light bulb went off in Hayes's brain. He stared at Bruce.

"I know the reason! It's that goddamned movie we watched last Friday night! Earle, you didn't do a good job taking us to a movie. You're fired! Rudy Hubbard, you've got the movie job now!"

Bruce smiled to himself. It was a job he was happy to be rid of, although he later joked that "Rudy never forgave me."

Now, though, Bruce was the one seeing that the Friday night movies were appropriate and, more importantly, that the Ohio State Buckeyes were prepared to play on Saturday afternoons. Following a legend like Hayes, especially in the fishbowl that was Ohio State football, was not a task envied by many of Bruce's peers. Most coaches would have much preferred being the guy who replaced the guy who replaced

Woody Hayes, rather than the one who stepped into Hayes's oversized shoes.

On the eve of the 1979 season opener against Syracuse, Bruce let it be known that he would not sever ties with the past but rather would embrace them when he invited Hayes to dinner with the team. Hayes had recruited all but two of the twenty-two projected starters for the team. But, Hayes declined.

"There's nothing they need from me—and if I came around, it probably would be misunderstood. Earle's doing a great job," he said.

Bruce's first team, with the charismatic and talented Art Schlichter at quarterback, took the heat off him in the simplest way possible. By winning. Expectations of outsiders were not as high as usual, as the Buckeyes began the season unranked. They moved to number 15 after beating Syracuse 31–8, the first of 11 consecutive wins that would vault them all the way to the top of the rankings. By midseason, it seemed no one could touch them. They beat Indiana 47–6, Wisconsin 59–0, Michigan State 42–0, Illinois 44–7 and Iowa 34–7 on consecutive weeks, setting up the season-ending showdown with Michigan in Ann Arbor, which they also won 18–15.

The win over the Wolverines in 1979 was Ohio State's first since 1975 and left Bruce with the feeling that all was fine in Buckeye Nation.

"It was the competition of the thing," Mike Trgovac said. "It was the same thing when we were getting ready to play Southern California. You respected their program so much, it was just about getting your asses out there and competing. It was kind of like two big-time nations who were really good, righteous nations getting ready to fight each other. You would try to kill each other for those three or four hours. But at the end of it, you would go back to being civilized."

The 1979 edition of the rivalry was played before a NCAA regular season record crowd of 106,255—the largest ever in Michigan Stadium history. Schlichter completed 12 of 22 passes for 196 yards as the Buckeyes broke what had been a 15-quarter drought with no touchdowns against Michigan by getting to the end zone twice in the second half.

The Buckeyes ended the season with an 11-0 record and a number one ranking. One bowl game could give Bruce the national championship in his first season—the national championship that had eluded the illustrious Hayes since 1968. Asked by reporters after the Michigan game if he ever expected to go 11-0 in his first season as Ohio State's coach, the burly Bruce, who resembled a teddy bear of sorts, broke into a toothy grin.

"Most certainly. I'm a positive guy," he replied.

The Rose Bowl opponent for the Big Ten champions was familiar—the University of Southern California, which was unbeaten as well but had one blemish on its record, a tie with Stanford earlier in the season. In a game witnessed by another huge crowd of 105,526 and yet another national television audience, the Buckeyes appeared in control as the game entered the fourth quarter. Leading 16–10, all the Buckeyes needed to do was hold off the Trojans in the final 5:21 and they would be national champs.

As on so many earlier occasions when Hayes's teams came close only to have the national title slip from their fingers, it was not meant to be. Southern Cal tailback Charles White, who had been difficult for the Buckeyes to contain all afternoon, suddenly became unstoppable. In a winning touchdown drive that covered 83 yards, White accounted for 65 of them on just two runs, of 32 and 33 yards. When he crashed into the end zone from the one-yard line with a mere 1:32 left to play, it was the Southern Cal contingent chanting, "We're number one!"

White ended up with 247 yards on 39 carries. Southern Cal coach John Robinson hailed the Buckeyes as "tremendous competitors. There were a lot of mistakes, even coaching mistakes, but it was still a great game."

Bruce added: "It was an excellent football game for us, except for SC's last possession. That was a great drive and they simply out-executed us. But on the whole, I was very pleased with our defensive play. USC is a very explosive team. They are everything they said they were."

Bruce was about to begin finding out how unforgiving Columbus fans were for perceived "coaching mistakes." Among other things, he would later be criticized for not showing enough emotion after the huge loss, which he of course found devastating. Fans also took issue with his comment that he was "very pleased" with a defense that had given up 247 yards rushing to one tailback.

Earle Bruce's honeymoon as Ohio State's head football coach came to a very abrupt, unfriendly end. Worse yet for him, the bar had been set high. He went 11-1 in his first season as Hayes's replacement and came within one point of winning the national championship. He was named Big Ten and National Coach of the Year. There wasn't much room left for improvement, but improvement would be expected.

With Schlichter back for more after what was only his sophomore season, the Buckeyes once again appeared to be on the brink of something great. But Schlichter already had a dark, dirty secret. The gifted athlete with the rifle arm who grew up on a farm just outside Washington Court House, a mere forty-one miles south of Columbus, was hiding a serious problem behind his growing celebrity status. Whenever he could get a little money together, Schlichter liked to gamble.

Schlichter later related that the betting began when he was a kid and he would wager nickels and dimes on card games. But by his sophomore year at Ohio State, he was sneaking off some afternoons to the nearby Scioto Downs horse track, where he would try to make $40 or $50 last an entire afternoon. By his junior year, the betting had begun to escalate—an afternoon at the track often required hundreds of dollars. Schlichter never fully explained where his extra spending money came from, and no one really pressed him on the issue. He was the star quarterback at Ohio State, for goodness sakes, and everyone had the right to blow off a little steam.

Earle Bruce certainly didn't seem to sense that Schlichter had a problem. Nor did anyone else say so publicly at the time, even though Schlichter would later admit that he began running up thousands of dollars of debt when he started supplementing his trips to Scioto Downs by betting with a local bookie on major league baseball and college basketball games by the time he was a senior co-captain in 1981.

Many years later, after Schlichter had been in and out of prison on various fraud charges related to his unquenchable thirst to gamble, a therapist who worked with him suggested that his problems stemmed from the fact that from the time he was throwing touchdown passes in Pop Warner football no one had really looked at him as a normal human being. Dr. Valerie Lorenz, the director of the center in Baltimore where Schlichter spent several weeks in counseling in 1997, said that Schlichter talked of a fractured boyhood relationship with his father—and of the need to be perceived as normal. In their sessions, Lorenz determined that what Schlichter really had needed in his earlier years was genuine affection, not hero worship.

He didn't get it at Ohio State. The passionate Bruce took to him like a second father and tried to give him the love that he craved. But it all revolved around football. And Schlichter hadn't been treated like any other football player, much less any other student, since his arrival on the Columbus campus in Woody Hayes's final season. It was Hayes, after all, who had promised Schlichter he would start at quarterback as a true freshman—in retrospect making Hayes's theatrical performance on the sideline prior to Schlichter's first game, when Hayes huddled up with both the freshman and veteran quarterback Rod Gerald, seem like a total sham. Some veteran players never forgave Hayes or Schlichter for putting Gerald, a two-year starter, on the bench; and some fans even went on to blame Schlichter for the conversion to a more passing-oriented offense that in their minds unleashed the dreadful chain of events that led to Hayes's demise in the 1978 Gator Bowl. It was, after all, a Schlichter pass intercepted by Clemson's Charlie Bauman that triggered the incident that brought Hayes down.

But in his final two seasons at Ohio State, Schlichter kept his emotions inside, and sought release through big games on the field and increasingly larger bets off it. It was his way of escaping reality, and as his debts mounted gambling became more and more appealing—so he bet even more, trying in vain to earn enough to settle old debts even as he was establishing new ones.

On the field, Schlichter showed few ill effects from his off-the-field sickness. In 1980, his junior season, the Buckeyes cruised into the Michigan season finale unbeaten in the Big Ten and with an overall record of 9-1. Ohio State's only defeat to that point had been a 17–0 loss to UCLA in Columbus early in the season. The Buckeyes were ranked fifth in the nation, the Wolverines tenth. But the promising season disintegrated along with an ineffective offense run by Schlichter, and a 9–3 loss to Michigan was followed by a 31–19 loss to Penn State in the Fiesta Bowl. That left the

Bucks with a record of 9-3, the first of what would be seven straight three-loss seasons under Bruce (six 9-3 records in a row, followed by a 10-3 mark in 1986 when they played an extra regular season game against Alabama in the Kickoff Classic).

As a senior in 1981, Schlichter's hopes to challenge for the Heisman Trophy were dashed by a sprained ankle that bothered him most of the season. He played through the injury, seeing to it that by the end of his career he had started every single game of his Ohio State career. But after opening the season with three straight wins, the Buckeyes lost back-to-back to Florida and Wisconsin, falling out of the national rankings for the first time since Bruce had taken over as coach. When they sneaked back into the top 20 at number 18 following three consecutive Big Ten victories, they lost at Minnesota 35–31 to fall out again.

Schlichter and the OSU offense rebounded for the annual pounding of Northwestern—this time by a score of 70–6—and the quarterback told teammates that he had no intention of going out a loser in the storied series against Michigan. With the game set for Ann Arbor and the Wolverines needing a victory to clinch a Rose Bowl berth, the upset wouldn't be easily pulled off. Michigan was an eight-point favorite.

Bruce brought in the big gun to get his team and fan base pumped for the contest. Since undergoing gall bladder surgery the previous May, Woody Hayes had kept a low profile. His weight had dropped from its usual 220 pounds to 158 when an abscess developed because a University Hospital surgeon had inadvertently left a surgical sponge in his abdominal cavity. Some friends later suggested that Hayes should have sued the hospital, but he never gave it any consideration and only asked that the sponge be removed in a subsequent procedure—prompting OSU president Harold

Enarson, the man who had signed off on his firing less than two years earlier, to send a letter of apology and appreciation for Woody's unique acceptance of the surgeon's life-threatening mistake.

Hayes made it obvious that he would rather turn his venom on the state of Michigan than an erring Ohio surgeon anyday. And Bruce put him to work before the 1981 Michigan game. On the Friday before the trip up north, Hayes, who by then had regained most of the weight he had lost prior to his surgeries, delivered a fiery speech to the Buckeye Boosters luncheon audience at noon. He then was asked by Bruce to do the same at the Senior Tackle ceremony a few hours later. Afterward, Bruce insisted that Hayes accompany the team to Ann Arbor for the latest showdown with their Big Ten rivals. Hayes agreed to do so.

As the game unfolded, it was as if Ohio State was merely hanging on, trying to avoid getting blown out. Schlichter's one-yard touchdown run gave the visitors a 7–3 halftime lead, but the Wolverines kicked a pair of field goals to move ahead 9–7 in the third quarter. Hayes had been assigned a seat in the totally unfamiliar territory of the press box. He was unaware of the universal rule that no cheering was permitted there, and proceeded to loudly whoop it up every time the Buckeyes made a big play—and moan every time something went wrong. Michigan officials and writers covering the Wolverines complained, but Hayes, who knew no different and probably wouldn't have cared even if he did, kept it up. Ohio State officials and writers covering the Buckeyes merely snickered.

When Schlichter and the OSU offense took over at the Michigan 20-yard line with eight minutes left, it seemed Hayes did not have much to cheer about. There was little reason to think the quarterback could pull off his quiet promise of an upset win. But on third-and-eight, he scrambled away from pressure and hit tight end John Frank for a key 11-yard gain, keeping the drive alive. Then he hit Gary Williams for 17 yards.

As the clock moved inside three minutes, the Buckeyes advanced to the Michigan six-yard line. The Buckeyes needed only a field goal to move ahead, but Bruce and Schlichter were determined not to settle for that. Schlichter stunned the capacity crowd at Michigan Stadium and the Wolverines' defense by rolling right behind big Vaughn Broadnax, who laid down a key block, and ducking into the right front corner of the end zone for a touchdown and a 14–9 lead that held up. There would be no trip to Pasadena for the team from up north.

When Schlichter led the Buckeyes to a 31–28 victory over Navy in the subsequent Liberty Bowl, it was his first and only bowl victory and seemed a fitting end to a storied college career. His career record was 36-11-1. He had become the first quarterback in school history to achieve All-American status as a sophomore. He set school records for passing yardage in a single season (1,816) and in a career (3,066)—by the end of his sophomore season. He went on to pile up 8,122 yards of total offense and accounted for 76 touchdowns. In a twist of irony, it was fitting that he ended his Big Ten career with the running touchdown against Michigan. Despite his reputation for being the passer who changed everything at Ohio State, where Woody Hayes had invented the "three yards and a cloud of dust" mentality, Schlichter actually proved to be adept as a running quarterback out of the option offense. He threw 44 touchdown passes in his career, and ran for another 32.

The National Football League beckoned, and Schlichter was chosen in the first round of the college draft by the Baltimore Colts. By midway through his rookie season, he had gambled away his entire $350,000 signing bonus. He allegedly made calls to bookies seeking to lay down bets on NFL games from pay phones in Baltimore's Memorial Stadium. When the league learned of his gambling, he was suspended in 1983. He was reinstated the following season, but soon thereafter resumed gambling. The Colts cut him in 1985 and he never played in the NFL again.

By 1988, when Schlichter filed for bankruptcy to shield himself from creditors, he claimed $1 million in debt. It was only the beginning of a downward spiral that would land him in a series of jails and prisons as he stole from family, friends, and unsuspecting scam victims over the next sixteen years to fuel his compulsive gambling addiction, possibly making his one wish come true: while behind bars, Art Schlichter would finally be treated like everyone else.

It didn't make him feel any better. In a 1996 interview with *People* magazine, he described how he felt after stealing money from his wife's purse to gamble. He also once was charged with stealing his father's credit cards to get $42,000 in cash to help cover bets.

"When you start stealing from your family and friends," said Schlichter, "you know it's only a matter of time before you're in jail or you put a gun to your head."

The roar of the Ohio Stadium crowds had never seemed further away.

10

Heart of a Heisman

A S ART SCHLICHTER was leaving Ohio State and descending into his personal hell, Earle Bruce was looking for ways to keep the program moving in pursuit of another national championship. Bruce already had learned that 9-3 wasn't quite good enough. The only way to get better was to recruit better players, and more of them. So Bruce made an offer in 1982 that a young assistant coach named Dom Capers felt he couldn't quite refuse.

Capers was an Ohio native, having grown up in tiny Buffalo, Ohio, in the southeastern corner of the state, and having played football at Mount Union College. Before he launched his own playing career, he would attend a high school football game every Friday night—and then would spend a good chunk of Saturday tracking Ohio State games as best he could.

"They didn't have all the college games on TV then, but you could get the Buckeyes on the radio," Capers said. "So I'd sit with my uncle and listen to the Ohio State games on the radio. Of course back then Ohio State was strong and probably a lot of their backup players could start at other places in the Big Ten. They used to just pound people. And Woody Hayes was the guy, the legend.

"Then on Sundays it was the Cleveland Browns. That was back when they had Jim Brown. That was how we would spend a weekend in Ohio then. The whole weekend revolved around following these football games, and we loved our teams."

By 1982, Capers was a fast-rising assistant who had coached at the University of Washington with Don James and Jim Mora, and also had made brief stops at Hawaii, San Jose State, and California before joining the staff of Johnny Majors at Tennessee. Bruce was well aware of Majors, having replaced him years before at Iowa State when Majors left to coach Pittsburgh. And by this time, Bruce also had become aware of Capers, who later would go on to become a head coach in the NFL with the Carolina Panthers and the Houston Texans.

"When I was in college football, I always said I would like to gravitate back toward Ohio State as an assistant coach," Capers said. "And I recruited Ohio from Tennessee. I recruited against Ohio State on a number of players, and I can tell you the players because it's probably how I ended up at Ohio State. Keith Byars and Jim Lachey were the two guys. I was recruiting them to go to Tennessee, and we had had Jim Lachey down to Tennessee for the summer camp and all that. They were the best lineman and the best back in the state of Ohio."

Bruce knew all of that. He was fearful of losing Byars, whom he hoped would be the next great runner in a long line of Buckeye backs, and Lachey, whom he wanted to pave the way for Byars and others with his great blocking. These were two players he felt he had to have. So the solution—or at least as Bruce saw it, one of the possible solutions—was to hire the assistant coach from Tennessee who had apparently made such inroads in recruiting them. Capers was close not only to both players, but to their families. Bruce knew of Capers's ties to Ohio. He called and offered him a job on his Ohio State staff, hoping that bringing Capers on board would mean that Byars and Lachey arrived right on his coattails.

"It was a touchy situation," Capers admitted. "Basically during the recruiting process, I got a call from Earle Bruce. If it had been any other place other than Ohio State, I probably never would have left Tennessee."

Capers went in to see Majors.

"I've been offered a job at Ohio State. I think I'm going to take it," Capers said.

Majors was not pleased.

"But you've been recruiting Byars and Lachey for us," he said.

"I tell you what, Coach. I will give you my word that I will not turn around and recruit Keith Byars and Jim Lachey for Ohio State. I will stay out of it."

Majors still was not pleased. He knew Capers would keep his word—having once called him "a definite favorite of mine" who "understands the importance of loyalty and has deep character"—but he also knew it wouldn't really matter. Once Capers was gone, so, too, were Tennessee's chances of landing Byars and/or Lachey.

Naturally, Byars and Lachey ended up following Capers to Columbus just as Bruce had hoped. Capers's first impressions of Bruce were favorable, but he sensed right away that Bruce was in an unenviable position.

A number of the other assistant coaches on Bruce's staff—Glen Mason, Randy Hart, and Fred Pagac, among others—had played for Hayes. Every once in a while, a group of assistants would get together and go over to the Faculty Club to meet Hayes for lunch.

"For a guy who grew up in Ohio and followed the Buckeyes, those are some of my fondest memories—of being able to just have lunch at the Faculty Club with Woody, because he was entertaining," Capers said. "You could tell the guy had so much charisma. You would wonder how he could come on so strong with certain players and, yet, after he had gotten after them, he could put his arm around them and bring them back. That's the key. A lot of coaches will get after people; but how come those people want to go to war and fight so hard for the guy because they don't want to let him down? Woody was the master at pulling that off, and we all wanted to pick his brain as much as we could and hear his stories.

"These guys that I coached with, they would laugh and tell stories. But you could tell that there was a tremendous amount of respect there. They respected the passion and the drive that he had to not only be the best he could be, but to try to get everyone around him to be the best they could be, too. And below all that was a sincere sense of caring about them as people, and for their families. I think that always came through. I think that was a tremendous buffer for him from the other side, in terms of him being such an aggressive guy, because there was always a motive behind what he was doing."

Bruce would use Hayes as a motivational speaker, sometimes having him speak to incoming freshmen about football and life; other times speaking at the Senior Tackle, the annual ceremony the week before the Michigan game in which senior players hit a blocking sled to symbolize the impending completion of their college playing careers. This was an emotional, long-standing tradition, and Hayes's fiery spirit often carried the day.

"One year when I first got there, Earle had him come in

and talked to the freshmen," Capers said. "It was an inspirational speech, and it was more about what you wanted to get
out of your life and your education and all that than it really
was about football. But he tied those things together."

Offensive lineman Scott Zalenski, who was at Ohio State
from 1980 through 1984, added of the occasional Hayes
speech: "He'd come around, and he'd speak to us—but only
at Earle's invitation. Otherwise, he pretty much stayed out of
the picture. But he would speak to us at a big game, like before the Michigan game. I think everybody realized what a
legend Woody was. He just had a way of talking that would
get you motivated; he just really caught and held your attention.

"You sort of hung on every word, just to hear what he'd
have to say. It was always a pleasure. I felt like if he talked for
three hours, I could just sit there and listen to what he'd have
to say and soak up every word. It was a real treat whenever
he came around."

There were many traditions that Bruce carried over
from the Hayes coaching era into his own. Pregame dinners
for home games, featuring the same types of large steaks and
pecan rolls favored by Hayes, were still held at the OSU Golf
Club before home games, followed by the usual Friday night
movie at Fawcett Center. And when players returned to their
rooms, they could expect a snack of chocolate chip cookies
and hot chocolate, or soda if they preferred, to be waiting for
them. On the morning of the annual Homecoming game
there would be the Captain's Breakfast, where team captains
would speak to the rest of the players about the upcoming
challenge, followed by a pregame walk, as a team, to the stadium. Even for road games, the coaches kept the pregame
ritual as close as possible to what they did before home
games—changing only the venues, not the ritual itself. What
might have seemed corny to outsiders provided a sense of

comfort to the players and coaching staff, as the routine became a settling respite each week before the fury that was to follow in the games. Thanks to Capers, and to Bruce's deft handling of the hiring of Capers, Keith Byars and Jim Lachey were soon to be part of it all.

The 1982 season began well with wins over Baylor and Michigan State, but then the Buckeyes dropped three in a row, to Stanford, Florida State, and even Wisconsin. The 6–0 loss to Big Ten foe Wisconsin in Ohio Stadium stung the most. The offense was so inept that Art Schlichter, now in the pros with the Baltimore Colts, took time away from his gambling addiction to meet with new OSU quarterback Mike Tomczak. Among other things, Schlichter talked to Tomczak about keeping his composure on the field (this was about the same time that Schlichter often would call a play in the Colts huddle and then forget what he had called seconds later because he was consumed with thinking about a bet.)

Whatever Schlichter told Tomczak, though, it worked. The Bucks, uncharacteristically unranked, won their last seven games to finish their customary 9-3. Included in the streak was a 24–14 win over favored Michigan, ranked number 14 in the nation, at Ohio Stadium; plus a 47–17 shellacking of Brigham Young, whose quarterback was Steve Young, in the Holiday Bowl. Capers still remembers the thrill of being part of the coaching staff that beat Michigan that year.

"It was incredible. It takes on a whole different meaning for you if you've grown up there, and if you've followed the Buckeyes from the time you were five, six, or seven years old," Capers said. "[Michigan] had [wide receiver] Anthony Carter and they were going to the Rose Bowl that year. But we beat them.

"Anytime you beat Michigan, you got a set of [miniature] Gold Pants. It's like a thing your wife could put on a locket or a chain around her neck. You put 'em in your drawer along with everything else—but it's an honor."

There were no Gold Pants handed out the next year, when Michigan, ranked number eight in the nation, beat Ohio State 24–21 in Ann Arbor. Jim Lachey played a key role in the loss. The Buckeyes were driving for what would have been the go-ahead touchdown when Lachey came off the field to talk with Bruce, who was sending in the plays via messenger guards. Bruce looked at Lachey hard.

"We're going to run your play," he said.

"What?"

"We're going to run your play. Lachey Right. Now get out there and run it."

It was a trick play, calling for center Joe Dooley to snap the ball to quarterback Mike Tomczak as usual. Only Dooley was then to take the ball right back from Tomczak and actually set it on the ground. The plan was for Lachey, who was unusually quick off the snap and very athletic for his size, to then pick the ball up and run for a touchdown. If it worked right, it not only would give the Buckeyes the lead but would do so in a fashion that Bruce believed would crush the Wolverines' spirit.

Lachey ran onto the field and called the play out in the huddle.

"Lachey Right. We're going to run Lachey Right," he stammered.

Scott Zalenski, the other guard, just looked at Lachey.

"Oh, no," Zalenski muttered.

"That didn't give me a lot of confidence," Lachey later confessed.

Michigan lined its nose tackle up in an off-set alignment that didn't help matters. The Buckeyes had never practiced the play against that particular defensive alignment, and it made the already nervous Lachey even more uneasy. He thought about calling a timeout, but didn't.

Dooley snapped the ball, took it back from Tomczak as designed, and set it on the ground—but then made a critical mistake. As he stepped back to block the nose tackle, he knocked the ball away with his heel before Lachey could pick it up.

"By the time I turned, the ball was seven yards away," Lachey said.

It might as well have been a hundred yards away. Michigan got there first and pounced on the loose ball, helping preserve the three-point win that sent them to the Rose Bowl. Earlier Big Ten losses to Iowa and Illinois relegated Bruce's boys to a fourth-place finish in the conference—the team's worst showing since Hayes's final year and only the second time since 1967 they had finished as low. It took a 28–23 win over Pittsburgh in the Fiesta Bowl to give Bruce his usual 9-3 record.

Joining the staff that year was another young assistant named Jim Tressel, who nearly two decades later would return to become the school's head coach.

"Thinking back about working with Jim, you could tell he was going to become a head coach," Capers said. "I just thought his values and all the things he believed in were good. Of course Jim and I had some things in common. He had played at Baldwin-Wallace, and I played at Mount Union in college. So we'd play each other every year. And his dad had been a longtime successful coach at Baldwin-Wallace. So he grew up having a father who was a very successful head coach, and he had a built-in mentor right there in his father. You could see right away that he had the background and the coaching ability to be something special."

Coach Woody Hayes was never shy when it came to letting others know exactly how he felt about what was transpiring on the football field.

(below) Tailback Archie Griffin, shown here breaking a tackle against Minnesota in a 1972 game, remains the only player in college football history to win two Heisman Trophies.

(above) Rex Kern (10), considered by Hayes to be the ultimate "mistake-proof quarterback," led the Buckeyes to an unbeaten record and the 1968 national championship. Blocking for Kern in this game against Michigan State in November of 1968, were fullback Jim Otis (35), left guard Tom Backhus (57), and right guard Phil Strickland (62).

Offensive tackle Dave Foley (70) and linebacker Dick Worden were co-captains on the 1968 team that capped a perfect season by beating O. J. Simpson and Southern California in the Rose Bowl.

This missed field goal by Michigan in 1974 preserved a 12–10 victory for the Buckeyes at Ohio Stadium and sent them to the Rose Bowl. It was representative of the many close games played in the series regarded as perhaps college football's most storied.

Tailback Keith Byars finished this memorable 67-yard touchdown run against Illinois in October of 1984 with one shoe on, one shoe off.

Hard hits like this one delivered on a Michigan receiver in 1987 made linebacker Chris Spielman a favorite Buckeye for the ages.

Earle Bruce wore what had become his trademark fedora for his final game as Ohio State's head coach. His players wore headbands with "EARLE" emblazoned across them and then went out to whip Michigan 23–20 in Ann Arbor.

Eddie George, shown here out-maneuvering Illinois in October of 1994, ran his way to the Heisman Trophy.

The term "pancake block" was invented for Orlando Pace, who flattened so many opponents that many regard him as the best offensive lineman to play for Ohio State.

John Cooper coached the Buckeyes for 13 seasons and had some great teams, but never fully understood the school's rich tradition and therefore never completely won over the Ohio State fan base.

(below) Tailback Maurice Clarett scores the game-winning touchdown in the Tostitos Fiesta Bowl, securing the 2002 national championship. Clarett later was at the center of a scandal that scarred the Buckeye football program.

Coach Jim Tressel holds up the 2002 national championship trophy.

Andy Geiger, who would step down as athletic director in the wake of controversy only six weeks later, still found reasons to smile at this news conference prior to the 2004 game against Michigan.

Ted Ginn Jr., who appears to be the next huge star in the making for the Buckeyes, returned this punt for a touchdown against Michigan in November of
2004.

Capers was on his own fast track to becoming a head coach, but his career would soon veer toward professional football. On his way out, he left Earle Bruce with a very nice present.

"The last guy I recruited there was Cris Carter," Capers said. "Cris played at Middletown High School. I practically lived at Middletown High School."

There were no limits then on how long a recruiter could spend on a high school campus, and Capers took full advantage. Carter's high school coach at the time was Bill Conley, who soon would end up on Ohio State's staff. Many times a high school coach's meal ticket to a big-time college program was his own high school star. But coaches also had to be prepared to work ridiculous hours that made any kind of social life outside of football virtually impossible. Capers, whose area of recruiting at the time was widespread, had a method of chasing down recruits that would have exhausted even many others in his own business.

"What I would always do is I would pick out my top five guys or so, and then I'd just live at those places. So I'd get to know all the faculty, I'd get to know their families, I'd get to know everybody in town," Capers said. "I probably saw Cris play all but three or four of his [Middletown] basketball games his senior year."

As good a recruiter as Capers was, he didn't always get every player he targeted. But he had a pretty good track record. Around the same time he was recruiting Carter, he also was working on tight end Alex Higden from Princeton High School near Cincinnati; Scott Leach from Bridgeport, Connecticut; defensive tackle Henry Brown from Andrew Jackson High School in Queens, New York; fullback George Cooper from Wyandanch High School on Long Island; and Tony Cooper from Circleville, Ohio, "who was supposed to be one of the best running backs in the state." Capers was busy.

"You'd just prioritize them. If you could get one guy, Cris Carter was the one you wanted to get—because he was the player of the year in the state," Capers said.

Carter eventually committed to Ohio State and went on to become one of the greatest receivers in the school's history. But it almost didn't happen. Shortly after Carter told Capers and others that he was coming to Ohio State, Capers decided to accept an offer to join Jim Mora's coaching staff with the Philadelphia Stars in the fledging United States Football League. After helping coach the Buckeyes to their 1983 Fiesta Bowl victory, Capers reluctantly informed Bruce that he was leaving.

Capers had about ten days before he had to report to training camp for the Stars, for they played in a spring league. Shortly after he packed up his belongings and headed to Florida for the Stars' camp, he received a surprising phone call one night. On the other end of the line was Bruce.

"Dom, you've got to help me out here. Cris Carter is now saying he's not sure he's coming here. He's saying he might even go to Michigan," an exasperated Bruce pleaded.

"What do you want me to do?" Capers asked.

"Call him. Call him for me and do whatever it takes to make sure he comes here to play for us," Bruce said.

Capers called Carter, who did not deny that he was wavering on his commitment to come to Ohio State.

"Michigan keeps calling and saying, 'Oh, we're losing Anthony Carter. We'd like you to come in and be Anthony Carter's replacement.' I have to admit it sounds appealing. Plus you're leaving Ohio State; why should I come?" Carter said.

Capers, no longer employed by Ohio State, went on the recruiting offensive nonetheless.

"Look, Cris, you gave your word that you were coming to Ohio State. You need to honor that commitment. I'm sorry I'm not going to be there, but you need to be a man of your word. And for an Ohio kid like yourself, it's absolutely the best move you can make."

It took more than one phone conversation, but Capers eventually persuaded Carter. In fact, the last conversation Carter had with the Michigan folks went a little differently than some of the previous ones.

"You shouldn't go to Ohio State. That's a running school. We'll throw it up here," a Michigan assistant told Carter.

"Ohio State is a running school because they don't have me. Once they see what I can do, they'll start throwing it," Carter replied.

To an extent, Carter was right. In a career that was cut short after three seasons, he amassed 164 receptions for 2,725 yards and 27 touchdowns—all Ohio State career records. The last player Capers recruited for the Buckeyes, and one of the best, paid dividends.

Keith Byars went on to have a productive career with the Buckeyes, marred only by an ill-fated finish. The former Dayton Roth High School standout played fullback in his first season, just to get on the field and gain some experience. But he longed to carry the football, and soon proved he could do it with the best of them. He was such a good blocker at fullback, however, that Bruce was reluctant at first to move him to tailback—and didn't do so until a teammate listed ahead of him on the depth chart suffered an injury in spring practice following Byars's freshman year.

By the following fall, Bruce realized that he was right in doing whatever he could to secure Byars's services for Ohio

State. He believed he had a future star on his hands. In fact, he was so confident that he soon grew sick of hearing about Oklahoma running back Marcus Dupree prior to an early-season game against the second-ranked Sooners in 1983.

"All we heard about leading up to that game was Marcus Dupree, and how great he was. Everybody kept talking about their guy, but we had Keith and I knew he was better than Marcus Dupree," Bruce said.

Bruce didn't hesitate to tell friends and fellow members of his coaching staff—and just about anyone else who would listen.

"You watch. We have a tailback better than Marcus Dupree. Keith Byars will make Marcus Dupree look sick. He'll run for more yards than Marcus Dupree."

The coaches may have believed him because they had seen Byars in practice every day; but most outsiders thought Bruce was at best overconfident in Byars, and at worst maybe a little off in the head. Dupree was everyone's preseason pick to challenge for the Heisman Trophy. Byars was a returning fullback. Yet as the game approached, Bruce did not back down from his comments.

Sure enough, Bruce was right. Byars outgained Dupree in the 1983 game against Oklahoma, helping the Buckeyes to a 24–14 victory.

It was the beginning of a remarkable two-year run for Byars before a broken foot would cut his college career short. Without a doubt, the most defining moment of his time with the Buckeyes came the following season, on October 13, 1984, in a game against Illinois at Ohio Stadium. With the Buckeyes trailing 24–7 late in the first half, and coming off a loss at Purdue one week earlier, there was little reason to believe Byars when a television camera panned on him on the Ohio State sideline after he scored his first touchdown.

"We're coming back, Dayton, Ohio! We're coming back!" Byars shouted into the camera.

Byars later explained his on-camera bravado to author Bruce Hooley for *Ohio State's Unforgettables*.

"I said what I said because I really believed it. I felt we were going to come back and win that game. Up until we scored our first touchdown, we were getting embarrassed in our own backyard. That just wasn't supposed to happen at Ohio State.

"Once I scored, the floodgates just opened. You could sense the whole mood in the stadium change. They put the camera on me, expecting me to say, 'Hi, mom.' Well, my mom was in the stands. She already knew I loved her. So I made a statement to all my friends and people watching all over the country. 'Hey, trust me. We're coming back.' And we did."

They did it in dramatic fashion. Byars rushed for five touchdowns and 274 yards—the five touchdowns tying Pete Johnson's school record and the 274 yards eclipsing Archie Griffin's single-game record of 246 against Iowa in 1973. Among Byars's touchdown runs was perhaps the single most memorable one in the modern Ohio State era—a 67-yarder in which he circled around the right end, cut back inside, lost his left shoe at the Illinois 35-yard line, and kept sprinting for the end zone without it.

"I just felt my shoe slipping off, but there was no way I was going to go back and get it," Byars said.

The one-shoe scamper produced his fourth touchdown of the day in Ohio State's remarkable 45–38 come-from-behind win, keeping alive its chances for a Big Ten championship and a trip to the Rose Bowl. After later losing 16–14 at Wisconsin, it took a 21–6 victory over Michigan to make all that happen. The loss left Michigan with a 6-5 record, which was their worst in Bo Schembechler's 16 years as head coach at the school. But Bo went down defiantly. Prior to the game, he had told referee Otto Kortz to be prepared to assist his team if the Ohio Stadium crowd of 90,286 got too loud while quarterback Chris Zurbrugg was barking out signals for the Wolverines.

With six minutes to go in the fourth quarter, and Michigan set to run the 14th play on a long drive, the crowd roared in a collective effort to help out the Ohio State defense. Zurbrugg motioned to the officials, who stared back at him blankly. Zurbrugg later said he attempted to call timeout, but that Kortz refused to grant him one.

"The crowd was really loud," he said. "My linemen couldn't hear. So I raised up and asked the referee for a timeout. He didn't give it to me. He just pointed at me to continue the play. The clock was running down, so I did."

And a Michigan lineman jumped off-sides. Schembechler was furious on the sideline. In the best Woody Hayes megaton imitation at Ohio Stadium, Schembechler inched fifteen yards onto the field screaming at every official within shouting distance. After the game, he continued his rant.

"Ohio State is a good team, but I concede nothing to them. We tossed away too many good opportunities and the officials did not help," he said. "But you can expect that in this league these days.

"The officials on the road have to protect the [visiting] quarterback. They [the Ohio Stadium scoreboard operators] flash it on the board for everyone to yell, and my quarterback kept trying to tell the official that they could not hear the signals. But they did nothing about it. They're bad officials. All the good ones have gone to the NFL, and they have no good young ones coming up. Who the hell wants to be an official? Would you want to stand out there and officiate games? Hell, no!"

Not with the wrath of Bo raining down upon you. In truth, the Buckeyes won the game because Bruce scrapped a three-wideout formation featuring the freshman Carter in favor of a Power-I running formation that put the ball more in Byars's hands in the second half. Byars scored all three of Ohio State's touchdowns and finished with 113 hard-earned yards on 28 carries. Helping pave the way for Byars all year was starting left guard Jim Lachey, who would be named first-team All-Big Ten along with center Kirk Lowdermilk and tackle Mark Krerowicz.

"This is something that I've dreamed about all my life—beating Michigan, winning the Big Ten championship, and getting to play Southern Cal in the Rose Bowl," Byars said afterward.

As the old saying goes, be careful what you wish for. Savoring a chance to finish 10-2 and on a high note instead of 9-3 and thinking about what might have been, the Buckeyes stumbled in their first Rose Bowl appearance since Bruce's first year as coach. Despite being heavy favorites—they were ranked sixth in the nation—the Bucks lost 20–17 to Southern California, who came in ranked eighteenth. That left them 9-3 again.

Byars not only led the nation in rushing with a school-record 1,764 yards (breaking another of Archie Griffin's records), but also in scoring with 144 points and in all-purpose yardage with 2,441. Byars himself thought he should have been a shoo-in for the Heisman Trophy. So did Bruce and others. But he had the misfortune of having his greatest year the same year that Boston College quarterback Doug Flutie, a fan and media favorite, threw a last-play, Hail Mary touchdown pass to beat the University of Miami on Thanksgiving Day.

"It was all about timing," Byars told Hooley years later. "Unfortunately, my [regular] season was over by then, and all the voters were sitting at home eating their turkey, watching that Boston College game [on television]. That was the last thing they remembered before the final vote, so it swayed things in Flutie's direction.

"I know in my heart I should have won that Heisman. Even today, I run into a lot of people who say, 'You should have won that Heisman,' and it means a lot to me. I may not have it in my living room, but I have that Heisman in my heart."

11

Mr. Buckeye

SOMETIMES a young man comes along who appears destined for certain pursuits in life. Such was the case with one of the freshmen during Byars's breakout junior season. Chris Spielman seemed born to play football at Ohio State University. Certainly he was groomed for it. His father, a longtime high school football coach at Canton Central Catholic, Canton McKinley, Canton Timkin, and Massillon, used to dress up Spielman in Ohio State gear and sit him in front of the television for Buckeye games. Young Chris loved nothing better than watching an Ohio State–Michigan game followed by Southern California taking on Notre Dame.

"Those were always the two biggest games we watched, but obviously the Ohio State–Michigan game was bigger. It was a family affair, I would say," Spielman remembered.

Asked how old he was when this tradition began, Spielman chuckled. "I don't even remember, really. Four, maybe? I'm sure I was dressed out even before I could remember."

When he was eight or nine years old, he ran into Woody Hayes at the Bob Evans restaurant in Canton. Hayes was in town recruiting Canton native Ray Ellis, who would play for the Buckeyes from 1977 through the 1980 season. Spielman's father knew Hayes well enough to go up and say hi and have Spielman and his brother get their picture taken with the legendary coach.

"I knew who Woody Hayes was. That was very exciting. I was like, 'What's he doing in Canton?' I do remember that thought that went through my head. I was like, 'I can't believe I'm in here seeing him get some biscuits and gravy just like the rest of us.' When you're eight, you don't think of a guy like that being human like everyone else. He seemed like he was more than that."

A decade later, Spielman was a celebrity in his own right around Massillon and Canton. He was an Ohio football legend before he even finished high school. Located a mere ten miles from the Pro Football Hall of Fame in Canton, the Massillon Tigers had long ago adopted the slogan that their school offered "the greatest show in high school football." It is a place where newborn baby boys receive miniature footballs from the athletic booster club after birth, before they leave the local hospital. Games were played in Paul Brown Tiger Stadium. Spielman, a high-energy linebacker, became such a local luminary that his picture was placed on the cover of a special edition box of Wheaties while he was still in high school.

It seemed a given that Spielman was going to play for Ohio State, even in his own mind. But in a testament to the willpower and calculating nature of the young man, Spielman wanted to visit some other campuses as well. So he took visits, by then limited to five for each recruit by the NCAA, to Penn State, UCLA, the University of Miami (Florida) and—gulp!—Michigan.

"I think you owe it to yourself to look at other places. There was never another place for me, but I wanted to look at the other places," Spielman said. "You know, you're eighteen years old and people want you. That's obviously flattering, so you kind of want to look at the other places that say they want you, too. But when push came to shove, deep down, I always knew it would be Ohio State. I just wanted to confirm that belief, I guess."

Spielman had watched from afar—or at least from nearby Massillon—and admired how Earle Bruce handled himself after taking over the program from Woody Hayes. When they met for the first time, Spielman came away even more impressed.

"My first impression was that he loved Ohio State—that he was passionate about football, and that he loved Ohio State. We had kind of the same types of personalities, so it was an easy connection."

While acknowledging that following a legend such as Hayes was difficult for any coach to do, Spielman noted that Bruce handled it about as well as any man could do.

"It makes it easier when you're undefeated, beat Michigan, and go to the Rose Bowl in your first year, which Coach Bruce did. That's not easy to do. He deserves a lot of credit for that, obviously."

At the same time, Spielman was reluctant to buy into the theory that Bruce's first season had spoiled Buckeye fans, who by Spielman's arrival on campus in 1984 were becoming increasingly dissatisfied with the 9-3 seasons Bruce kept churning out. Spielman said that he understood the fans' desire for more than a nine-win season. In fact, he felt the same way; he just didn't blame Bruce every time something went wrong.

"No, I don't believe the fans were spoiled or the expectations were set too high—because that's Ohio State," Spielman said. "When you come into these circumstances, the standard has been set and the rules are in place. It's not like an expansion NFL team. You are expected to win every game you suit up for. You expect to win every game. Those are the standard expectations at Ohio State."

It didn't take Spielman long after his arrival to begin making himself known. He quickly earned a starting spot as a true freshman, only to suffer a sprained ankle during the second week of fall practice. He then aggravated the injury in a preseason scrimmage, and Bruce decided not to start him in the season opener. This infuriated Spielman, who felt as if he could play through any pain—and did not want to begin his Ohio State career on a sour note.

"I couldn't practice the whole week, so I didn't start because I didn't practice. I felt like I was ready to play. We were playing Oregon State and they were hanging in there and making it closer than it needed to be," Spielman said. "I've always been a guy where if I have a question, I'll go to the decision-maker. And Earle was the decision-maker. So I got behind him and got in his ear."

It was more like Spielman stalked Bruce on the sideline. Wherever the coach went, Spielman followed. Bruce had his headset on most of the time, so Spielman shouted at him as they strolled the sideline together.

"I'm here to play. I earned my job. Put me in!" Spielman yelled again and again.

By the end of the first quarter, Bruce had heard enough. He put Spielman in. On the very first play he was on the field, Spielman made a tackle—the first of 546 he would make as a Buckeye.

"I never did know for sure if he heard me. He had his headphones on. But somebody heard me," Spielman said. "Fortunately, when I finally went in, I did all right. It felt like this is what I was destined to do. I was like, 'So here is my time; let's go!'"

His play as a reserve in the first half was impressive enough that Bruce ordered linebackers coach Bob Tucker to start Spielman in the second half.

"All he did then was go out and make the first 10 tackles [in the third quarter]," Bruce later said. "He played a heck of a game."

Making tackles is what the intense, fiery Spielman did best. He had a nose for the ball, and although his speed in the 40-yard dash could be questioned, his instincts for getting from one side of the field to the other by using any advantage possible could not. He would cock his head one way, anticipating a play to go to one side or the other, and lean his body in that direction ever so slightly even before the ball was snapped. Rarely did he guess wrong when he was reading an opposing formation or tendency. Playing with heart might be a cliché for some; for Spielman it was the only way he knew how to conduct himself on the football field. He went all-out, all the time.

Teammates at Ohio State and later in the NFL would talk about how Spielman "owned" the defensive huddle. They hung on his every word. They wanted to show that they, too, could play as hard as he did. Another football cliché states that the great players play every down like it might be their last. Cliché or not, Spielman knew no other way.

"Turnovers! We have to have turnovers! Hit somebody HARD and let's create some turnovers!" Spielman would preach to his defensive brethren in the huddle. And then he would go out and hit someone, oftentimes jarring the ball loose; other times it simply sent the message to the ball carrier that if he came anywhere near him again, he was going to knock his block off. He loved to get inside their heads in this manner.

Any opposing coach or player who underestimated him risked painful reprisal. Faster ball carriers rarely got the drop on him. Spielman seemed to know where they were going before they did, and he would get there first. Then he would position himself at the best angle to deliver the sure-handed tackling blow with the best leverage.

Later, when his OSU playing career was over, some NFL scouts failed to grasp the essence of all this. He wasn't drafted until the second round because many scouts looked past the fact that he was as pure a football player as there was, and studied only his size and speed in the 40. They declared him too small or too slow, or both. They would later feel foolish for failing to see what was right in front of their eyes: a man destined to dish out punishment on the football field. No one prepared harder or hit harder, or made fewer mental mistakes.

And Spielman was tough. More than once he hit an opposing player so hard, he also knocked himself silly. On one such occasion, he sauntered back to the huddle slowly, a little wobbly. On the next play, he didn't pursue the ball with his usual gusto, leaving observers to wonder what was wrong. Suddenly, Spielman sunk to one knee on the field—and puked his guts out. Then he bounded up and was ready to play again, arguing with trainers who came out to escort him off to make sure he hadn't given himself a concussion.

In the off-season, no one worked harder in the weight room or at conditioning. Spielman may have been a mere six feet, if that, and no more than 215 or 220 pounds when he arrived at Ohio State. But it was a hard 215 pounds, and when he left four years later it was an even harder, more well-sculpted 240. But then, Spielman never was caught up in numbers—except the ones that judged success or failure on the scoreboard.

"There are guys walking the street who can bench 400

pounds, run a 4.5 40, and jump out of the gym," he said once. "You've got to have something other than that. What do you bring to the table that is special, that sets you apart from anybody else? That's what is important."

Spielman's first season would rate as his most special, although he couldn't have realized it or the turmoil that would follow at the time.

"It was my first experience of playing in the Michigan game," Spielman said of the 21–6 victory in Columbus in 1984. "I played in the Massillon-McKinley game [in high school], which is a whole story in itself. But it was that game times ten. The excitement, the tradition and the pageantry, it was all good. I looked around and I was like, 'Wow. I get to do three more of these. That's pretty cool.'

"It also clinched the Big Ten title and a shot to the Rose Bowl for us. I thought we were going to win the Big Ten and go to the Rose Bowl every year I was there."

As it was for Byars and the rest of the Buckeyes, the trip to the Rose Bowl that year was a letdown for Spielman.

"That was a game we should have won. I give USC credit. They weren't a great team, but they were a good team. Jack Del Rio was a linebacker for them at the time, and they had Duane Bickett playing for them at the time. Joey Browner played for them at the time. They had just a lot of good players who ended up being good NFL players.

"I thought we had 'em. We were going for a touchdown, but had a couple penalties at the end and they ended up pulling it out. It was disappointing. It was very disappointing—because I thought that '84 team was as talented as any team I played on. If you look at the players that were on that team for us, a lot of them ended up being pretty good NFL players over the years."

There were other big games during his career, however. His favorite may have been during the following season, when Iowa came to Columbus ranked number one. The Hawkeyes had Heisman Trophy candidate Chuck Long as their quarterback, and he was coming off a game in which he had boosted his Heisman candidacy by throwing for six touchdowns and 399 yards. Columnist Burt Graeff of the *Columbus Citizen-Journal* wrote, tongue-in-cheek of course, that Long might be able to throw for 1,000 yards against an Ohio State secondary that had been suspect at times.

The Buckeyes seized on this and other perceived slights. Colleges aren't supposed to care about or discuss betting lines, but somehow it came to the Ohio State players' attention that they were listed as two-point underdogs in their own house. They hadn't lost at Ohio Stadium in 19 games, which was the longest home winning streak in the country at the time. The way the eighth-ranked Buckeyes figured it, only the 31–28 loss at Illinois four weeks earlier kept the game from being number one versus number two in the nation—and they were more determined than ever to prove they were better than they had shown that day.

Spielman was particularly incensed by all the negatives being tossed around about the Buckeyes.

"It's like a stab in the heart," he said. "But on Saturday, we're going to pull the knife out."

Spielman and his linebacking cohort Thomas "Pepper" Johnson met with *Sports Illustrated* writer Hank Hersch for a dual interview prior to the game. Hersch described them as "Ohio State's salt-of-the-earth and pepper inside linebacking duo," and later wrote of the scene thusly:

> "You can't let the great quarterbacks like Chuck Long set up and pick you apart," said Johnson, a cocksure senior who nevertheless talks softly. "You have to make them play great."

"Dare them to," added Spielman, a sophomore to-
bacco dipper.

"It's not a matter of what they do on offense . . ."
started Spielman.

" . . . it's what we do on defense," finished Johnson.

Spielman spat. Johnson glared. And the seeds were
sown.

All of this was swirling in the minds and hearts of the Buckeyes when they sat down that Saturday for the Captain's
Breakfast, the players-only event where leaders can speak
their minds. On this occasion, it was Byars who stepped forward to deliver a message none of them would ever forget.
This was to be Byars's crowning season. A senior, he had entered it as a favorite to capture the Heisman Trophy not only
in his heart but to carry it away to his living room. By this
time, though, that dream was shattered along with a broken
bone he had suffered on the outside of his right foot during
fall camp. Byars had tried to play with the injury, but had
reinjured the foot the previous game against Minnesota and
already knew he could not get on the field for Iowa after
missing the entire week of practice.

"Guys, I don't get to go out there today. But you do. You
get to do what I can't, and that upsets me because I want to
be out there so badly," Byars said.

Then, the usually softspoken Byars's voice rising, he
punctuated his closing comments by slamming a fist onto the
table in front of him—which sent two lunch trays flying and
a glass of water flying back up into Byars's tormented face.

"Let me tell you something: I will be out there with you
today in spirit. I can't be out there with you physically, but I
will be with you in spirit. I will be with you wherever you go on
that field, and I will be a part of everything you do. So don't let

me down! Do it for me! Do it for Ohio State University! Do it for the state of Ohio! Let's beat these guys to prove everybody who said we couldn't wrong! No one comes into the Horseshoe and beats us, I don't care what they're ranked!"

Spielman and Johnson, among others, jumped out of their seats. Byars had them so pumped up they wanted to get the game started right then, right there.

"You could see how desperate he was at the Captain's talk at the pregame meal," Spielman said. "He was very emotional about it, and I think that resonated with a lot of guys.

"The lunch trays and the water glass went flying. But it wasn't fabricated. It was sincere and true. You can see that's the passion and emotion that a lot of Ohio State players have, and probably more so from the kids who are actually from the state of Ohio. And Keith was from Dayton. He grew up with this."

Johnson added of Byars's speech: "He said he was going to be in every one of our shoes, on every one of our shoulders and in our hearts. It gave me some chills."

Iowa and Chuck Long had no chance in the game that followed. In front of an Ohio Stadium record crowd of 90,467, Long wasn't even the best quarterback on the field. That was Jim Karsatos of Ohio State, who hit flanker Mike Lanese for gains of 19 and 21 yards to help set up a 28-yard field goal by placekicker John Spangler on Ohio State's very first possession.

The final score of 22–13 wasn't indicative of Ohio State's dominance on that chilly day when rain was mixed with light snow, none of which helped Long's repeated attempts to get the Iowa passing game going. Spielman seemed to be everywhere, as did Johnson. Each registered 19 tackles. Spielman added two interceptions, and would have had a third if he had not dropped Long's first attempt of the game.

"I think that game was, for me, like the movie *The Per-*

fect Storm," Spielman said. "This was the perfect football game for me. It was just a game where everything seemed alive, even more so than normal at Ohio Stadium that day.

"Iowa was ranked number one. They had a Heisman Trophy candidate playing at quarterback in Chuck Long, who I later played with in the NFL in Detroit and teased about how I took his Heisman Trophy away that day. I thanked him all the time for the two picks [interceptions]. I was riding the guy about that day for a long time after the fact."

Even Woody Hayes took note. Though he wasn't in attendance after recovering from yet another heart attack, Hank Hersch reached him by telephone afterward to see what he thought of the Buckeyes' big victory.

"That Spielman, boy, he's a real football player. And that Johnson, he hammers you, too. Boy, they can hit," he said excitedly.

Praise from Hayes still meant something.

"Anytime a man and a coach of that stature says something nice about you, you certainly are humbled for lack of a better word," Spielman said. "And I guess, too, as a player over the years you learn that you're never really as good as people say you are, and you're never really as bad as people say you are. But when Woody says it, that obviously means something more."

At one point, Earle Bruce thought that Spielman's perfect game would be part of a perfect season. But that all changed with Byars's preseason injury and the early loss to Illinois. Even after the big win over Iowa, the Buckeyes failed to capitalize on the momentum—stumbling against Wisconsin and losing at sixth-ranked Michigan 27–17 to conclude the 1985 regular season.

"I thought we had a shot to win everything with him as a senior," Bruce later told author Bruce Hooley of Byars. "He was so good. A healthy Keith Byars playing like he was as a junior, we could have gone undefeated."

Spielman wanted it for Bruce as much as for himself. But another promising season was dashed the following year, 1986, when the Buckeyes opened the season by losing to Alabama in the Kickoff Classic and then followed that 16–10 loss with a 40–7 shellacking at the hands of Washington that dropped them all the way out of the national rankings. It was the first time since 1894 that the Buckeyes had begun a season 0-2, and alumni who were growing agitated about Bruce now had plenty of ammunition with which to blast him. After Bruce finally won one, the critics weren't quieted. Mayor Dana G. Rinehart even referred to Columbus as a city that some referred to as "the future former home of Earle Bruce."

Nine consecutive wins followed, but then came another devastating loss to Michigan with a trip to the Rose Bowl on the line. The Buckeyes still tied for the Big Ten title, but were sent to the Cotton Bowl instead. Years later, Spielman recalled the 26–24 loss to Michigan that year as the worst defeat he absorbed in his four-year Ohio State career. It was made more difficult to handle because of the uncharacteristic brashness the Wolverines displayed before the game. Normally low-key and reserved, senior Michigan quarterback Jim Harbaugh had broken with both his usual personality and the pregame tradition of keeping quiet so as not to agitate the opponent by guaranteeing victory.

"We don't care where we play the game," he said. "I hate to say it, but we could play it in the parking lot. We could play at twelve noon or at midnight. We're going to be jacked up."

Trailing by two with 1:32 to play, the Buckeyes still had a chance to shut Harbaugh's yap. But on third-and-10 from the Michigan 36-yard line, quarterback Jim Karsatos fired a pass to Cris Carter, his dynamic wide receiver, on a button-hook pattern that went for only eight of the yards necessary for a first down. Critics howled long and loud about Bruce's supposed lack of wisdom for calling a pass play where the route would end before reaching the first-down marker, and he took the heat afterward.

"The play depends on the coverage," he said almost inaudibly in the postgame news conference. "It could go 10 yards."

But it didn't. On fourth-and-two from the Michigan 28, Bruce consulted with special teams coach Randy Hart on the sideline. He was considering calling on placekicker Matt Frantz to attempt a 45-yard field goal into a ten-mile-an-hour wind. It would be the longest field goal of Frantz's career if he succeeded.

"Can he make it from there?" Bruce asked Hart.

"Yes, he's capable of it. I think he can," Hart answered.

Bruce decided to give Frantz that chance to be a hero. Instead, the kick—though plenty long enough—sailed wide left. And Bruce was the goat for not doing something different.

On the other side, Coach Bo Schembechler called it the wildest of his 18 games against Ohio State—but that may have been a comment made in the heat of the moment, without proper reflection. Regardless, Michigan was going to its eighth Rose Bowl since Schembechler's arrival. Bo was so happy that he finally forgave Harbaugh for his bold and seemingly foolish pregame prediction.

"I'd'a said it myself if I had any guts," a grinning Schembechler added.

Spielman was an emotional wreck in the Ohio State locker room.

"That was a real tough loss," Spielman said. "But they had a good thing going. They were able to run the ball on us. We were able to get a turnover, a fumble, in the last minute of the game and we had a chance to seal it there at the end with a field goal. It just didn't work out.

"We would have run the table on our Big Ten schedule and would have gone to the Rose Bowl, and this was after starting out 0-2 that year. We lost in the Kickoff Classic to Alabama and went out to Washington and got smoked. Then we came back and won all our other games. So, yeah, that was a tough one. That was probably the toughest loss I had as a Buckeye."

Spielman was named a finalist for the Lombardi Award following the regular season and asked Bruce to accompany him to Dallas for the ceremony. Bruce was reluctant to do so at first. He was busy trying to prepare himself and his team for a Cotton Bowl appearance against Texas A&M. When he finally did agree to go, he couldn't help commenting to reporters that Fred Akers, his counterpart at Texas, had just been let go after waging a losing battle against some powerful alumni. Akers often had been compared to Bruce because Akers had replaced the legendary Darrell Royal at Texas, another of the nation's most storied programs, and had found it difficult to operate in the previous coach's shadow, despite winning most of his games. His career record at the school at the time of his firing was 86-31-2.

"I was reluctant to go [to Dallas] because I saw what was happening to coaches in Texas," Bruce joked. "My winning percentage is only about 75 percent. Hey, that's why you're seeing more coaches go into the cattle business—because cattle don't have alumni."

His comment was more telling than most people knew. He was having his own troubles satisfying the demanding Ohio State alumni crowd. He also wanted to beat Texas A&M badly in the Cotton Bowl because he didn't have much professional respect for the Aggies' colorful coach, Jackie Sherrill. In fact, he suspected Sherrill of cheating, as did many others in the college football community. Furthermore, Sherrill had made big-name enemies—ticking off Penn State coach Joe Paterno, a man Bruce admired greatly. When a reporter once suggested jokingly to Bruce that he could probably get more people to love him if he was a little more "jazzy, like Jackie Sherrill," Bruce bristled.

"I don't want to be a Jackie Sherrill," he said. "I'll be an Earle Bruce, but I don't ever want to be a Jackie Sherrill. You can tell him I said that, because I'd tell it to his face. I can go look in the mirror and feel good about myself."

In many ways, the Texas A&M Aggies were a reflection of the brash, cocky Sherrill. Certainly their quarterback, Kevin Murray, appeared to be. When Murray and Ohio State quarterback Jim Karsatos accompanied their coaches to various pre-bowl festivities, Karsatos took an immediate dislike to his A&M quarterback counterpart.

"When you go to these bowl games, they have a lot of these event-type things that the starting quarterbacks really end up spending time together at because the coaches usually take the quarterbacks or the team captains or whatever to these press conferences. He was incredibly arrogant," Karsatos said of Murray.

"One of these events that we went to they brought out these footballs and we were supposed to throw 'em out into the crowd kind of as a gift. I ended up hitting a chandelier, trying to throw it into the back. He was just kind of smug in his response to that."

So Karsatos and Bruce felt good after what transpired in the subsequent confrontation against Murray and Sherrill in the Cotton Bowl. Although Spielman didn't win the Lombardi Award (he would win it following the next season), the Buckeyes finished the season by soundly beating Texas A&M 28–12. Spielman said the defense felt it had lost the Michigan game, so it was determined not to let that happen again.

"We didn't feel good about it and we wanted to do something about it," said Spielman, who spearheaded the defensive turnaround that featured five interceptions by picking off two passes himself. One he returned for a touchdown, as did the Buckeyes' Michael Kee.

Karsatos was particularly pleased with how the Bucks won. Texas A&M came in averaging 440 yards per game, but was held to fewer than 300 as Murray continually was harassed into making critical mistakes in the passing game.

"I just didn't have a good feeling for him, so when he threw those five interceptions and two that went [back] for touchdowns, I couldn't have been happier," Karsatos admitted. "I don't like people who are way into themselves. When they fall on their faces, I think it's rightly deserved."

Karsatos said later that he wasn't surprised when the Buckeyes handled Sherrill's Aggies with relative ease.

"We smoked 'em. We were ready to play and we were a team. We were pretty tight at that point in the season, because it had been a long season. And their guys were already looking at going to the pros."

For once the Buckeyes seemed concerned with how they looked. This was the game when Bruce caused a stir by chucking his usual OSU ballcap for a fedora with a scarlet feather sticking out of it. He completed his new look by wearing a stylish charcoal-colored suit in place of his usual Ohio State football gear.

"I thought it was about time for a change in image," said Bruce. The *Cleveland Plain Dealer* couldn't resist adding that Bruce's "image in the past has been likened to oatmeal."

The Buckeye players also came out wearing gaudy red shoes.

"We wanted to do something to make the players look flashy," Bruce explained.

Regardless of his intentions, it was the Spielman-led defense that enabled the Buckeyes to go out winners in their final game of the season. All five of the interceptions came in the second half, breaking open a close game. Spielman snared the first, dropping back into coverage and picking off a pass intended for Texas A&M tight end Rod Bernstein, which he then returned 24 yards for the first touchdown in his three-year OSU career.

"Maybe it was the red shoes," he joked later. "I might wear them from now on."

Bruce was set to wear the fedora from then on. He thought it had brought him good luck. He also thought the immediate future was rosy for his Buckeyes, who would return most of their key players the following season.

He had never been more wrong in his life.

Woody Hayes stayed busy in his "retirement," but a stroke he suffered in May of 1985 while on an airplane en route to a speaking engagement in Vancouver was the beginning of a series of health setbacks from which he would never fully recover. He was flown back to Columbus on the private jet of prominent businessman John Galbreath after the stroke, and spent the next several weeks undergoing treatment and therapy at University Hospital.

Champ Henson, the former Ohio State fullback, provided him with a red cane—and during his recuperation Hayes frequently was spotted walking slowly along Cardiff Road, near his home, with the aid of the cane. Hayes no longer could drive his truck, and he was seen less frequently at his office, which had been moved to a windowless first-floor location. He had another heart attack shortly thereafter, and began suffering from complications such as leg ulcers.

In January of 1986 he flew by a private plane arranged by OSU President Edward Jennings to New Orleans to accept the Amos Alonzo Stagg Award and a standing ovation at the American Football Coaches Association convention. Schembechler met him at the plane and stayed at his side most of the visit. While there, the frail and obviously ailing Hayes sat at a table and greeted a long line of coaches from around the nation who simply wanted to shake his hand. He had a kind word for almost every one of them.

But then Mike Trgovac came through the line. The former Michigan standout's playing career had been cut short by injuries, and he was beginning his coaching career. After two years as a graduate assistant under Schembechler at Michigan, Trgovac now was a full-time assistant on the coaching staff at Ball State University in Muncie, Indiana. It had been nearly a decade since he and Woody Hayes sat alone in the basement of his parents' Youngstown home.

Once in front of Hayes, Trgovac swallowed hard and stuck out his hand.

"Woody, I don't know if you remember me. I'm Mike Trgovac. I ended up going to—"

Woody cut him short.

"Goddammit, I remember you! You're Mike Trgovac. Your dad's name is Ed. Your mom's name is Jackie, and, you sonofabitch, you went to Michigan!"

Trgovac was stunned.

"I was like, 'Wow!' This is ten years after he recruited me and he said it just like that. I didn't even get done saying what I was trying to say and he laid that on me," Trgovac said. "He was failing in health a little bit at the time. I'm pretty sure he wasn't joking. He still sounded a little bitter to me. It didn't sound like he was going to be having me over to his house for any Sunday dinners.

"What was amazing to me, though, was not only did he remember my name and all the circumstances around trying to recruit me—but he remembered my parents' names. That was impressive."

It also was a little scary. Trgovac moved on as quickly as possible.

Less than three months later, Wayne Woodrow Hayes passed away. He had been in and out of the hospital more than anyone other than his wife, Anne, realized over the final few years. He had had a pacemaker installed on one trip, and had continually battled complications related to his diabetes. But he rarely complained.

In the last week of his life, he agreed to be roasted by a Columbus organization, but only if Bruce was roasted along with him. Then Hayes called old friends, such as Lou Holtz, Bill Mallory, and Schembechler, and gruffly ordered them to be at the event, regardless of whatever else those busy men might have had scheduled. Holtz even flew in from Arizona, where he was hosting an alumni event for Notre Dame, the school where he was now head coach, and then flew right back to Arizona after the roast.

When Hornung of the *Columbus Dispatch* informed Hayes of the personal sacrifice Holtz had made to get there, Hayes openly wept. Schembechler had to postpone an appearance in Dayton to make the roast, and did so only after

Woody promised the he would introduce Bo at the rescheduled banquet in Dayton a couple days later. Hayes agreed, and fulfilled his promise as usual. He died two days later, on March 12, 1987. It was less than one month after his seventy-fourth birthday.

Thousands, perhaps even millions, mourned his loss across the state of Ohio and elsewhere. At Ohio Stadium, bouquets of flowers began dotting the field on and around the huge scarlet and gray O at midfield. Single red roses were laid on the field as well. One family left a picture of a baby wearing an Ohio State sweatshirt, with a football at the boy's feet.

More than 1,400 people crowded into First Community Church for the first and more private of two memorial services. Delivering the eulogy was none other than former President Richard Nixon, who concluded by saying:

> Two thousand years ago, the poet Sophocles wrote,
> "One must wait until the evening to see how splendid
> the day has been." We can all be thankful today that
> in the evening of his life, Woody Hayes could look
> back and see that the day had indeed been splendid.

The second, more public memorial service was held at Ohio Stadium and was attended by more than 10,000, even though it was during weekday working hours and most Ohio State students were off campus on spring break. Schembechler spoke there, calling Hayes "a great friend of mine" and "the greatest football coach the [Big Ten] conference ever had."

Bruce also spoke, recalling how he had arrived at Ohio State many years earlier hoping to become a great running back—only to have his dream shattered by a severe knee injury. And how Hayes followed him home and urged him to return with the offer of making him a student-coach. He applauded Hayes for caring about his players long after their playing days were over.

Chris Spielman drove to the memorial service with Fred Pagac, who had played for Hayes and was in the midst of a nineteen-year run as an assistant coach at the school. While moved by Hayes's death, Spielman was consumed more by the prospects of the life that lay in front of him. Then he looked over at Pagac, and saw that he was sobbing.

12

Out of the Firing and into the Hot Tub

WITH HEAVY hearts, the Buckeyes returned to the field for the 1987 season. They had finished the previous year strong, taking care of business against Southwestern Conference champion Texas A&M in the Cotton Bowl. Meanwhile, Bruce was being wooed by the University of Arizona. Knowing that he wasn't happy any longer at the school he loved so much, tired of dealing with demanding alumni, Arizona pursued him vigorously. And Bruce liked much of what they offered. A couple years earlier he had considered the head coaching position at Missouri. He even had gone so far as to visit with school officials, keeping the visit quiet. But the romance with Arizona was something different. It was too public for anyone to ignore, and the level of resentment toward Bruce in some powerful circles reached new heights. Bruce very nearly took the Arizona job, backing off only when OSU athletic director Rick Bay and Bruce's Ohio State assistant coaches talked him out of it.

Much of their reasoning centered around the considerable talent that the Buckeyes had returning that year. Bruce may have been unhappy, but he wasn't stupid. This might be his best chance to capture a national championship at his alma mater.

Chris Spielman certainly had every reason to think his senior year could be very special indeed. He had finished his junior year with a school record 105 solo tackles. Add in his assists and he was in on a remarkable 205 stops on the season. But before his senior season could start, he and Bruce were delivered some shocking news. Cris Carter, who figured to be the focal point of the offense in what would have been his senior season as well, was declared ineligible by the school when it was disclosed that he had signed with notorious sports agent Norby Walters, who had a reputation for being unscrupulous.

Carter was the brash, talented kid who ultimately did more to help the Ohio State offense evolve than any quarterback who had ever played there, Art Schlichter included. He routinely made one-handed grabs that left teammates agape in practice, then often followed them up with circus catches in games. Bruce considered him a team leader, too. In an unusually tight game against perennially awful Indiana in 1986, Carter stood up in the locker room at halftime and glared at his listless teammates.

"Y'all better wake up out there! We're not losing to these guys as long as I'm here!" he shouted.

They didn't in large part because of an acrobatic one-handed grab Carter made that set up a key Ohio State touchdown. Another time, in the Citrus Bowl against Brigham Young in 1985, Carter actually went up and made a spectacular one-handed catch of a ball that quarterback Jim Karsatos thought he was throwing away. Years later, Karsatos still occasionally watched film of what he insists is the greatest catch he has ever seen at any level of football. Then again, it was the by-product of hard work and extra practice.

"We would do this thing after practice called the Scramble Drill," Karsatos said. "It was kind of exhausting because I'd run around and their [the receivers'] job was to run to an open space. Basically the idea of it was that if I was rolling right or coming out of a certain play and I ended up scrambling, I knew what their reaction was going to be and where they were headed. Cris would sit out there with me and do that all day.

"And that's kind of what happened in the Citrus Bowl game. I got chased out of the pocket and was rolling right. I was getting chased by Jason Buck, who was way faster than I was. I was getting near the sidelines and I thought, 'Let's not take the sack here. Let's just throw the ball away.' I saw Cris kind of tiptoeing the sidelines and I thought, 'Well, I'll just throw this way over his head and we won't get intentional grounding and we can come back for the next play.' So I wind it up and let it go high and outside, and Jason kind of rolled me out of bounds."

As he rose from the ground, Karsatos was stunned to find Buck glaring at him, swearing.

"You sonofabitch, I can't believe you completed that pass with me knocking your ass down like that," Buck glowered.

"What are you talking about? I threw that ball away," Karsatos said.

"No, you didn't. He caught it."

Karsatos still couldn't believe it.

"He caught *what?*"

Eventually the quarterback figured it out. Shaking his head in disbelief, he ran back to the huddle to call another play.

"When I finally saw it on film, he was tiptoeing the sidelines and he jumped up and caught the ball left-handed by the point of the football at least a yard out of bounds. Then he somehow levitated back in bounds to get both of his feet

in bounds. I swear to this day that he actually levitated to get back in bounds. When I saw it on film, it just blew me away."

There was no doubt that Carter was a rare talent. But he suddenly wasn't going to be around for the 1987 season.

"When we lost Cris," said Spielman, "that changed everything. People ask what went wrong for us that season. Well, that's what went wrong. We lost Cris Carter."

It showed right away, but the Buckeyes got away with disguising it for a while. They beat West Virginia and Oregon, then forged a 13–13 tie with fourth-ranked Louisiana State. The offense struggled in the Big Ten opener, but the Bucks held on for a 10–6 win at Illinois.

The bottom dropped out on October 10, 1987, when Indiana came to town for a visit. With no Carter and no Byars, there was literally no offense for the Buckeyes, who gained only 10 yards rushing in the second half. Carter was right about one thing. The Buckeyes would never lose to Indiana as long as he was around. But once he left, it didn't take long for the Hoosiers, who hadn't beaten the Buckeyes since Woody Hayes's first season as coach in 1951, to cash in.

Worse yet, the usually woeful Hoosiers beat the Buckeyes at their own game and in large part because they were coached to near perfection by Bill Mallory, the former Ohio State assistant who had served on Hayes's staff with Bruce. On Indiana's first two touchdown drives, the Hoosiers ran it right down the Buckeyes' throats, oftentimes trying to neutralize Spielman's great lateral play-making ability by simply running straight at him with extra blockers. The Hoosiers played nearly flawless football, committing no turnovers and few penalties. Mallory even credited a lesson learned from Hayes for making the upset possible.

"We brought a referee in to work our practices Tuesday and Wednesday," Mallory said. "Woody did that, and I learned a lot from him. He was a great man."

Bruce no doubt agreed with Mallory's methods, but was greatly embarrassed by the end results. There was no disputing that Mallory's team had been better prepared on this day than his own.

"It's the darkest day I've seen in Ohio State football," Bruce declared.

There were more dark days ahead for Bruce, who was under increasing pressure from the alumni and an administration that seemed to be pandering more and more to them. His sole ally in the OSU hierarchy seemed to be athletic director Rick Bay, who couldn't understand why so many people openly despised a man he figured they didn't really know.

"Why Earle has a problem with popularity I have never quite understood, because everybody who knows him likes him," Bay told *Sports Illustrated*'s Hersch. "Maybe he needs to get out more. I always hate coming to work on Wednesdays because the letters that were written at halftime on Saturday get to me about then."

The vast majority of his players liked him. They thought him a little "quirky" and even "silly" at times, according to Karsatos, his starting quarterback in 1985 and 1986. But they certainly liked him, and enjoyed his occasional attempts to relax the mood—such as when he surprised them with the fedora-and-suit attire prior to the Cotton Bowl the previous year. "We had kind of reached this crescendo and we're putting on all these red shoes, and all of the sudden Earle shows up in this suit and this hat. We had never seen him like that before, you know," Karsatos said. "So it was almost like a comic effect."

The public rarely got to see the light side of Earle Bruce. And he was demanding of his players, but fair. At the same time, he seemed to sense when it might be time to do something off-kilter to calm everyone down. Once, he paid a physical price to do so.

"I remember one day when he challenged [running back] Vince Workman to a 40-yard dash," Karsatos said. "Earle used to be a sprint champion in the state of Maryland. For years, he held the record and all that. And so he challenged Workman to a 40-yard dash, and we all go out there to watch.

"They line up on the 40-yard line and take off, and about 20 yards down he pulls a hamstring. He fell down like a sack of potatoes. I mean, the whole team just lost it . . . broke down laughing, rolling around on the ground. The trainers rush out; Earle's moaning on the ground. Oh, it was funny.

"But I mean, he was serious about it. He was trying. He was running really hard. But he was, what, well into his fifties? He wasn't going to beat anybody. It was hilarious. We never knew if he was doing it as a joke to try to loosen people up or not. You would think not because that wasn't him, but then again it had the right result."

Meanwhile, rumors that were no laughing matter swirled about Bruce, covering everything from accusations that Bruce had told off some prominent alumni to whispers that Bruce had a gambling problem and had enabled Art Schlichter in his early days as a gambler by accompanying him to the Scioto Downs racetrack. Still others charged that, like Woody Hayes before him, Bruce had intimidated and even struck players during practices. But the most universal claims were a combination of vaguely perceived sins: that Bruce wasn't colorful enough, didn't press enough flesh with enough enthusiasm at alumni functions, and wasn't willing to act like he liked someone when he didn't—no matter how much they contributed to the university. Other school administrators hinted that Bruce was balking at more stringent academic guidelines that the school was trying to impose on incoming recruits and other student-athletes. Oh, there was the other issue that he hadn't won enough, either.

Assistant coach Bob Palcic was added to Bruce's staff in June of 1986, just in time for all the fun of 1987. He was coming from the University of Arizona, and vividly recalled the horror of his first night in Columbus.

"I turned on the radio, and in five minutes people were calling up and screaming, 'Why can't Nine-and-Three Earle win?!!' This was in June. I'd just come from Arizona, where we went 8-3-1 and were heroes, and here they want to get rid of a 9-3 coach? Unbelievable."

But true. The gambling rumor gained further momentum when Richard Celeste, then the governor of Ohio, publicly hinted at it. Though Celeste later apologized, both the mayor of Columbus and the governor of Ohio were now on record as disapproving of the way Earle Bruce was conducting his business as Ohio State's football coach.

Bruce never denied some of the charges leveled against him. Like Hayes, he occasionally would get physical with some of his players during practices. He also made no secret of his disdain for certain alumni. But he insisted that he cared deeply about the education and well-being of his players, and he drew the line at the gambling charges.

"That was kind of crazy," he would say years later. "I'd go to the track, but I'm not addicted to gambling. And from what I know about it, going to the track is legal."

What really mattered at this point was what was happening on the field, not off it. The Indiana debacle was followed by a narrow 20–17 win at Purdue and a 42–9 thrashing of Minnesota at Ohio Stadium, but then disaster struck in the form of consecutive losses to Michigan State, Wisconsin, and Iowa by the combined total of 10 points. The Iowa loss was the backbreaker, coming in the final seconds. It was after that loss that Spielman said he and the rest of the players finally realized that their coach was in some serious trouble and might lose his job.

"I don't know. Again, you're a young kid. You've got your own issues. But I think after we lost the Iowa game at home on a play we never should have gotten beat on, we all realized the situation," Spielman said. "We were in a defense that in my opinion we shouldn't have been in, and Marv Cook caught a pass from 20 yards out with no time left and ran it in. Guys missed tackles or whatever, and ball game over. I was like, 'What? That's my last home game at Ohio State? And it ends *like this?*'"

Making matters worse, there were reports of some powerful alumni in their suites at Ohio Stadium openly rooting for Iowa, so as to hasten the demise of their despised Bruce. The last-second loss left Bruce's Buckeyes with the unheard-of Big Ten record of three wins against four losses with only the game against Michigan remaining, and with an overall record of 5-4-1.

Bruce remained proud and defiant. At his usual weekly media luncheon the following Monday, he declared: "I'm staying at Ohio State."

Then it started getting messy. President Edward Jennings and the university's board of trustees decided they could stand it no longer. On orders from the trustees, Jennings went to Bay and instructed him to tell Bruce that he was fired as coach—but to wait until after the upcoming Michigan game to do the dirty deed. Bay refused, and subsequently resigned in protest. Then Bay leaked the story to the press in an effort to drum up support for Bruce. Jennings countered by appointing Jim Jones as the new athletic director with the clear understanding that he would do so only if Jones agreed that his first action would be to fire Bruce.

Jones agreed, and because Bay already had leaked the story, OSU officials felt they had no choice but to go ahead and make their decision public—before the Michigan game was even played. It left Bruce a lame-duck coach going into the biggest game of the season, but there was no way he wasn't going to coach it. In some ways, he considered it the biggest game of his life. Spielman and the rest of the players rallied around him, with the idea of "winning one for Earle." Spielman said what amazed him was how Bruce simply went about his usual business that final week on the job.

"I think he's genuine and he's honest. And like I've said, the thing I always liked about him was his love for the university. That was never clearer or came through any more than when he was fired the Monday before the Michigan game," Spielman said. "He came in and mentioned that he was fired and he obviously was upset, but he never let that get in the way of normal preparations for the Michigan week. He wanted his players to enjoy the Michigan experience, and we got to. So that to me showed a selfless attitude about what it is to be a head coach, that your team is way more important than you are; that the feelings of the team are more important than the feelings of any one individual."

Spielman said there were some mixed emotions as the Buckeyes prepared for the game. They felt both anger over Bruce's dismissal and excitement about playing Michigan. But he said Bruce's message and the way he went about preparing them eased any collective concerns that they had.

"What better way to show our loyalty to him than go out and play a great game? We can't do anything about that decision; it's not like we were making the decisions for the university. What we could control was that we could go out and send the guy out a winner on the road in Ann Arbor, which was kind of a special way to do it. And we were able to do that."

Playing an inspired game, the Buckeyes beat Michigan 23–20. Spielman said it was as if he was in a trance afterward. He doesn't even remember what Bruce said to the team in the locker room after it was over. But he does have a vivid recollection of one thing.

"The only thing I really remember after that game was watching the team carry him off the field. And I kind of stood back, out of the way, and watched that in Ann Arbor—which, I think, for him there would be no better way to end his career at Ohio State. It was very special. That was probably my fondest memory of playing at Ohio State."

Yet Spielman resisted the urge to run into the middle of the mob of Ohio State players to help hold Bruce high. He held back instead, working the fringes of the inner circle, taking it all in mentally.

"I just wanted to kind of absorb it—because it was my last game also. I just wanted to hang back and watch it from a distance. I wanted to see it and absorb everything from that moment—the sights, the sounds, the smells. It was the final time not only for Coach Bruce, but the final time for myself in an Ohio State uniform."

The Buckeyes were extended an invitation to play in the Sun Bowl, but the administration declined. Spielman said that the players didn't mind.

"We didn't have a coach. There wasn't an interim coach named," he said. "Besides, winning like we did at Michigan, I think that was a good way to end it."

Bruce's messy firing almost overshadowed all else, which was a shame. Spielman ended his career with 546 tackles. Only Marcus Marek, who had played for Bruce from 1979 through 1982 and made 572 tackles, and Tom Cousineau, who had played for Hayes from 1975 through Hayes's final season in 1978 and made 569 stops, had piled up more in their careers. His 29 tackles against Michigan as a junior tied the school record first set by Cousineau in a game against Penn State in 1978. For the kid who grew up in Massillon, where Bruce once had coached the legendary Tigers, it was quite a career.

"My four years at Ohio State were the greatest of my

life," Spielman said. "There have been so many great, great players throughout Ohio State history, and it's been going on for so many years. To have the God-given ability and to be a part of it was a gift. You come from a family where when you get something that's really cool, you appreciate it.

"So why it was so special to me was because I embraced everything about it. Everything. Whether it was the Gold Pants, the pecan rolls at the dinner at the golf course the night before the game, movie night, the smell of the locker room on a Friday . . . whatever it was. I embraced it all and absorbed it.

"I was a guy who was honored to be a Buckeye. Everything about it meant the world to me."

With Bruce gone, the Buckeyes needed a new coach. Times had changed since the days of Woody Hayes and his series of one-year contracts. Hayes not only had refused to sign anything but the one-year deal, but had routinely turned down raises, insisting that any extra money the university wanted to dole out should go to his hardworking assistants, whom he declared needed it more and probably deserved it more than he did.

When Bruce first took over for Hayes, he, too, began signing a series of one-year contracts. But this was out of step with other major universities and led, among other things, to Bruce occasionally entertaining outside offers from other schools, such as with Arizona and Missouri. When Ohio State went to hire a new basketball coach in 1986, the administration knew it couldn't attract top talent by saying, "Well, our football coach operates on a year-to-year basis, so you can, too." Gary Williams eventually was given a five-year contract to coach the team, causing administrators to rethink their position on the football coach. Bruce then was awarded a three-year contract.

Welcome to the real big time, Ohio State. When the next two years didn't go as planned, there was a problem. Bruce still had two years remaining on his contract after losing to Michigan on the ill-fated missed field goal attempt in the final seconds in 1986; after it all fell apart in 1987, he still had one year remaining. So when he was fired, Bruce initially responded by filing a $7.45 million lawsuit against the university for wrongful dismissal. He eventually settled out of court for $471,000—roughly the equivalent to one-year's worth of work after the yearly income for television and radio shows, a Nike contract, speeches, and a summer camp were added to his annual base salary of $87,120.

So when the Buckeyes needed a new coach in 1988, school officials knew it would take big bucks to get their man. The board of trustees was determined to hire someone who wasn't an Earle Bruce clone. Woody Hayes, yes, if they could. But Bruce already had proven that repeating the magic Hayes once brought to the university was difficult. The key would be to hire someone dynamic who could reenergize a program that was fast losing recruits to other schools because it was suddenly perceived to be in turmoil.

Enter John Cooper, who upon first glance seemed to be everything the crazed alumni were looking for. At fifty-one years old, Cooper was a fast-talking, grinning coach who was relatively fresh off a victory over Michigan in the Rose Bowl on January 1, 1987. That meant a whole lot in Columbus, where they had just fired a coach fresh off his fifth victory over Michigan in nine tries. Cooper's win came as coach at Arizona State, which had whipped the Wolverines 22–15 in the Rose Bowl following the 1986 season. In a twist of irony that wouldn't be fully appreciated until later, his latest big win at Arizona State had come over Air Force in the Freedom

Bowl—completing a 7-4-1 season that he attributed to "heavy graduation losses" from his Rose Bowl squad a year earlier.

It was precisely the type of excuse that more rational, or at least less harried, Ohio State faithful never would have accepted from one it was now willing to call its own. Yet Mr. Cooper came to town, and Columbus at first embraced him. Or at least certain people did. And Cooper raced into the city with his arms held wide open, palms held outward, looking to be lathered with their love and much, much more.

Shortly after his arrival, Cooper signed endorsement deals with a local supermarket chain and, infelicitously, a hot tub company. He made plans to build a luxurious home on a lot that alone cost $150,000, an outrageous sum to the conservative Columbus crowd. He said that his wife, Helen, would design the new custom home.

"You hire me, you hire my family," he boasted.

To others in rural Ohio, who worked on farms or in grimy factories or foundries, Cooper was too much, too fast. Ed Sidwell, a young man who had moved to Galion, Ohio, from St. Louis when he was thirteen years old, remembers how he embraced Ohio State football after making the move with his family. He had watched and admired the likes of Keith Byars and Cris Carter, Mike Tomczak and Tom Tupa, Chris Spielman and Jim Karsatos, and even the now embarrassing Art Schlichter. By 1988, he was attending Ohio State and admitted that he was one who had grown tired of Bruce's monotone approach to football and the world. Sidwell soon would talk himself onto Cooper's football staff as one of Cooper's first student-coaches, just months after Cooper was hired on December 27, 1988.

Sidwell remembers Cooper's initial assault on the collective Columbus psyche.

"Upon his arrival in Ohio, one of the first impressions people got of him was when you saw him with his family on

TV doing commercials for this hot tub company," Sidwell said. "I mean, you just got out of a Woody Hayes era, you just got out of an Earle Bruce era, who was Woody Junior. And of course Paul Brown and people like him were part of the tradition before that. I mean, this is ultraconservative Ohio State.

"And now you've got a guy, his wife, his beautiful model daughter, and his chiseled, skinny son jumping into a hot tub in their bikinis and swimsuits. There were only a very few selective people who ever saw Earle or Woody in anything less than their skivvies—and you had to be riding on the team bus to have that privilege, if you could call it a privilege. And here John Cooper was all over central Ohio, advertising hot tubs. He was like a duck out of water in Columbus, Ohio.

"And he did it right away. Right away he started sponsoring grocery stores, Jack Nicklaus's chain of Golden Bear. He signed a shoe contract, signed a contract with the hot tub company. So you knew right away that he was exploiting his celebrity. And right away you also had the impression that he was kind of putting himself ahead of Ohio State University.

"And mind you, for people who went to Ohio State University, it's Ohio State University first and anybody else second."

Cooper had his reasons for trying to cash in right away. He had been led to believe by university officials that he would more than make up the financial difference of a modest base salary of $98,000 with outside endorsements. His deal with the school included separate contracts for radio, television, and other obligations, but he felt he needed to supplement those to make more than the $400,000 his predecessor had been making annually—and what he felt he deserved. After all, he had left behind a $300,000 annual package at Arizona State, where he also had been given a $500,000 home at half-price.

In other words, Cooper was a modern-day coach used to perks. He also received a five-year contract at Ohio State, something Hayes and Bruce had never been offered. That Cooper could coach seemed to be documented in his 82-40-2 record in 11 seasons as a head coach at Tulsa and Arizona State. Word on the street was that he could have stayed forever at Arizona State, where his three-year record was an impressive 25-9-2.

But this was Ohio State. Earle Bruce had been fired despite a record of 81-26-1 over his nine seasons. The 81 victories were the most of any Big Ten conference coach during that stretch. And one fact that OSU ignored when hiring Cooper was that, despite the Rose Bowl win over Michigan (which admittedly was one more Rose Bowl win than Bruce ever managed), Cooper didn't always fare well in the big games. In three years at Arizona State, he had never beaten archrival Arizona.

While filming the hot tub and supermarket commercials, Cooper also sought to put local media and alumni at ease with his homespun style in interviews and fund-raising functions. He was entertaining, but he turned off folks by poking a little bit at the Buckeyes' program—stating matter-of-factly that his Arizona State boys would have whipped them, too, as they did Michigan in the 1987 Rose Bowl.

"We had a great team," he told them. "I didn't outcoach Bo [Schembechler] in that game. I had a better team. I think the whole Pac-10 has more speed and better athletes than the Big Ten."

He was entitled to his opinion, of course. But he would have been smarter to keep his mouth shut. Even when

Cooper tried to give the impression that he was aware of Ohio State's football tradition, he sounded out of touch.

"I went after this one," Cooper said of the Ohio State job. "This is *the* Ohio State University. There are no others. What a tradition! I mean, Archie Griffin won two Heismans and he works right down the hall!"

Cooper unveiled a three-part plan to reinvent the Buckeyes' program. First, he wanted to recruit better players, particularly in-state. (He boasted that his Arizona State program had produced more NFL players in recent years than Ohio State had.) Second, he wanted to start redshirting more freshmen. ("Tom Tupa, Chris Spielman, and Greg Rogan would all be back this year if they hadn't played as freshmen," he explained.) And finally, he planned to place a new-and-improved emphasis on weight training. ("Last year, only three players on the team could bench 400 pounds. At Arizona State, we had at least a dozen," he claimed.)

While many in the Ohio State family began stealing questioning glances at themselves, wondering if the school had hired the right man for the job, Cooper kept grinning. He couldn't believe his good fortune.

"I've bounced around chasing my dream," he said. "But it's right here. You can't get a better coaching job than this."

13

Ferrets and Failures

I T DIDN'T take long for Cooper to display one of his strengths shortly after his arrival. He was a master recruiter. And he didn't mind telling people about it. In an interview with Rick Telander of *Sports Illustrated* in August of 1988, Cooper happily recounted his first few hours as Buckeye coach.

"I left Anaheim at midnight on December 30 after the Freedom Bowl, flew here [to Columbus], met the board of trustees when I arrived, announced to 500 people at a press conference at noon that I was the new coach, and then started calling recruits."

Within moments, he informed Telander, he had persuaded quarterback Kirk Herbstreit, a top recruit from Centerville, Ohio, to attend Ohio State—just by calling him on the phone. Cooper went on to describe how it had been like that for weeks, going "a hundred miles an hour, twenty-four hours a day" right up until the national letter-of-intent signing day on February 10. He pulled out a calendar to illustrate how he wouldn't slow down even in the so-called off-season and how, during the season itself, his schedule would be so packed with media and booster functions that, on Thursdays, he "would try real hard to do a little coaching." It was a joke, but it wasn't that far from reality, according to Ed Sidwell, who would spend six seasons working on Cooper's Ohio State staff.

"I was amazed because I had a predisposed opinion of Ohio State's program and Earle Bruce and, of course, prior to him Woody Hayes. Very stern, very conservative. In control," Sidwell said. "And John was very aloof and very standoffish. Very much an administrator, a delegator. And really kind of stood on the sidelines, twirling his whistle, knowing when the media and the cameras were out there at practice with their cameras pointed at him. He knew when to go off across the field, blowing his whistle and yelling at somebody. Typically it coincided with when the media was out at practice. The [assistant] coaches did all the coaching."

Cooper was smart enough to surround himself with some of the best assistant coaches in the business. He hired Bobby Turner, who later coached running back Terrell Davis for the Denver Broncos in the Super Bowl; Frank Falks, who coached Barry Sanders in Detroit; Jerry Sullivan, who would become offensive coordinator for the Arizona Cardinals; Larry Coyer, who would become defensive coordinator for the Broncos; Ron Zook, who would briefly become the head coach at the University of Florida. Larry Coker, later the head coach at the University of Miami (Florida), would be on Cooper's staff in 1993 and 1994.

Cooper not only was smart enough to hire a great staff, but he also was perceptive enough to quickly realize the flap he had gotten himself into over the hot tub and supermarket commercials. He decided that they were not worth the extra pocket change he was making from them.

"Promptly after all the criticism about the hot tub, he definitely put that stuff aside," Sidwell said. "He canceled the run of the commercials. In fact, he took a huge pay cut in sponsorships and endorsements. Basically he cut all the fat except for his TV and radio show—and really reduced his income by about a quarter. So I think he got the message, and I think he got it very clearly that that's not how you do it at Ohio State."

On the field, it began well enough for the new coach. He won his first game against Syracuse and was carried off the Ohio Stadium field waving a scarlet towel over his head. But then the Buckeyes lost four of their next five games. They finished Cooper's first season with a 4-6-1 record—Ohio State's first losing season in 22 years—after losing 34–31 to Michigan in the season finale. The Buckeyes' seventh-place finish in the Big Ten was their worst since 1959.

The team rebounded the next season to go 8-4, and suddenly Bruce's 9-3 finishes weren't looking so bad. Included in that 1989 season was a memorable 41–37 win over Minnesota in which the Buckeyes overcame a 31–0 first-half deficit. But even that game seemed typical of what folks were coming to expect of Cooper's talented but often misdirected teams. They turned the ball over four times in the first half, helping spot the Golden Gophers their big lead. Then in the second half they were marvelous, with quarterback Greg Frey throwing for the remarkable total of 327 yards after the half.

"I told them to get out there and fight for their lives," Cooper said afterward. "That [first half] was probably the worst half I've ever been associated with. The second half, because of the result, was probably the best."

The Buckeyes began the 1990 season with victories over Texas Tech and Boston College, setting up an Ohio Stadium showdown with Southern California that conjured up memories of past glorious Rose Bowl encounters. The Buckeyes, who hadn't been ranked in the top 10 nationally since the fifth game of Bruce's final season, had creeped up to number

15 in the Associated Press top 25 (which expanded from the top 20 one year earlier). They were favored over Southern Cal, which was ranked 18th.

As the game went on, though, the visitors gained the upper hand. With time running down and USC seemingly in command, Ohio State scored to pull within 35–26. The Buckeyes' only chance was to recover an onside kick, score, and then do it again. But, hey, they were the Ohio State Buckeyes. Many of them on the sideline resolved not to give up.

Cooper was not one of them. A violent thunderstorm was approaching the stadium. He was concerned for his and his players' safety, plus that of the fans. He called over the lead official.

"Listen, we're getting ready to try an onside kick here," Cooper told him. "If we don't recover it, why don't you just call the game? I don't like the looks of the storm we've got developing here."

The official looked back in surprise, but agreed to do so. Ed Sidwell was sitting up in the press box with some other Ohio State coaches when the deal went down.

"It started thunderstorming real bad. They stopped the game with about two minutes and some change to go; we were down by nine points. And he called the game," Sidwell said. "Well, in defense of John Cooper, and I've got to back up a minute here and say that no matter how much I think John Cooper was not the right coach for the Ohio State head job, I did respect him as a good, decent human being and a family man. I will say that.

"But with that particular night, and again in defense of John, there were lightning strikes hitting everywhere, all around the stadium. I was up in the booth and I had a pretty good view of it, across the horizon and over the horizon. They [the lightning bolts] were dropping everywhere and the rain was coming sideways."

So Cooper did what he thought was right. But again, he lacked the ability to understand why Ohio State fans and alumni would never comprehend his motives. They were absolutely furious with Cooper for giving up before a game was over, figuring that if even they hadn't been able to pull out a miracle victory, the least they could have done was send the right message to the players by going down fighting.

"The reason why it was so big for John Cooper was it added insult to injury," Sidwell said. "Nobody wanted to like John Cooper by that point anyway. The only thing John could have ever done to make people like him was to beat Michigan and win the Rose Bowl, which John never did. He eventually did them both on separate occasions; but he never did them both in the same season. And John Cooper, until he could accomplish that, he couldn't have done anything right.

"Now if Lou Holtz had done something like that at South Carolina, I believe he could have gotten away with it. But from day one, the media and the alumni had it out for John Cooper. And a lot of it had to do with stuff that he brought on himself. . . . John did not have enough knowledge of the tradition and the history and the mentality of Ohio State and its alumni when he took the job."

The losses to Michigan were piling up, despite the fact that Bo Schembechler had stepped aside in 1989—taking his 21-year record of 194-48-5 and a total of 13 outright or co–Big Ten championships with him. The pressure was mounting on Cooper to end the losing streak to the Wolverines and begin building that type of legacy for himself at Ohio State. And another situation was about to develop that would test his character as head coach.

■

Cooper was at his best recruiting, not on the sideline. That much was evident when he pulled running back Robert Smith out of Euclid High School in the Cleveland area and brought the talented freshman to Ohio State in 1990. Northeast Ohio was not an Ohio State hotbed at the time, and Cooper knew it. Michigan, in fact, was recruiting more high-profile players out of Cleveland than Ohio State.

Smith had been the bright spot on an otherwise ho-hum 7-4-1 Ohio State team in 1990. As a true freshman—Cooper apparently didn't believe in redshirting true freshmen any more than Bruce had when he elected not to do so with Chris Spielman and others—Smith had broken Archie Griffin's 18-year-old freshman rushing record with 1,126 yards. Looking to capitalize in the recruiting game on this success in any way he could, Cooper even persuaded school officials to schedule one game at cavernous Cleveland Stadium the next year. Again, this did not go over well with Ohio State traditionalists, who would much rather have seen the Buckeyes pound Northwestern in the familiar Horseshoe.

By this point, Cooper's job already was in trouble. A 23–11 loss to Air Force in the Liberty Bowl—the same Air Force team he had beaten in the Freedom Bowl in his last game as Arizona State's coach four seasons earlier—had kicked a movement into gear that seemed inevitably headed toward his dismissal. Unless, of course, he could beat Michigan and go to a Rose Bowl.

University president Gordon Gee, who had publicly discussed awarding Cooper a contract extension early in the 1990 season, now backed off that position. In a private meeting with Cooper, he gave the coach what amounted to an ultimatum: have a big year or prepare to leave. Cooper complained that not giving him a contract extension after discussing it publicly hurt him in recruiting, where he was beginning to make strides in areas such as northeast Ohio. But then, Cooper did not mind pleading his case publicly when he thought it helped his own cause.

"We've got to produce this year," he said at one point. "President Gee and the athletic council and pretty much everyone who has anything to do with my future have indicated that."

With that in mind, Cooper decided to hire tough-guy Elliot Uzelac as his new assistant head coach–offensive coordinator. A former head coach at Western Michigan and Navy who most recently had been offensive line coach at Indiana, Uzelac was hired with the idea that he was a Type-A personality who would instill discipline and toughness on the football field. Players had admitted that Cooper's practices, never as tough as Woody Hayes's, had gotten even softer. Uzelac changed that immediately by making more rigorous drills part of each practice, and Cooper gave him free rein to do so.

"To be honest with you, Elliot was the perfect mold for Ohio State," Sidwell said. "Very disciplined, very stern, very tough coach. A very much up-in-your-face coach—and a lot of players resented that. He was many of the things that John Cooper was not. But to work with Elliot, he was a tremendous coach."

Uzelac did not tolerate laziness and did not always accept team physicians' perceptions of player injuries. According to an account in *Sports Illustrated* magazine, when offensive lineman Mike Huddleston suffered a severely sprained ankle during spring practice in March of 1991, team doctors ordered him to stay off the ankle for two weeks. Yet several days later—just three days before the annual spring game—Huddleston told the magazine that he was summoned to Uzelac's office.

"If you're not willing to play with pain," said Uzelac, "I'm not sure you can be a starter for me."

Huddleston said that he figured he'd better try to play in the spring game "even though I was limping and I couldn't run or cut as fast as I needed to."

During the game, another player rolled onto Huddleston, spraining his knee and making his ankle sprain worse. As he looked around in pain while he lay on the ground, one thing crossed his mind.

"Uzelac never even walked over to see how I was," he said.

Huddleston told the magazine that he became further aggravated when none of the coaches called to inquire about his condition for several days afterward.

"I decided I didn't want to play for these people," Huddleston said.

So he quit. Huddleston said he never heard from the coaches again, and read in a local newspaper the following August that he had left the team "because of personal reasons."

Some observers thought Uzelac was particularly tough on Robert Smith, believing that former offensive coordinator Jim Colletto, who had left to become head coach at Purdue, had "coddled him." Smith, on the other hand, was the rare student-athlete who professed to be more interested in becoming a doctor than in carrying a football for Ohio State to secure a lucrative future in the NFL. He took his premed studies very seriously.

About the same time Huddleston was reading about his own demise in a newspaper, on August 15, 1991, Smith was in his dorm room supposedly studying for a test in inorganic chemistry, a summer school course in which he was uncharacteristically struggling. His final exam in the course was two weeks away, and he was worried. For perhaps the first time in his life, he might fail.

Uzelac, performing bed check along with Sidwell,

knocked on the door. His first knock came just before the usual ten o'clock curfew when the players were in their version of preseason training camp.

"I happened to be doing bed check that night in the dormitories with Elliot, and Elliot's standard was always firm, but fair," Sidwell insisted. "He would say, 'Lights out!' And knock on the player's door. The player would answer the door, and he would say, 'Okay, lights out in ten minutes' or whatever time it was until ten o'clock.

"He comes to Robert's room, and this one particular night we knock on Robert's door—and he's in there playing with his ferret that was his personal pet."

Yes, Smith said he was studying. But it looked to the coaches as if he was playing with his ferret.

"Coach, I've got some extra studying to do. Can I keep the lights on a little bit?" Smith asked.

"Yeah, okay, Robert. I'll give you until 10:30. Keep the lights on until 10:30," Uzelac responded.

Sidwell added: "He probably had about forty minutes left from the time we knocked on his door until the time lights needed to be out at 10:30. We made an exception for him. And then, I'm going to say a couple of weeks later—I'm not certain—but when the summer grades came out, Robert had failed. Robert all of his life had gotten nothing but straight As. He was a 4.2 student [in high school]. And I really think, in my opinion, Robert needed to blame somebody for him failing this particular chemistry course. And I believe Elliot was the scapegoat on this.

"Robert went out to the press and made it very clear that Elliot was telling the players in so many words—and I'm paraphrasing—that school is not important; football is first; to hell with your studies; it's Ohio State football. Which I never witnessed and can't confirm. All I can confirm is the night that Elliot cut an exception for Robert, giving him extra study time before lights out—which he did not do for anybody else.

"Next thing you know Robert says, 'I'm outta here. I'm quitting. If Elliot stays, I'm quitting.' And it became really ugly. And, of course, John Cooper was caught in a tight spot—because here he had a kid who really had won the alumni over with being Rookie of the Year in the Big Ten. John was looking good because he had not only a big player on his team, but he was winning games and he had taken that player out of an area where they hadn't been recruiting well. So Robert's presence on the roster helped John look good—especially after an embarrassing start for John."

Smith contended he had been studying for his chemistry exam when Uzelac told him to turn the lights out. Uzelac and Sidwell contended otherwise. Smith met with Cooper and delivered his ultimatum, telling him that Uzelac had said, in effect, that Smith took school "too seriously" and that he should consider cutting classes if it meant getting to football practice on time. Cooper refused to believe that Uzelac was guilty of such a thing, which Smith then took to mean that the head coach thought he was lying.

The running back said he was taking his game and going home. He threatened to transfer to John Carroll, a Division III school that was just a short commute from his home in Euclid. There was one catch, one trump card that Cooper kept in play. He did not revoke Smith's scholarship even after Smith quit the team.

Cooper steadfastly defended Uzelac—at first. But Uzelac seemed stunned to be caught in the middle of the firestorm, and the resulting tension appeared to play a role in chest pains that he suddenly began experiencing on the practice field. On August 29, he underwent an emergency angioplasty to clear a clogged coronary artery.

The Buckeyes went on to have a big enough year to keep

some of the heat off Cooper. They won their first four games and six of their first seven, but without Smith their offense wilted late in the year. The regular season ended with an embarrassing 31–3 loss to fourth-ranked Michigan, now their master for four straight years. Another loss followed to Syracuse in the Hall of Fame Bowl, giving Cooper an 0-3 record in bowl games.

Cooper's self-professed dream job was becoming nightmarish.

Prior to the following season, Smith approached Cooper. After sitting out an entire season, but still on scholarship, Smith technically was a redshirt sophomore. He still had three years of playing eligibility left—and plenty of time to pursue that medical degree.

"What will it take to bring you back?" Cooper asked Smith.

Smith's eyes narrowed. He was very clear on this point.

"I'm not coming back if Elliot's still my coach. I won't play for you if he's still around," Smith replied.

Cooper's version, offered later to author Alan Natali for a book ironically entitled *Woody's Boys,* was that he eventually placed Smith and Uzelac in a room and told them to work it out. He said that he pulled Uzelac aside beforehand and told him what he expected.

"I asked him to patch it over, because I wanted the kid back on the team," Cooper said.

Then Cooper left the room, Smith and Uzelac again took to arguing about who was right and who was wrong, who said this and who said that. Smith stormed out of the room, again reiterating on his way out that he couldn't, or at least wouldn't, return if Uzelac remained his top offensive coach.

Sidwell and the rest of the coaches could sense the tension in the Ohio State offices as the drama unfolded.

"John was faced with a dilemma: bring back the rookie running back of the year in the Big Ten, but you've got to fire your offensive coordinator. It was very clear," Sidwell recalled. "Next thing you know Robert's back on the team and Elliot's fired."

Uzelac has never talked publicly about what transpired.

"But the rest of us, we observed it and we knew what happened," Sidwell said. "Elliot chose to take the high road and say nothing but great things about Coach Cooper and the entire situation. But the rest of us knew.

"Even in very private conversations over a beer, Elliot always chose to take the high road, which I really respected. Sometimes I would even try to fish it out of him, and he wouldn't give it to me. And I really respect him for that. At the same time, the rest of us around it knew what happened. And a lot of us lost a lot of respect for Coach Cooper at that time."

Smith didn't, of course. He appreciated the fact that Cooper had chosen player over professional colleague. So when a local sportscaster began railing on Cooper for not only the losses, but for the alleged losses of many great traditions previously associated with the program, Smith jumped to his beleaguered coach's defense.

"People say Woody Hayes did this, Woody Hayes did that," Smith said. "I'm not one for the tradition thing, and I don't give a shit what Woody Hayes did. I don't think it's fair to compare coaches of different eras. It was a great era in Ohio State football [under Hayes]. But it's time for Buckeye fans to wake up and smell the coffee. Woody Hayes is dead."

With friends like that now covering his back in Columbus, Cooper needed no more new enemies. But they were now piling on after the whistle, and would keep coming.

Robert Smith had another big year for the Buckeyes in 1992, helping them to an 8-3-1 record. The one tie was 13–13 against Michigan at Ohio Stadium, marking the first time Cooper had been able to avoid losing to the Wolverines. Anything less, and rumor had it that OSU president Gee was ready to pull the plug on Cooper. But an uninspiring 21–14 loss to Georgia in the Florida Citrus Bowl followed. Meanwhile Smith decided to pursue a career in the NFL after all and left Ohio State following the season.

"The fallout from it really is kind of three-fold," Sidwell said years later. "A) you had to bring a kid back and fire a guy and turn his whole personal life and job situation upside down, just for a kid, to help you win ball games; B) John Cooper had to jeopardize his integrity and lost a lot of respect in the meantime; and C), and here's the biggest, after Robert Smith put so many people through hell to go to a school for a medical degree, he left early right after that season to go to the NFL and left his education [behind]. Now he's since gone back [to his studies] and I think he actually even worked toward it when he was in the NFL. But after making it so clear that it was education first and football second, he left after his second year at Ohio State to go into the NFL."

The successful recruiting at all costs did seem to pay off when, the following season, the Buckeyes ripped off eight consecutive wins to start the season, capping the streak with a 24–6 thrashing of Penn State at Ohio Stadium. It was the Buckeyes' third consecutive win over a ranked opponent— after they had entered the year with a cumulative record of 2-8-1 against such foes under Cooper.

The Buckeyes were now ranked third, their highest

ranking in the Cooper era. In fact, after they whipped Northwestern 51–3 in the season's fourth week, they had returned to the top 10 for the first time since early in Earle Bruce's final season. If they could win the next two games against Wisconsin and Indiana, Ohio State would clinch a Rose Bowl berth before they even had to face Michigan at the end of the season. Wisconsin, however, was ranked 15th in the nation and had beaten Cooper 20–16 the previous season for the first time in five meetings since he had become OSU coach. The game also would be played on the Badgers' home field in Madison.

"It's going to be showdown time in Madison," Cooper pledged.

Ohio State guard Jason Winrow added: "Every team we play is in our way to get to the Rose Bowl. We're not going to let anybody stand in our way."

It sounded good, but the Bucks fell flat in the showdown. They settled for a 14–14 tie. Then a hard-fought 23–17 victory at 19th-ranked Indiana placed even more importance on the season finale at Michigan. In seasons past, Cooper had tried to downplay the Michigan game ever so slightly, calling it "a big game" but hinting that perhaps it wasn't the be-all and end-all that Ohio State fans always made it. Again, he simply did not understand the depth of the history of the program he was in charge of running.

This time, there could be no denying it was a monumental game. With a win, the Bucks would secure sole possession of the Big Ten title and the Rose Bowl berth that went along with it. A loss, and they would tie for the title with Wisconsin—but Wisconsin would go to the Rose Bowl. Despite Cooper's intentions of lessening the pressure on his players by his statements to the press that the Michigan game was more or less just another big game, the nature of the practices that were set up during Michigan week made it clear that it wasn't Northwestern they were getting ready to play.

"When we would play Michigan, we would hype it up so big," Sidwell recalled. "A lot of the Michigan players I coached later in the NFL, their attitude was entirely different. But the attitude that we took going into the Michigan game was that it was so big, it was bigger than life. Bigger than anything you can do or ever will do.

"Hell, when I would run the scout team for Michigan week, we would actually wear Michigan-colored jerseys. Our equipment manager would order blue jerseys. We would get blue-and-maize tape and cover their helmets to look like Michigan helmets. They would give me a Michigan cap and a Michigan jacket. And everything we did was Michigan. We would dress our players up to look like Michigan players. It was that crazy.

"We put too much hype, too much emphasis on that game. You're at Ohio State. You don't need to say too much about it. They used to pipe in the Michigan fight song our entire practice. I don't think John made too much of the Michigan game. I think everybody there at Ohio State made too much of the Michigan game, including some of the alumni coaches."

Some, however, tried to slow the runaway hype train. Assistant coach Fred Pagac, who had played for Hayes and approvingly described Woody's practices as "war," suggested backing off.

"We need to quit making so much emphasis on this one game," Pagac told the other coaches.

Sidwell added: "I think John was trying to say the same thing to the media, but it was directed more toward the players—because when we would go into the Michigan game, we'd come out of the tunnel and their rear ends were so puckered you couldn't drive a penny nail through their butts. I'm serious. And typically, from my experience in the six

Michigan games I coached in, it was the sloppiest game Ohio State played all year long—because [our players] were just so wound up in the hype that they couldn't relax and get into a groove and play a good game."

All of which explains what happened to the Buckeyes in 1993. Going in ranked fifth in the nation, playing against a struggling Michigan team coached by Gary Moeller that already had four losses and was unranked, Ohio State fell and fell hard. They lost 28–0 in inexplicable fashion. It was Sidwell's final year on Cooper's staff, and not the way he had hoped to go out against the Wolverines.

"Hell, we went in my last year and we were favored by touchdowns. We go up to Ann Arbor and people are already making their plans for Pasadena—and we get whipped 28–0 by an average Michigan team. It was awful."

But it had become routine at Ohio State under Cooper, whose record against Michigan dipped to an unfathomable 0-5-1. Cooper kept saying that it was the team, not himself, that was losing to Michigan. Win as a team, lose as a team, that was his theme.

Sidwell didn't quite see it that way as he headed out the door to begin coaching as an NFL assistant with the Washington Redskins. He blamed Cooper for most of Ohio State's problems.

"It was my opinion that John just didn't have the backbone to make tough decisions one-on-one regarding the players. It was easy with the coach, because he brought you in and he could get rid of you in a hiccup and replace you. With the players, it was more difficult. It was my impression that John was intimidated by the players and didn't want to confront discipline one-on-one with the players," he said.

"And he wanted to hire coordinators and position coaches who could take care of their own players. Which, for some people's philosophy of management, that's perfectly fine. But I believe that in football, unlike in some other organizational structures or hierarchy, it all comes from the man up top—all the way down.

"And I think that the Ohio State program was a reflection of its head coach all the way down. We had some of the best talent in the six years there. Some of the best talent that has gone on to be pros, top draft picks, year after year. And yet we could never outright win a Big Ten, we could never go to a Rose Bowl—and we certainly could never contend for a national championship."

14

It's a Heisman, by George!

THE FOLLOWING year, in 1994, John Cooper finally pried the Michigan monkey off his back, at least temporarily. Playing at Ohio Stadium, in a season marred by earlier miscues, the Buckeyes held off the Wolverines 22–6 in the regular season finale in front of a boisterous crowd of 93,869 at the old Horseshoe. No one even seemed to care much when they failed yet again to follow up that big win with another—losing to sixth-ranked Alabama 24–17 in the subsequent Florida Citrus Bowl to finish the season 9-4. Nearly forgotten was the embarrassing 63–14 loss at top-ranked Penn State earlier in the season, in a game that the Buckeyes had hoped to use to show they were close to returning to college's elite few.

The landmark win over Michigan did not come without a price for the usually mild-mannered Cooper, who was nursing a sore right hand after delivering a punch to a blackboard in the Ohio State locker room at halftime. If it was designed to light a fire under his listless troops, who nonetheless led 12–3 at the time, it worked.

"That got a real spark under us," offensive lineman

Korey Stringer said. "Coach Cooper came in, and he was as excited as I've ever seen him. He was so fired up, the next thing you know, he hauled off and knocked the blackboard out. He put a good dent in it, too."

Tailback Eddie George added: "That really showed us how much he wanted to pull out the victory. He's usually laid back and calm. He's not usually into emotional speeches, but that definitely pumped us up."

Woody Hayes would have been proud. But then, that was neither the compliment Cooper sought nor appreciated. He just wanted to do his own thing, which he displayed in his postgame comments when reporters mentioned how he must have been pleased to have finally conquered the team from up north on his seventh attempt.

"I don't look at it like I beat Michigan," Cooper said. "Just like in past years, I didn't really feel like I had lost to Michigan. Our football team beat Michigan today. This football program beat Michigan—and it was an outstanding Michigan team."

The Buckeyes did so with the sort of offensive daring that had been missing from many of their previous encounters with the Wolverines under Cooper's command. Scott Terna's first-quarter punt pinned Michigan at its own one-yard line, and when quarterback Todd Collins stumbled while retreating from center shortly thereafter, Ohio State had a gift of a safety and a 2–0 lead.

Plus they got great field position following the free kick after the safety, needing to drive only 40 yards for a touchdown. But that score would not have occurred if Cooper hadn't ordered his team to go for it on fourth-and-one from the Michigan 31. He did, though, and Eddie George barreled through for a six-yard gain and the key first down that kept the drive alive.

Another fourth-down conversion on a pass from quarterback Bobby Hoying to wide receiver Joey Galloway kept alive a 64-yard first-half drive that produced Josh Jackson's 26-yard field goal and a 12–0 lead six minutes before the blackboard punching. But that punch occurred because Cooper was furious with his defense for giving up a field goal just before halftime—and when placekicker Remy Hamilton of Michigan hit another one in the third quarter, suddenly it was 12–6 and the momentum seemed to be shifting. The next time Hamilton attempted a field goal, however, it was blocked by Ohio State defensive back Marlon Kerner, and Mighty Mo swung the Buckeyes' way for the remainder of the day.

Once again, Cooper had dodged a bullet. A loss and everyone was certain he would have been sent on his way. Instead, he was hailed as a hero as he hadn't been since he had arrived in Columbus six years earlier. For once, he basked in the glory of it all, if only briefly.

"Some people say you have to be dead or be gone to be appreciated around here, and that may be true," Cooper said. "I'm not gonna tell you that I haven't had some times when I figured, 'I need this? How much more can I take?' But I came up the hard way; you gotta be thick-skinned to coach here, there's no question."

His reward for sticking it out until he—er, the program—finally beat Michigan was a new five-year contract. But that wasn't awarded to him by athletic director Andy Geiger until an incensed Cooper, who thought his one Michigan win was worth more than the mere two-year extension initially offered, visited with Louisiana State about its vacant head coaching position.

Right around the time Cooper was landing his first contract with Ohio State in 1988, an event was taking place that would help the coach seven years down the line. Young Eddie George, then fifteen years old, was being sent away from his hometown of Philadelphia to Fork Union Military Academy in Virginia by his mother, Donna. All Eddie wanted to do was play football. He hated school, and his grades, always poor, were only getting worse.

Donna George decided to do something about it. As much as it pained her, she sent him away. Eddie was stunned when she delivered the news and resisted going, but she would hear none of his whining.

"This is what you need. This is what you're going to get," she told him.

They both cried the day he left. It would be years before he understood why he had to go.

"I was hardheaded, and I didn't listen," he said. "Before it got worse, my mom had to send me away."

Fork Union was a very strict place, instilling just the kind of discipline the younger George desperately needed even if he didn't yet grasp why. He had to rise promptly at 6:00 A.M. each morning. Drill instructors were always on his case to make sure he followed the school's many rules, ready and willing to punish him with chores such as sweeping and waxing floors.

But they had a football team at Fork Union, too. And this is what George lived for. Life on the football field wasn't any less demanding. There were even more rules that had to be followed, without exception, if you wanted to play, and at first the coaches had to convince George of this.

"You can achieve any dream you want. But first you have to change your attitude," they told him over and over.

George gradually began to listen. He started working harder not only in the classroom and on the football field, but in the weight room. He became, in his words, "a fitness freak," spending any free time he could doing extra workouts on his own. As his size and strength grew, and his defiant attitude toward authority figures softened, he developed into a punishing running back who in his last two seasons at Fork Union rushed for 2,572 yards and 37 touchdowns.

That was more than enough to grab John Cooper's attention at Ohio State. And Cooper knew how to grab a young man's attention when it came to recruiting him to come and play football for the Buckeyes. Long gone were the days when education was the foremost thing mentioned. What got them now was the lure of the NFL, where a professional career could bring millions of dollars. Cooper could help them get there, and they all knew it. If they forgot, he would remind them.

Once at Ohio State, it was slow going at first for George, who again had to force himself to be patient and work hard, waiting for his chance. His first two seasons, in 1992 and 1993, he carried the ball a total of only 79 times—although he did score eight touchdowns. By his junior season, he was the featured tailback and pounded out 1,442 yards on 276 carries while scoring 12 touchdowns.

Though the NFL beckoned, George bucked a growing trend and decided to stay in school for his senior season in 1995, sensing that he and the Buckeyes might just accomplish something special. He was right. With George carrying the ball an average of more than 25 times per game, usually behind the crushing blocks of mammoth left tackle Orlando Pace, the Buckeyes reeled off 11 consecutive victories. George rushed for 219 yards in the second game of the season, a 30–20 victory over Washington at Ohio Stadium. It was the first of 12 consecutive games of 100 yards rushing or more. When he added 207 yards two weeks later in a 45–26 conquest of Notre Dame, his name was politely added to the watch list for Heisman Trophy hopefuls.

Then came the game against Illinois at the Horseshoe on November 11, 1995. With 92,639 looking on, George went nuts. When it was over, Ohio State had a 41–3 victory and George had a school-record 314 yards rushing, including a 64-yard sprint to the end zone on Ohio State's first play of the second half for a 24–3 lead.

And to think the Buckeyes were worried going into the game because Terry Glenn, a former scout-teamer who had evolved into a game-breaking threat at wide receiver, was out with a shoulder separation. It turned out that all quarterback Bobby Hoying had to do was hand off the ball to George, even though a week earlier the same Illinois defense had held Iowa to a mere 20 yards rushing. The Illini were led by linebacker Kevin Hardy and defensive end Simeon Rice, who would go on to be the second and third players taken in the next NFL draft.

"Looking at the film [beforehand], I wondered how we were going to get even 20 yards," George said modestly.

Instead, his 314 yards shattered Keith Byars's previous game record of 274. Cooper said it legitimized George's stature as a serious Heisman Trophy contender.

"Big No. 27, wow, he came to play today and did a great job with every opportunity he had," Cooper told reporters. "If Eddie George isn't the finest football player in the nation and deserving of a Heisman Trophy, I don't know who is."

But that was an individual matter. The Buckeyes were on a roll as a team, too, and had their sights set on something bigger. They outscored their last five opponents before the Michigan game by the cumulative total of 216 points to 62—and 28 of those points came in the second half of a home game against Iowa when Cooper benched his starters, including George, after running up a 56–7 halftime lead.

Suddenly, the Buckeyes were in the hunt for a national championship again, and Eddie George's name was being circulated along with those of a pair of quarterbacks—Nebraska's Tommie Frazier and Florida junior Danny Wuerffel—as a Heisman favorite in what many suggested could be the closest Heisman voting in history. The Bucks were ranked number two in the nation, with only nemesis Michigan remaining on the regular season schedule. But the game was to be played in Ann Arbor, and Michigan had a good team, too. The Wolverines were ranked 12th and seemed more dangerous now that they were being coached by Lloyd Carr, who was in his first year after Gary Moeller had been forced out despite 23 seasons at the school, mostly as Bo Schembechler's trusted assistant.

It seemed to be yet another setup for a letdown on the Ohio State end. And in this regard, Cooper's team was all too predictable yet again. They went down 31–23, losing yet another shot at the Rose Bowl in the process. Fans were disappointed to learn that for the second year in a row and for the third time in four years, they would be drinking orange juice again—no doubt with some vodka mixed in to ease their pain—at the Florida Citrus Bowl. Naturally, the Buckeyes lost there, too, dropping a 20–14 decision to Tennessee to close the once promising season at 11-2. Only John Cooper, it seemed, could go 11-2 at Ohio State and leave everyone with a horrible taste in their mouths about it.

The pain of the disappointing season was eased somewhat when George was named the Heisman Trophy winner. Despite the close vote that had been predicted, he won by a landslide to become the Buckeyes' fifth Heisman winner— their first since Archie Griffin won the only back-to-back awards, in 1974 and 1975. Only Notre Dame had more Heisman winners in its storied history. George had put up the right kind of numbers to accomplish it: 1,927 yards rushing and 24 rushing touchdowns, averaging a gain of nearly six yards every time he carried the ball. He led the nation in scoring, and set a school record for pass receptions by a running back with 47 for 417 yards and one additional touch-

down. He finished his Ohio State career ranked second behind Griffin with a total of 3,668 yards rushing.

When the announcement that he had won the Heisman
was made at the Downtown Athletic Club in New York City,
George's mind immediately flashed back to all the hard work
he had put in since his mother had shipped him off to Fork
Union Military Academy against his will but for the betterment of his development as a young man and a football
player. He dropped his head into his hands.

Archie Griffin, sitting directly behind George, pumped
his right fist into the air. George then rose slowly and hugged
the other finalists before turning to the two other people who
had accompanied him to New York: John Cooper and his
mother, Donna. Then he hugged them, too, saving his mother
for last.

Without question, Cooper now had the players with which to
pursue national championships. They often were leaving
school early in pursuit of the NFL dream that Cooper openly
advertised, but there were enough who stayed long enough to
win big over the stretch that began with George's senior season. They reeled off 11 wins in a row to start the next season,
too, and Cooper's best player that year was Orlando Pace, the
6-foot-6, 330-pound mountain of a left tackle who mowed
down every opponent in sight.

As a freshman the previous year, Pace had earned a
starting job on the first day of training camp when coaches
marveled at his rare mixture of size, speed, and athleticism.
One season later he blocked his way to the Lombardi
Award—the first sophomore to ever win. Pace joked with others that he felt like he also "could always say I got a piece of
Eddie's Heisman, too."

Cooper insisted that "he's played his position as well as anyone else I've ever coached. . . . I can't say for sure whether he's the best player in the country, because I haven't seen everyone play. But I know this: he's the best I've seen."

And from Lou Tepper, the head coach at Illinois: "In my eight seasons at Illinois, he and Tony Mandarich have been the two most dominant offensive linemen we've ever played. It's rare that an offensive lineman can make you change a game plan. Those are the only two who have caused me, as a defensive coordinator and then a head coach, to say, 'Wow, when we pass-rush, we want to avoid him at all cost.'"

Longtime OSU assistant coach Fred Pagac compared Pace favorably to John Hicks, who had paved the way for so many of Archie Griffin's yards back when Pagac was playing tight end for the Buckeyes. Others went back further and compared Pace to Jim Parker, who had won the Outland Trophy in 1956 while blocking for another Heisman Trophy winner from Ohio State, Howard "Hopalong" Cassady. Parker then embarked on an NFL career that took him all the way to the Pro Football Hall of Fame.

By his junior season, the coaching staff had come up with a way to keep track of Pace's blocking efficiency. During film sessions, they tracked how many times he knocked opposing defenders flat on their backs, calling them "pancake blocks." He registered the remarkable total of 80 pancake blocks that year. Cooper figured having tangible evidence of what Pace was doing might influence Heisman Trophy voters to cast their ballots for Pace. The school's public relations department even made up refrigerator magnets that displayed a stack of pancakes with Pace's name on top of them to distribute to Heisman voters.

More importantly, with Pace blocking in 1996, Cooper figured it finally would be his year. And for a long while, it was. The Buckeyes began the season by crushing Rice 70–7 and followed that up with a 72–0 rout of Pittsburgh. Next up was a spectacular 29–16 win over Notre Dame in South Bend, in Cooper's 100th game as Ohio State head coach.

"It doesn't get any better than this," Cooper gushed afterward. "Not many teams come in here in this environment and beat an outstanding team like Notre Dame."

The Irish were ranked fifth in the nation at the time. When the Buckeyes followed that up a week later with a 38–7 thrashing of fourth-ranked Penn State, everyone but Pace admitted they were a little shocked.

"I'm not surprised by this," he told reporters. "Penn State's a little undersized. I knew we could compete with anybody in the nation. If they're number four and we beat them like that after beating Notre Dame when they were number five, I guess we're number one."

Actually, the Buckeyes rose to number two, where they would remain for most of the season. In another 48–0 rout of Illinois, Pace cleared the way for several breakaway runs by starting tailback Pepe Pearson and the Buckeye backs—once knocking the final defender out of the way some 50 yards downfield.

The Buckeyes kept right on winning—until they met up with Michigan, of course. This time they played with their first Rose Bowl since Cooper's arrival already clinched, but the result was the same. Michigan won 13–9, again tarnishing a fantastic season.

An unlikely hero emerged in the Rose Bowl, however. After being benched by Cooper in favor of Stanley Jackson, quarterback Joe Germaine rallied the Buckeyes to a 20–17 victory over previously unbeaten Arizona State by throwing a nine-yard touchdown pass to wide receiver David Boston with 19 seconds left. It was sweet vindication for Germaine, who had grown up in Mesa, Arizona, and had wanted to attend Arizona State but was told by ASU coach Bruce Snyder to forget it because he was committed to another quarterback by the name of Jake Plummer. On this day, Germaine bested Plummer, giving Cooper his biggest non-Michigan win, over the school he used to coach.

Everyone in Columbus felt great about that. But Michigan still rankled. Cooper's record against the Wolverines was now 1-8-1.

Pace won the Lombardi Award again, becoming the first player in college football history to capture the award in consecutive seasons. This time he took the Outland Trophy to go along with it, and also finished fourth in the Heisman voting—the highest such finish for an offensive lineman since John Hicks of Ohio State had finished second twenty-three years earlier. And then, despite having one more year of eligibility remaining, he took his game to the NFL, where the St. Louis Rams made him the number one overall selection in the next college draft.

Cooper, meanwhile, was becoming increasingly frustrated that so many Ohioans could not seem to look past his woeful record against Michigan. He had, for goodness' sakes, just completed a stretch in which he'd won 22 of 25 games; he was 14-0 against everybody else besides Michigan in the Big Ten over the previous two years. Shouldn't that count for something?

Instead, his critics harped on the fact that he agreed to give Archie Griffin's No. 45 jersey to incoming linebacker Andy Katzenmoyer, who had requested it. Never mind that Cooper first checked with the ever-pleasant Griffin, who said he wouldn't object as long as Katzenmoyer performed in a manner on and off the field that would make the former two-time Heisman Trophy winner proud. Katzenmoyer obliged at least on the field (he was the target of ridicule off the field when he took golf, music, and AIDS awareness classes in summer school in order to stay eligible to play football) where he racked up tackles at a Chris Spielman–like rate.

Cooper kept winning with startling regularity the next two seasons. But 1997 ended with yet another loss to the Wolverines, this time by a 20–14 count to a Michigan team ranked number one in the nation. The record for the season dipped to 10-3 when defeat was followed by a loss to Florida State in the Nokia Sugar Bowl, and some alumni increased their grumbling about Cooper.

But every time it seemed Cooper was in trouble, he would stage rallies everywhere but in Ann Arbor (or in Ohio Stadium on any day when the maize-and-blue were in attendance). Oftentimes Cooper did his best work behind closed doors—and not only with recruits, but with school administrators.

"To know John you need to understand the fact that he's as clever as a fox," Ed Sidwell said. "And where he's good— really, really good—is when the athletic director or the president or trustees confront him and call him one-on-one into their office. John could sell a pair of white gloves to a woman eating a ketchup popsicle. I'm not kidding you. He is the cleverest fox in the whole world.

"I really think it carried over into recruiting. But he could do it with trustees, presidents, chancellors. He could take any situation that obviously all directions pointed toward him, and he could take those arrows and point them in fifty other directions. And by the time you walked away after hearing his explanation, you would say to yourself, 'Wow! That made perfect sense.' And then you'd have to shake yourself and say, 'Wait a minute!' He was very good at that."

With the wolves, and the Wolverines of course, at his door again in 1998, Cooper nearly delivered everything that could have secured his future. But again, he was one win short. This time, in his tenth year at the helm of the Buckeyes, he beat Michigan 31–16 before 94,339 at Ohio Stadium—and for a brief moment even his critics ignored his dismal record against the Wolverines.

A cynical reporter from the *Cleveland Plain Dealer* noted that Cooper stood at midfield after the rare win over Michigan, "ready to have his portrait painted. His arms crossed, his head cocked skyward taking it all in." Then the reporter wrote: "This wasn't an everyday feeling—heck it wasn't an every-other-year feeling—for Cooper. He tasted the joy of becoming a father more often than that of beating Michigan."

So the shots came even in victory now. Meanwhile, the Buckeyes would have gone undefeated and to the Rose Bowl that year, but didn't because of an earlier 28–24 loss to Michigan State at home after an 8-0 start. Again, they were so close, yet not there in the national championship picture. But they had another win over Michigan, and the 24–14 triumph that followed over Texas A&M in another Nokia Sugar Bowl appearance solidified their stature as one of the top programs in the country once again.

Cooper had accomplished much. Ohio State remained an established college football power, as it had been before his arrival but had not been in his early years. He had doubled his win total against Michigan, leaving his record at 2-8-1 but less noticeable because everyone always remembers what you do last. He had even won two of his last three bowl games.

But he still wasn't Woody Hayes. And despite what Robert Smith once said about it, people in Columbus still cared about that and about a coach's record against Michigan.

15

Back to the Future

THE BUCKEYES faltered badly the next season, dropping their final three games—including what was becoming the traditional loss to Michigan under Cooper. The late-season slide left them with a 6-6 record. In the Big Ten they finished 3-5 and tied for eighth. Although Cooper kept telling anyone who would listen that he had been coaching for thirty-seven years and had always been a winner, those kinds of numbers simply aren't tolerated at Ohio State.

There were other problems as well. Cooper's teams seemingly were becoming more undisciplined off the field as well as on it. An increasing number of players were getting into academic trouble or making local news because of minor scrapes with the law. Alumni were clearly disgruntled—only this time the angered mob included more than the usual alumni who bought tickets and contributed money to the university and thought that gave them the right to yell at the coach. Included now was a growing number of former players who were disenchanted with the way Cooper kept them at more than arm's length.

Each year the former players would hold an alumni golf

tournament at the Scarlet and Gray Course. Each year under Cooper, attendance at the tournament was dropping. Cooper treated the tournament as an inconvenience rather than as a recruiting tool to help keep younger players connected with older ones, as had traditionally been the case. One year, Cooper even called the course to make sure no beer would be served at the tournament—because he said it wasn't in the budget.

"Any of the traditional alumni events where the guys came back to either be with the team or just to be with ourselves, like where we have the alumni golf tournament, that thing was losing interest because he really didn't want to do it and didn't spend much time on it," said former quarterback Jim Karsatos, by then a member of the radio broadcast team. "He never canceled the event, but he didn't make it a priority. He and his coaches would show up and kind of play together. They didn't mingle with the former players at all."

It was typical of Cooper's aloof management style and his inability to grasp the rich history of the program, despite the fact that he was about to embark on his 13th season as its head coach. Instead of embracing former players and using them to help build a bridge to the future, he shunned most of the ex-players, especially those who had played for Hayes and Bruce. At first it only puzzled most of them; by the turn of the century in 2000, as it continued to escalate, it exasperated and infuriated them.

"Being with the radio crew, I was still around the program closely," Karsatos said. "But yes, I would say the other guys very definitely felt shut out when I talked to them."

Cooper kept his job for one more season. This time, it was clear that the only way he could survive was to put together a huge season—one that would include a victory over Michigan at the end of the year. When the Buckeyes began the season 5-0, it looked as if Cooper might be on his way to dodging yet another firing squad. But then the Bucks lost to Minnesota at Ohio Stadium, and again at Purdue two weeks later. Now it seemed clear that he would be gone if he couldn't beat Michigan in the regular season finale.

Alas, Cooper couldn't get it done. Despite going into the contest as the favorite and playing at home, he lost yet another one to the Wolverines 38–26. When a 24–7 thumping by Lou Holtz and South Carolina followed in the Outback Bowl, athletic director Andy Geiger gave Cooper the bad news. The only one who seemed surprised was Cooper himself.

In the weeks leading up to the Outback Bowl, starting wide receiver Reggie Germany was kicked off the team when it was learned he had a 0.00 grade point average; leading rusher Derek Combs was held out of the starting lineup after missing the first bowl practice in Tampa; and one of the team's offensive linemen, Tyson Walter, sued another, LeCharles Bentley, for $50,000 in the wake of an on-field fight during practice the previous spring. This stuff seemed straight out of a real-life *Animal House*. The perception was that Cooper not only had failed to beat Michigan on a regular basis, but that he now had completely lost control of the program as well. That perception and reality collided somewhere pretty close to the truth.

At the news conference announcing his firing at the Woody Hayes Athletic Center, Cooper fought back tears and feigned disbelief at his fate.

"It's the only thing I've ever done in my life," said the sixty-three-year-old Cooper, who said he had hoped to coach at least one more season. He made the point that this was the first time he had been fired in thirty-eight years in the profession. While the tears welled up in his eyes, school officials planned to make the wealthy Cooper even wealthier. The university agreed to pay $1.8 million to buy out the last three years of his contract, which had paid him more than $1 million annually.

During Cooper's tenure in one of the theater-style team meeting rooms there was a plaque on the wall that listed the "Program Goals" of the coach in supposed order of priority:

- Earning academic degrees
- The Big Ten title
- The Rose Bowl
- The national title

At the end of his tenure, the tally on these goals was not very impressive, leaving Cooper with a muddled legacy at best. Academics, especially late in Cooper's tenure, were considered a joke by many of the players whose main goal was merely to stay eligible long enough to pursue their real dream of playing in the NFL. In 13 seasons, Cooper's teams tied for two Big Ten titles, won one outright, and played in just one Rose Bowl. And despite twice finishing as high as second in the Associated Press national rankings, they never got within more than a two or three weeks' sniff of a national championship before they had to play Michigan or try to beat somebody in a bowl game. His record in bowl games was 3-8. He was even worse against Michigan, going 2-10-1.

But the biggest mistake he made might not have been losing so often to Michigan. It might have been not putting beating Michigan every year on his list of things to do when listing "Program Goals." It revealed his lack of understanding of the Ohio State tradition. One story from early in his tenure in 1991 illustrated that all too clearly. It displayed Cooper's failure to connect with the deep Ohio roots that ran in every direction from the Ohio State program, except for under his own feet.

The event was Paul Brown's death in 1991. This was the passing of a true Ohio football legend. Paul Brown was the man who once had coached at Ohio State; the man who had helped build the legendary Massillon High School program into the perennial powerhouse it had become (where the college-style stadium now bore his name); the man who coached the professional football team in Cleveland so adeptly that it was named after him, the man who was elected into the Pro Football Hall of Fame in Canton in 1967—before he spent the last eight years of his career building and coaching a new pro team, the Cincinnati Bengals, in another corner of Ohio. Everyone knew Paul Brown and what he meant to Ohio football; everyone but John Cooper, apparently.

"If you're from Ohio and you know what Ohio is on every level of football, you know this man and what he means to the sport," said Ed Sidwell. "In my opinion, Ohio is the birthplace of football. And when somebody says 'football' in the state of Ohio, they think of Paul Brown. I mean, you're talking about a guy with ties to Massillon, Ohio, the Cleveland Browns, Ohio State University, the Cincinnati Bengals. He *was* Ohio football."

Sidwell was there when, shortly after Brown's passing, Cooper leaned forward during a regular staff meeting and asked "in all seriousness, in very melodramatic fashion" if his assistant coaches thought he should attend Brown's funeral. "To which some of us really wanted to jump out of our seats and stomp our feet and say, 'What are you, crazy? Of course you have to be there!'" Sidwell said.

Sidwell, being one of the younger coaches in the room, was relieved when a couple of the older coaches such as Fred Pagac and Bill Conley spoke up.

"Oh, Coach, you catch the quickest plane you can—and

you make sure you sit in the front row where everyone can see you so that everyone knows Ohio State University is represented by its head coach," one said.

"Absolutely. This is Paul Brown. This is the guy who paved the way for everybody in this room," the other chimed in.

Cooper nodded. The rest of the coaches stole glances at each other in a mixture of relief and disbelief. Cooper went to the funeral as advised and made sure he was seen by the entire state of Ohio.

"But he had to ask that. Can you believe that?" Sidwell said. "And when I say that the guy did not have any knowledge of the tradition and the history, not only of Ohio State, but of the state of Ohio, that is what I'm talking about. He was the wrong guy right from the beginning for the Ohio State job."

Yet he held the job for 13 seasons and finished with a record of 111-43-4. Only Hayes coached longer and had more career wins, with his record of 205-61-10 in 28 seasons. Under Hayes, however, discipline was the watchword for the Buckeye players. Not so under Cooper, whose laid-back management style and lack of holding individuals accountable for their personal actions (including, at times, himself) had eroded the level of internal discipline on the team until it bordered on the nonexistent.

Former Ohio State defensive end Mike Vrabel, contacted in Pittsburgh where he was now playing in the NFL for the Pittsburgh Steelers, said that the team's lack of discipline, obvious though it was, shouldn't have fallen on the head of the dismissed head coach.

"You can only do so much as a coach. If a kid doesn't care, he doesn't care," Vrabel contended.

Reached by phone from his home in Bonita Springs,

Florida, Earle Bruce was asked what he thought of Cooper's firing.

"His record is good. Beating Notre Dame twice is good," Bruce said. "But I guess if you're talking about being remembered at Ohio State, you've got to talk about the Michigan games and the bowl games."

Once that discussion began, Cooper had no defense.

By this time, Earle Bruce had moved on to coach Colorado State, where he was fired in 1992 after admitting he had committed NCAA violations regarding days off for his players and off-season coaching, and for the open admission that he had struck players during practice. Colorado State officials said Bruce had punched at least nine players "with a closed fist in unprotected areas of their bodies." Bruce didn't deny it.

"But I didn't hit anybody that whole last year," he later told a reporter. "I'm not denying hitting. [Grabbing] a guy's facemask, or hitting him in the stomach. But beat a guy up? It's like this: you're talking about football. It's a contact sport."

Bruce was a dinosaur, from a bygone era. By 2000, he had gone on to coach for two Arena League teams only because he still enjoyed coaching. He also served as an analyst on Buckeyes football broadcasts for a Columbus radio station, where he often criticized his successor. As the school geared up for its latest search for a new coach, someone asked Bruce what he thought.

"You know the best way to be a success in Columbus, Ohio, as a football coach? Want me to tell you? The only way is to be dead or retired. Then you're great." He laughed loudly.

The candidates for the job were numerous, and most were fairly obvious. There was Glen Mason, the former Ohio State assistant who now was head coach at the University of Minnesota; Fred Pagac, the respected assistant who had served faithfully not only on Cooper's staff but also on the staffs of Bruce and Woody Hayes, after having played for Hayes; Chris Spielman, whose lack of coaching experience made him a long shot but whose zest for the game and popularity with fans at least earned him an interview for the job; Tyrone Willingham, the head coach at Stanford, was an attractive African-American candidate being mentioned; Oakland Raiders coach Jon Gruden (a Dayton, Ohio, native) and Oregon head coach Mike Bellotti were initially attractive candidates as well. There was one more candidate, perhaps less known than the rest, who quickly emerged as one of the favorites.

Shortly after the firing of Cooper, Karsatos and some other former players, such as Spielman and Jim Lachey, met with one another to discuss who they thought the school should hire. Spielman may have wanted the job, but quickly realized that his interview was little more than a courtesy call. Karsatos had played quarterback for two years when Bruce was the head coach and had always been impressed with Bruce's position coach, Jim Tressel, who since had gone on to become head coach at Youngstown State, where he won four Division 1-AA national championships.

In his two years as quarterbacks coach at Ohio State, Tressel had worked on a staff with Mason, who was the offensive coordinator, and Pagac, who was then in charge of outside linebackers. Tressel had grown up a Buckeyes fan. His father, Lee, had even played at Ohio State briefly for Paul Brown in 1942 before enlisting in the Navy during World War II. Lee Tressel eventually returned to Columbus to earn his master's degree from Ohio State. Later, when he was coaching at Baldwin-Wallace, the elder Tressel mimicked many of the things that Hayes did at Ohio State. He even taught a coaching class at Baldwin-Wallace where he used a textbook written by Hayes. Jim Tressel heard his father talk often of Hayes in glowing terms, even before he played quarterback under his dad at Baldwin-Wallace.

"My dad loved Woody Hayes. . . . If Woody watered down the AstroTurf, so did my dad. If Woody ran a certain play this way, so did my dad," Tressel later wrote in the book, *What It Means to Be a Buckeye*.

Every year, Jim Tressel would see little of his father during the football seasons. But the Baldwin-Wallace season always ended before the annual Ohio State–Michigan battle, and Lee Tressel made it a point of sitting down with his family to watch The Game each year. It was something young Jim always looked forward to.

Jim Tressel had met Hayes in 1976 when Tressel came to Ohio State to study coaching quarterbacks with George Chaump, who was then the quarterbacks coach on Hayes's staff. Tressel had long ago read Hayes's book *Hotline to Victory*, and readily admitted studying him. In 1981 when Tressel's father was dying, Hayes found out about it and drove to Cleveland "to be with him all hours of the night," Tressel later wrote. There was no doubt that Jim Tressel's bloodlines ran scarlet and gray.

"When Coach Cooper was leaving and a group of us were kind of putting together our wish list, you didn't hear Coach Tressel's name right out of the box," Karsatos said. "Now you would have if you had asked us. We thought he would be an ideal candidate because he's a very good football coach, he's been in the Ohio State system, he's an Ohio guy, he understand the importance of what football is to the people of Ohio. He was very well respected. At Youngstown

State, he was well respected within the community.

"And, you know, listening to the press and listening to the people in general, people would talk about how a coach from a small program, even though he won championships, wouldn't be able to coach at an Ohio State level. . . . Well, all of us know that football is football. It really doesn't matter what level you're at; if you can coach guys at your level and win championships, you can coach at any level. It really doesn't matter."

An Ohio newspaper editorial listed five criteria that the Buckeyes should be looking for in their new coach. They were:

1. A coach who can beat Michigan. (Woody was 16-11-1.)
2. A coach who can take the Buckeyes to the Rose Bowl. (Woody went to eight, including four in a row from 1972 to 1975.)
3. A coach who can win national championships. (Woody won five—in '54, '57, '61, '68, and '70.)
4. A coach who can win Big Ten championships. (Woody won 13.)
5. A coach who is passionate and bleeds scarlet and gray. (Woody wrote the book.)

Interestingly, the Ohio State media guide and some of the more generous Ohio media were now giving the Buckeyes full credit for winning a national championship under Hayes in 1970, when, in fact, the only organization that proclaimed them as such was the little known and barely recognized National Football Foundation. The rest of the nation, even then, used the Associated Press writers poll and United Press International coaches poll as their national championship measuring sticks—and after the Bucks lost that year to Stanford in the Rose Bowl, AP dropped them all the way to fifth in its final poll, while UPI had them ranked second. Hayes's last true national title had come in 1968.

But the implications were clear. After a departure from tradition in hiring Cooper, the native of Powell, Tennessee, school administrators wanted to hire someone who would take them back to the future. The days were gone when Hayes and Bruce could slug players in practice and get away with it, but there was an obvious need for a hard-line coach who would instill old-school values and a sense of discipline while melding the traditions of years past with some of the modern-day methods of managing a big-time college football program.

Reporter Rusty Miller of the Associated Press wrote a story describing how Cooper had alienated many former players and fans, mentioning that some never forgave him for mistakenly referring to Ohio Stadium as "Buckeye Stadium" during one of his early and ill-timed television commercials. The next head coach would have to know the difference and, more critically, understand the importance of getting all the subtle things right. Former OSU quarterback Dave Purdy told Miller: "I was hoping, just like a lot of the ex-players, that they would find somebody who had Ohio ties. I think anybody who's coached in this area, who grew up and played in Ohio, definitely knows the significance of the Michigan game and the traditions at Ohio State."

The finalists were rather quickly narrowed to Glen Mason and Jim Tressel. To some, Mason was the more solid candidate. He had the Division 1-A head coaching experience Tressel lacked; plus Mason had played for Hayes. But there were those, like Karsatos, who backed Tressel and believed that if he could win big at the Division 1-AA level, he could do it at the Division 1-A level as well.

Proponents of Tressel pointed out that in 15 seasons at

Youngstown State, he had won more than 70 percent of his games and four national titles. Opponents pointed out that John Cooper won 70 percent of his games as well—but they could say nothing about the national titles. Lesser competition or not, Tressel had delivered something at Youngstown that Cooper hadn't at OSU.

Tressel also graduated nearly 60 percent of his players, who often said that the coach regularly kept tabs on how they were performing academically and whether they were attending classes. In the 2000 season, twenty-eight of his players earned grade point averages of 3.0 or higher. In Cooper's final seasons, the graduation rate for Ohio State players had dipped to 28 percent, one of the lowest in the Big Ten. Still, there were those who doubted that Tressel would be able to exert the same close watch and influence in academics at OSU, which was a considerably larger operation than the one at Youngstown State.

In the end, OSU president William Kirwan and athletic director Andy Geiger, after a frenetic but rather swift sixteen-day national search, decided on Tressel over Mason. They settled on one of Ohio's own who had made his coaching name less than 200 miles from Columbus and had a deep respect for the rich traditions and history of Ohio State. Geiger announced that Tressel had signed a five-year contract starting with a base salary of $700,000, plus a $100,000 signing bonus. His salary would increase $100,000 per year so that by the fifth year he would be making at least $1.1 million—but he also could earn extra by reaching incentives such as certain bowl games and winning a national championship.

"My issue of coming to Ohio State really had nothing to do with contracts," Tressel said. "It would have been tough to take a one-year contract, but you know what? I would have done it. Woody did it twenty-eight times."

It was precisely the right thing to say at precisely the

right time and place. Tressel also talked of building strong re-lationships between the faculty and his players. He stressed building a bond with the past, the importance of improving the overall academic picture of the program, and the impor-tance of establishing trust and teamwork.

"Team is the key to anything," Tressel said. "If we can reach our potential, if we're unselfish, if we care about one another and if we build relationships with everyone, there is nothing we can't do."

At the news conference announcing his hiring, Tressel spoke for nearly thirty minutes about how much the Ohio State job meant to him. He grabbed everyone's attention.

"It is with tremendous excitement and humility that I accept this challenge and responsibility as the head football coach at the Ohio State University," Tressel began. "While touring campus this week, three words constantly appeared: tradition, people, and excellence. Our task will be to uphold and build upon the storied past of Ohio State football, while developing each individual to reach his full potential on and off the field. This must all be done within the framework of the team, as we seek the standards of excellence of our great state and institution."

Shortly after accepting the job, Tressel met with Kar-satos and many other former players and asked a simple question.

"What's needed here? What can I do to bring all the guys who played here back into the fold?"

That's a good question, Karsatos thought. But it's even better to hear that the new coach is concerned enough to ask it.

"I don't think it was the intent of the school to hire somebody to bring back the traditions that we had. I think that was Tressel's idea—because when he came in, he and I sat down for quite a while when he moved into his new office. He asked the alumni guys a lot of questions," Karsatos said. "He made a very concerted effort to remind all the alumni guys that he was interested in keeping them closer to the program—by inviting guys to practice, by having the Tunnel of Pride and having former guys come back to be captain. Because he understands the importance of tradition and of having those types of things.

"He's a football historian. He knows the history of Ohio State and of college football in general."

The Tunnel of Pride actually was begun in 1995 when Cooper was still coach, but it was the brainchild of ex-Buckeye quarterback Rex Kern and Geiger. In an effort to commemorate Notre Dame's visit to Ohio Stadium for the first meeting between the two schools in nearly 50 years, Kern and Geiger reached out to former Ohio State players who were attending the game and asked them to form a human tunnel for the current players to run through as they came onto the field. But whereas Cooper merely seemed to tolerate this, Tressel embraced it. The Buckeyes now run through the Tunnel of Pride every other year when Michigan visits the Horseshoe, and Tressel loves the opportunity to have the current Buckeyes rub shoulder pads with the great Buckeyes of the past.

At the first alumni golf tournament Tressel held, not only was there plenty of beer and not only did the head coach mingle with everyone before, during, and after the event, but Tressel also made sure one of his assistant coaches was positioned on each hole. He also instructed his players to attend the dinner afterward and then made sure they stuck around to meet many of the former players. Cooper had never done any of that. Dave Foley, one of the captains on the 1968 national championship team, was one who had felt alienated during Cooper's tenure.

"I don't know Cooper well enough to say he's a good guy,

a bad guy, or something in between," Foley said. "But one of the things that Tressel has done that I think is fantastic is that they invite all the old players back, and the whole coaching staff is there for that golf outing. There is one coach or one member of the staff on every hole—and they don't move. So your foursome would go around, and me, as an old football player, I would get the chance to meet the offensive line coach at some point.

"It was a scramble [golf format], so maybe for one hole the coach would hit a drive and you'd play as a fivesome. Then maybe the next hole the coach might not be a golfer, but he'd hit a putt for your group and you'd still talk football with him. He might be the running backs coach. So all of us old guys got to meet this guy and say, 'Hey, Coach, how are the running backs looking?' It was such a simple thing, but it's exactly the kind of thing that was needed to get the old players reconnected to the program. Think about it. Every guy that went back had a chance to physically say something to every one of the coaches. What a great way to build camaraderie, eh?"

Karsatos pointed out that it helped build bridges from one generation of Buckeyes to the next, but that perhaps most important of all it taught the younger players currently in the program to respect the history of Ohio State football. Now they could put faces with the names of the previous greats they had always heard about, or at least that they had been hearing about since Tressel's arrival.

"The team comes out for dinner [at the golf outing], and we get to mingle with the guys and sit around and talk," Karsatos said. "You know, the young players don't see [how important this is] today. But they see how much the alumni guys care—and I guarantee you that the relationship between the young players of today and the alumni guys is so much better than during Cooper's era. No disrespect to John, because he just didn't get it, but the alumni guys have so much that they can give to these younger players. And the younger players during Cooper's era had no respect for the alumni guys. None. They didn't know the tradition. They hadn't seen any film. They didn't read the history. They knew nothing, so they had little or no respect.

"I'm down there a lot [at practices], so I see these guys. But the first couple of weeks now [each year under Tressel], they're calling me Mr. Karsatos. It makes you feel a little old, but it's a sign of respect. When an honorary captain comes to flip the coin at the beginning of the games and to speak to the team before games, these kids know who it is. Even a guy who played before they were born, they still know who he is—because that's what Coach Tressel teaches. He's like, 'This is who this guy is, and here is some film. Learn about him.'"

Tressel also talked about improving the academic picture for his players on the day he was hired.

"The first thing we've got to do is create relationships across the board," he said. "We've got to make sure that the athletic academic support area knows that we are going to back everything that they're doing and learn what still needs to be done. . . . We had our first discussion about the importance of class with the team this afternoon. I explained to the team something my dad used to always explain to us: there is only one reason to miss class, and that's a death in the family—your own."

The new coach even mentioned that his own son, Zak, a junior pre-veterinary major at Ohio State, had been unable to attend the news conference announcing the hiring of his father as the Buckeyes' coach because he had a physics class. Again, all the right words seemed to be tumbling out of Jim Tressel's mouth.

That night, he attended the Ohio State basketball game at Value City Arena, the new basketball venue that replaced

St. John's Arena. At halftime he stepped up to a microphone and introduced himself to the sellout crowd. Then he proclaimed, "I can assure you that you'll be proud of our young people in the classroom, in the community, and, most especially, in 310 days in Ann Arbor, Michigan."

Jim Tressel had arrived as Ohio State's new head football coach.

16

Champions . . . And the Cloud of Clarett

DREW CARTER, a wide receiver who was about to enter his sophomore year, and quarterback Steve Bellisari, who was preparing to enter his senior year, were sitting in the stands at Value City Arena in Columbus when Tressel made his bold prediction at halftime of the Ohio State basketball game on January 19, 2001. They immediately exchanged concerned glances, not sure at first what to think about Tressel's soon-to-be famous Michigan "guarantee." They didn't really know the man yet, had only met him briefly, and upon first glance they had thought he appeared rather conservative.

"But that was not a conservative statement," Carter said. "We just looked at each other and were like, 'Wow, this guy really means business.' And then it dawned on us, 'Well, I guess now we have to back that statement up.'"

First there was much work to be done. Despite Cooper's reputation as a recruiter, Tressel wasn't convinced at first that there was enough talent on hand to immediately put the Buckeyes back on top in the Big Ten. But he kept talking about playing together as a family, about putting trust in one another and doing all the right things. Then one day early in his first August training camp, an obviously distraught Tressel called his players together.

"I just want you all to know that today I lost my best friend, my mother, Eloise. She had been diagnosed with pancreatic and liver cancer. I just thought you should know. I had really hoped that she would live to see me lead you guys onto the field in Ohio Stadium. She loved her Buckeyes," said Tressel, his words breaking with emotion. Then he broke down crying.

Again, this new coach surprised his players. But for many of them it was a revelation. Cooper had coached them at a distance akin to arm's length or more. They were closer to their position coaches than they were to the head coach under Cooper's reign. Now this coach was letting them inside his personal life. He welcomed their consoling embraces, and in turn immediately let them know that his door was always open. They felt they could come and talk to him about anything.

Tressel would grieve for his lost mother through his entire first season, oftentimes struggling with her loss in private. But his players grieved with him for a woman they never knew, for a man they had only begun to know.

His first season began with a 28–14 victory at the Horseshoe, but it wasn't very impressive. It came over Akron, a team Buckeyes fans were accustomed to whipping by at least five touchdowns. That was followed by a narrow 13–6 loss at UCLA, a team ranked number 12 in the country, and already critics started wondering about the offense Tressel was running. Victories at Indiana and at home over number 14 Northwestern were followed by a home loss to Wisconsin, another unimpressive win, 27–12 over San Diego State, and still another loss, at Penn State. After seven games, the record was 4-3. Wins over Minnesota and Purdue were followed by a 34–22 loss to Illinois—both at Ohio Stadium—

and suddenly it was time to travel to Ann Arbor to try to make good on the guarantee of the previous winter.

It did not look promising. The Buckeyes were 6-4 and hadn't played consistently well all season. Bellisari, the starting quarterback and a two-time team co-captain, had been arrested on drunken driving charges less than forty-eight hours before the Illinois game. Tressel immediately suspended him "indefinitely" and would not let him participate in Senior Day at Ohio Stadium prior to the Illinois game, which is when seniors are introduced to the crowd along with their parents in an emotional ritual before their final home game.

But since the day he had been hired, Tressel had focused on this game at Michigan. Although no one ever located a planner with the days marked off, Tressel could recite without hesitation how many days it was until the Michigan game every single day of the year. Every Saturday during spring practice, he had the players watch a quarter of the previous season's 38–26 loss to the Wolverines and then dissected why they had blown a 9–0 lead to embarrass themselves at Ohio Stadium.

"It was all about why didn't we win, what mistakes were made, what blown assignments cost us. He's real specific on things," senior defensive tackle Mike Collins said. "With Coach Cooper, this week was just another week. With Coach Tressel, Michigan has been here since he's been here. The counting of the days and weeks, the mistakes we made last year, going over what it's going to take to win in the Big House this year. He's made that his emphasis."

Tressel said he realized how important the game was to himself, and by extension to his players and staff and to the entire state of Ohio. Just to remind his players, he began an annual tradition by bringing in Earle Bruce to talk to his players beforehand.

"I know full well how exciting this game is," Tressel told reporters. "I know what it means to these guys. I know what it means to all the guys who have ever played in The Game. And I know what it means to college football. It's been one of the toughest, cleanest, best rivalries in the history of college football."

He paused to let that soak in—within himself and with others.

"Here I am a part of one of the great sporting events that there are each year, that the eyes of the world watch," he said. "I take that responsibility with a lot of seriousness."

He recalled one of the Michigan games from when he was an assistant on Bruce's staff, when he was coaching receivers and one of them lined up wrong, getting called for a penalty that negated a big play.

"You feel like you let the world down," he said.

He was determined not to feel that way after his first game against Michigan as Ohio State's head coach. But he didn't back away from the guarantee. And he said he wasn't worried about Michigan coach Lloyd Carr using it against him to get the Wolverines pumped even more than usual for The Game.

"No one needs bulletin board material when it comes to Ohio State–Michigan," he said.

Tressel opened himself up to some criticism by reinstating Bellisari on the team and saying he could suit up for the game. But after Bellisari issued a public apology, Tressel was asked where the senior stood on the depth chart.

"As I stand here today, I guess he'd be number four," Tressel replied, indicating that he would be behind Craig Krenzel, Scott McMullen, and even scout team quarterback Rick McFadden.

Krenzel—a native of Sterling Heights, Michigan, no less—was a sophomore preparing for his first college start in the most unlikely of places under difficult circumstances. McMullen had started the previous week against Illinois when Bellisari was suspended, but Krenzel had relieved him in the second half and led the Buckeyes on three drives that resulted in a missed field goal and two touchdowns. Furthermore, Bellisari and Krenzel were roommates.

The game plan at Michigan, however, did not require the quarterback to have a big day throwing the football. Relying more on big plays by the defense and a strong running game by tailback Jonathan Wells before Wells had to leave with leg cramps, the Buckeyes wasted no time jumping on top. On Michigan's first possession, quarterback John Navarre overthrew tight end Shawn Thompson. Ohio State's Mike Doss intercepted and returned the ball to the Michigan four-yard line, setting up the first of three Wells rushing touchdowns three plays later.

On fourth-and-one in the second quarter, with the Buckeyes still leading 7–0, Tressel decided to go for the first down from the Michigan 46-yard line. Wells burst through the line and didn't stop running until he was in the end zone. Later in the same quarter, Ohio State's Darrion Scott deflected another Navarre pass attempt into the hands of teammate Tim Anderson for an interception, setting up yet another touchdown run by Wells.

The Wolverines, who had entered as the favorites with an 8-2 overall record and a 6-1 record in the conference, suddenly looked panicked on their own home field. With a Big Ten championship and a trip to the Rose Bowl slipping away from them, Coach Lloyd Carr inserted backup quarterback Jermaine Gonzales for the struggling Navarre. On his second play from scrimmage, while operating out of the shotgun formation, Gonzales let the snap get past him. The ball bounded out of the end zone for an Ohio State safety, and just like that it was 23–0 Buckeyes.

Michigan rallied in the second half, but Ohio State held on for a 26–20 victory. Tressel became not just an immediate hero, but a legendary part of the Ohio State–Michigan lore for having backed up his guarantee. Krenzel completed 11 of 18 passes for 118 yards.

"I am so proud of these kids," Tressel told reporters (and by extension all OSU fans) afterward. "I didn't promise this win. I promised you would be proud of us. I think whether we won this game or not, you would have been proud of us."

There was more pride to be had straight ahead, but some shame to share, too.

Maurice Clarett arrived on the Ohio State campus early the following spring. Tressel had come across the running back by chance while attending a nephew's high school game in Youngstown. Tressel's nephew was playing for a team from Berea. Clarett, only a freshman at the time, ran for 246 yards against them.

"Holy smokes. This kid is good," Tressel muttered to himself.

Clarett already was, and he knew it. When the college recruiters started calling shortly thereafter, Clarett made it clear that he wanted to be on the fast track to the NFL. In a story later recounted by then–Notre Dame assistant coach Urban Meyer to *ESPN the Magazine*'s Tom Farrey, an incident involving Clarett in 2000 illustrated that the kid wanted to control his own destiny as well. Standing in the Notre Dame locker room after a 27–24 overtime loss to Nebraska, Meyer turned to Clarett.

"Well, what do you think?"

"I want to come to Notre Dame," Clarett stated flatly.

"Well, that's great. We'll count on it," the surprised Meyer replied.

"No, you don't understand. I want to come to Notre Dame right now."

"But . . . you're a junior. You can't do that."

"I'll graduate early. Skip my senior year."

"But Notre Dame has never done anything like that," Meyer protested.

"If you don't take me," Clarett said, "I'm going to Michigan."

So Notre Dame started working on it, but then Coach Bob Davie got fired and the plans to bring Clarett in early were nixed. Meanwhile, Tressel was hired to replace the fired Cooper at Ohio State, and suddenly Clarett was thinking he might look pretty good in scarlet and gray. Clarett had attended Tressel's football camps in Youngstown and had gone to Youngstown State games. Tressel was tight with Thom McDaniel, Clarett's coach at Warren G. Harding High School, where Clarett had transferred as a sophomore.

Tressel agreed to let Clarett get a jump on his college career by enrolling at Ohio State early, and right away Clarett made a quick impression on his new teammates-to-be in spring practice after Tressel's first season.

"He came in and started talking trash about how he was going to take the running back position over," said Chris Gamble, who would become the first two-way starter at Ohio State in forty years by starting at both flanker and cornerback in the coming season. "And he didn't care if one of the other running backs was standing right there. He would tell them right to their face, 'I'm here to take your job.'"

He was right, too. After suffering a thumb injury that set him back during spring practice, Clarett came back in the fall ready to show that he belonged. It had been a tumultuous off-season for the team. Tressel kicked linebacker Marco Cooper off the team after Cooper's arrest on drug and weapons charges. Tight end Reggie Arden pleaded guilty to drunken driving charges, and then fullback Brandon Joe was suspended for all three weeks of training camp and the season opener against Texas Tech after getting arrested for driving under the influence. Tressel was supposed to be cleaning up the program, but some of the off-the-field problems seemed to be getting worse.

Clarett, meanwhile, was soaking up the Ohio State atmosphere. Standing next to Drew Carter in the tunnel, bouncing up and down as he prepared to run onto the Ohio Stadium field for his first game before 100,037, Clarett could not contain his excitement.

"I've waited all my life for this," he told Carter.

It looked like it when he ran 175 yards on 21 carries for an average gain of 8.3 yards every time he touched the ball against Texas Tech. He scored three touchdowns, two of them coming on electrifying runs of 59 yards and 45 yards. It was the greatest opening day rushing performance by a true freshman in Ohio State history, and the Buckeyes rolled to a 45–21 victory.

"I think it's just time for Ohio State to earn its respect back," Clarett told reporters afterward. "I think we lost it for the last couple of years, and I think it is time for us to put our foot down and say, 'This is Ohio State. We're back again.'"

Clarett said he gained a surge in energy and emotion simply from attending the team's pregame pep rally with the band in St. John Arena.

"It was my first time going to that," he said. "You just kind of felt the energy from the people screaming and hollering."

A 51–17 win over Kent State followed the next week,

with Krenzel, now installed as the full-time starter at quarterback, connecting on 12 of 14 passes for 190 yards. Then Clarett turned up his game a notch, rushing for 230 yards in a 25–7 romp over Washington State in front of the largest crowd—104,553—in Ohio Stadium history. Suddenly, the kid was looking like something very special.

The next week, though, Clarett sat out with a knee injury that required arthroscopic surgery, and the Buckeyes struggled at Cincinnati in their first road game against an in-state opponent since 1934. Krenzel had to scramble for a touchdown with 3:44 left and the defense then had to fend off four passes to the end zone at the end of the game to hold on for a 23–19 victory. Twice Cincinnati receivers dropped winning touchdowns in the end zone.

"We got a little lucky," senior safety Mike Doss said in an understatement.

But the Bucks were 4-0, and they made it 5-0 when Clarett returned only twelve days after knee surgery to rush for 104 yards and three touchdowns the following week in a 45–17 rout of Indiana. Teammate Cie Grant, a linebacker, summed up what Clarett had done by simply calling him "Maurice the Beast."

Against Indiana, word soon got around that Clarett had run so hard that he popped the stitches on his right knee. Soon local merchants would be churning out souvenir T-shirts with "Maurice the Beast" printed on them. They would be instant hot sellers. Clarett said he took pride in displaying his toughness.

"If you saw [the University of] Miami last year when they won the national championship, they were a tough team," he said.

Meanwhile, Clarett was enjoying an increasing number of perks off the field as folks started talking about him fueling an Ohio State national championship bid. Many of his classes were independent study, which he figured required him to show up the last two or three weeks of a ten-week course to do the required work. He rarely attended one African-American and African studies class, and his grades were beginning to slip.

As with other players—and as with other major programs that dealt with uninterested student-athletes—the Ohio State coaches directed Clarett to a string of tutors to help him improve his grades. Later, he would contend that they did much of the work for him, which Ohio State officials would steadfastly deny.

But the controversy would come later. For now the Buckeyes were winning on the field, and Clarett, whom teammates noticed was driving a different new car every few weeks, seemed extremely happy on and off the field. The cars supposedly were loaned or leased to Clarett courtesy of friendly boosters at the Car Store and McDaniel Automotive in Columbus. Clarett would later contend that the boosters even drove vehicles down to campus for his personal use.

More big games followed. He rushed for 140 yards and two touchdowns in a 27–16 win at Northwestern, despite losing three fumbles. He went for 132 yards and two touchdowns as the Bucks crushed San Jose State 50–7, to move to 7-0 in front of another record Ohio Stadium crowd of 104,892.

The wins kept coming—19–14 at Wisconsin, 13–7 over Penn State, and 34–3 over Minnesota, the last two before huge crowds at Ohio Stadium. Clarett lasted only one series before a shoulder injury sidelined him against Penn State, but not before he would gain 39 yards on four carries to become only the second freshman in school history to gain over 1,000 (the other was Robert Smith, who had gained 1,126 in 1990).

That set up a Big Ten showdown on the road against

Purdue. This time Clarett wasn't the hero. Krenzel hit wide receiver Michael Jenkins from 37 yards out for the game's only touchdown with 1:36 left. Gamble's fourth interception of the season sealed the 10–6 win with 45 seconds left, and the Buckeyes were 11-0.

"It feels almost like we're kind of destined," Jenkins said afterward.

Next was a 23–16 overtime win at Illinois in windswept, cold Memorial Stadium. The Illini tied it with a field goal on the last play of regulation, placing the Buckeyes' perfect season in jeopardy. Playing without the injured Clarett once again, the Buckeyes pulled out the win in OT on the strength of Maurice Hall's eight-yard touchdown run and some solid defense.

Now Michigan was up in this remarkable season. Ranked second in the nation and playing before still another Ohio Stadium record crowd of 105,539, the Buckeyes' offense received a boost from Clarett's return. Krenzel kept mistakes to a minimum and the defense again made enough big plays to produce a tight victory. This time the score was 14–9, setting up a national championship showdown with the heavily favored Miami Hurricanes in the Fiesta Bowl.

Fans stormed the field and carried the triumphant Krenzel off on their shoulders. Tressel led the throng in a thrilling rendition of "Carmen Ohio." Maurice Clarett waved a towel over his head and hugged everyone in sight.

Six weeks later, the Buckeyes won their first national championship since 1968 by defeating Miami, the defending champions, whose 34-game winning streak was snapped. Clarett scored the winning touchdown on a five-yard run in the second overtime, and then Cie Grant, the senior linebacker who gave Clarett the "Maurice the Beast" moniker, forced a hurried and errant pass by quarterback Ken Dorsey on fourth down on Miami's final possession to secure the 31–24 victory.

"Everyone should cherish this, because you're never guaranteed to come back here," Grant said. "The last team to do this at Ohio State was in 1968. Look at all the great players who have come and gone in between."

Never had truer words been spoken. Tressel beamed.

"We've always had the best damn band in the land. Now we've got the best damn team in the land," he said.

Clarett was held to 47 yards rushing on 23 carries, but made up for his dismal day with one of the greatest hustle plays in school history when he caused and recovered a fumble by Miami's Sean Taylor after Taylor intercepted Krenzel in the end zone.

Buckeyes everywhere rejoiced. Former assistant coach Dom Capers, by now the head coach of the Houston Texans in the NFL, was on vacation at a resort in Mexico with his wife, Karen, sitting by the pool rooting on Ohio State. He promised "all these Mexican guys" who started gathering around that he would give them Texans hats and T-shirts if they'd join him in rooting for the Buckeyes.

Archie Griffin, now an associate director of athletics at his alma mater, was in attendance of course and marveled at how many Ohio State fans made the trip to Sun Devil Stadium to witness a night none of them would ever forget.

"We only had 16,000 tickets to sell, but somehow our fans got their hands on a whole lot more. It seemed like you looked around that stadium and saw nothing but scarlet and gray. I was absolutely blown away by how loyal our fans were," he said.

Jim Karsatos called the game from the Buckeyes' radio booth. He couldn't hide his emotions and didn't attempt to.

He was pleased for Tressel, even though he had often dis-
agreed with some of his play calls during the 14-0 season.

"He has his own philosophy," Karsatos said. "He had his
own way of coaching players and calling football games and
managing football games. And to that degree, he and I have a
little bit of a disagreement. But the reality is he wins, and I
have a lot of respect for the way he gets things done.

"He drives me nuts half the time. But in the 2002 season, as much as I got frustrated with play calling and decisions and stuff like that, the reality was that whenever it
came down to crunch time, I never got nervous. And the
team never got unsettled. They were always in control, and
they always thought they had a chance to win the football
game—and that starts with him."

The joy everyone was feeling was soon to be soiled by
none other than one of the stars who had helped to make it
happen.

Buckeye Nation was so ecstatic about winning the national
championship again that it seemed to have forgotten the
boorish and childish behavior of Clarett during the week
leading up to the Fiesta Bowl. Clarett had asked school officials if he could attend the funeral of a childhood buddy in
Youngstown, and initially they said yes. But there would be
paperwork to fill out to make sure giving Clarett a plane
ticket under the circumstances was not an NCAA violation.
Clarett was given the paperwork, but never filled it out. So
just hours before he was to board his plane, school officials
told him he couldn't go.

Clarett was furious. He called the school officials "liars."
He later knocked on Tressel's hotel room door, crying over
the injustice of it all. Tressel tried to console him, but told

him that he couldn't go without first filing the paperwork. By then, it was too late. The funeral of his friend went on without him.

Soon the next season would go on without him. Clarett was still borrowing cars from the Car Store, and on the night of April 16, 2003, took out a 2001 Monte Carlo that had just been purchased at auction. He drove it to the Ohio State workout facility the next day, and while he was inside, he learned that the car had been burglarized. He called Tressel, asking what he should do.

"Call campus police and report the crime," Tressel told him.

Clarett met a campus policeman at the car and proceeded to tell him that the car had been loaded with televisions, radios, and compact discs, along with some $800 in cash. The police report listed the following items that Clarett said were stolen: cash ($800), various audio components ($5,000), clothing ($300), two CD cases with a total of 300 CDs (estimated at $15 per CD, or $4,500), and a black leather wallet. The total: more than $10,600.

Clarett said the car was borrowed and that many of the items weren't his, so he did not file an insurance claim. But soon he received an urgent call from the athletic department, telling him the NCAA wanted to talk with him. They suggested he bring an attorney.

The NCAA wanted to know about the break-in; they wanted to know how the kid could have been driving a borrowed car with all that stuff supposedly in it. They asked about an $800 credit card purchase he had made for clothing at Macy's department store. About this same time, the *New York Times* reported that Clarett and other Ohio State players had received preferential academic treatment.

On July 29, news of the Monte Carlo break-in finally became public. The next day, Tressel and athletic director Andy

Geiger announced that Clarett couldn't rejoin the team until questions about his eligibility were addressed. By August 22, he was told he was on a "multi-game suspension." Two weeks after that, Geiger said that Clarett would not play at all for the Buckeyes in 2003 because he had not been truthful with NCAA investigators and he had taken illegal benefits from boosters without the coaching staff's knowledge.

It was the beginning of an ongoing saga that for a time directed attention away from another terrific season, as the Buckeyes went 10-2. But for the first time in three years under Tressel's command, Michigan beat Ohio State in the season finale. With no Clarett, running the football was a problem all year. Not only did they no longer have him, but they had been unable to recruit a top running back because during the recruiting season all the top running backs had little or no interest in coming to a place where it appeared a sophomore-to-be was entrenched as the starter and star, perhaps for up to three years.

Clarett applied for but was ruled ineligible for the NFL draft. He said nothing for nearly another eight months before hooking up with *ESPN the Magazine* for an exclusive interview during which he claimed Tressel lined him up at least initially with some of his various cars, and that he and other student-athletes were given preferential academic assistance and summer jobs where they made big money to do little or nothing. He said that boosters had lined his palms with frequent "hundred-dollar handshakes" during the national championship run of 2002, when his popularity in Columbus reached rock star status.

Geiger said Clarett was lying, and that he had displayed a pattern of lying since coming to Columbus. He questioned ESPN's motives for printing the interview, which, in turn, sent ESPN into overdrive with its vast network of television and print reporters in an all-out effort to defend its integrity and the journalistic right to pursue the truth. Tressel said nothing and tried to coach his team through another season. He wondered if Woody Hayes had ever had to deal with anything remotely close to this kind of modern-day mess.

Other players hinted that there might be something to some of what Clarett charged, but Chris Gamble called it "crazy" for Clarett to "bring all that back up." Of the aggressive boosters, Gamble added: "They were around. But I didn't even want to talk to those guys. I was never a guy who wanted to get into all that stuff because I didn't want to get into any kind of trouble." The other players confirmed only that tutors sometimes helped them a little more than required or than what was supposed to be permitted, and that the cushy summer jobs were available if you wanted them. The NCAA came back on campus to investigate, and suddenly Maurice Clarett, the kid who helped the Buckeyes win a national championship and had been the toast of the town only two years earlier, was Public Enemy Number One in Columbus. They should have known that anyone wearing No. 13 was cursed.

Jim Karsatos summed up the general feeling in the community by commenting: "I don't have time in my day to worry about that kid. Honestly, I always thought he'd be a problem. He turned out to be a problem, and it's not worth your time or mine. He's wasting everybody's time—and good riddance."

Chris Spielman also was quick to jump to Tressel's defense.

"I consider Coach Tressel a friend. I do a radio show [in Columbus] now and we can sit around and argue about offense and defense, Xs and Os. That's the fun part about football," Spielman said. "But when somebody comes out and questions someone's character, and his ethics, then I think that's unfair. Especially since none of the stuff Clarett said has ever been proven.

"So when a guy is forced to defend himself after the NCAA was just in here for sixteen months investigating and found nothing wrong, I'm a little disappointed that it's getting the play that it's getting. But that's the world we live in in sports today, with the Internet and competing magazines and TV and radio and all that.

"Coach Tressel is doing fine. He's got nothing to hide. He's confident in his staff and in himself that they do things the right way—and I believe him."

One former assistant coach at several prominent Division 1-A schools commented that situations similar to what appears to have happened with Clarett were becoming all too common in college football.

"So many of these kids think of college ball only as a means to the end of getting to the NFL, and nothing more," this assistant said. "They aren't coming to your school looking for an education. And if a kid comes to your campus with his hand out, there will be some booster somewhere in town willing to put something in it. The head coach, he can't possibly keep track of everything that's going down. He's trying to coach his team. There aren't enough hours in the day as it is. He simply cannot control what all the boosters do, or what a kid is going to do who arrives with the mentality that he's going to have his hand out looking for off-the-field perks."

As for the academic side of today's student-athlete, this former assistant, who now coaches in the NFL, laughed and added: "What's the old saying? You can lead a horse to water but you can't make him drink. We used to have to go to kids' dorms or houses and drag them out of bed to get them to go to class. But you can't do that for them every single day. If they don't want to go, sometimes they're just not going to go and there's not a damn thing you can do about it."

At Ohio State, the glory is found on the field. As Tressel embarks on a new set of modern-day challenges that no doubt would have left Woody Hayes throwing right jabs at the air and smashing his wristwatch and glasses on the ground in frustration, the games are still being played. Even as Clarett aired his accusations in November of 2004, there was one place Tressel could find solace.

It was on the sideline in the Michigan game. Even though they entered as underdogs with an uncharacteristic record of 6-4 and were playing a Michigan team that had won eight in a row overall and 13 straight in the Big Ten, the Buckeyes pulled off a 37–21 upset for Tressel's third win in four games against the despised Wolverines.

And suddenly all appeared to be just fine again in Columbus, Ohio.

The tranquility brought on by another win over Michigan was short-lived for Tressel and Buckeye fans. Less than one month later, Tressel suspended quarterback Troy Smith for the MasterCard Alamo Bowl because Smith "had violated team and NCAA rules and standards." Smith had replaced Justin Zwick as the starter earlier in the season and had given the team a lift over the final five regular season games, having amassed 386 yards of total offense in the win over Michigan with 241 yards passing and another 145 yards rushing. It was the third highest single-game total yardage output in Ohio State history.

"All of our players, including Troy, know they have a number of responsibilities to fulfill in order to have the privilege of playing at Ohio State," Tressel said. "Troy has not fulfilled those responsibilities and therefore will not be able to play in the Alamo Bowl."

Led by Zwick and the versatile Ted Ginn Jr., a receiver who can line up all over the field and appears to be the Buckeyes' next big star, beating Oklahoma State in the Alamo Bowl was no problem. The final score of 33–7 included four field goals by placekicker Mike Nugent, pushing Nugent past Pete Johnson on the top of the Buckeyes' all-time scoring list with 356 points.

Andy Geiger, the embattled and increasingly bone-weary OSU athletic director, said that the university had petitioned the NCAA to allow Smith's reinstatement for the 2005 season, but that Smith would miss at least the 2005 season opener. Prior to the Alamo Bowl, Geiger shed light on what had occurred to lead to Smith's suspension. He even admitted for the first time that maybe there was a significance to some of what Clarett had said after all, but he continued to insist that the Ohio State coaching staff and the athletic department had been duped along with everyone else. He also insisted that the school's program did not have a "systematic or widespread" problem.

What had happened with Smith sounded familiar when compared to at least some of what Clarett had charged. Robert Q. Baker, a forty-six-year-old man who used to run a business in Columbus and shared a luxury suite with other businessmen at Ohio Stadium, had handed over illegal benefits, presumably cash, to Smith. Then Baker had allegedly bragged about it to employees, leading Geoffrey Webster, an attorney for Baker's former company, Poly-Care Services, to call the Ohio State athletic department to report the transgression.

Poly-Care Services employees had told Webster that Baker had boasted about giving an envelope to an Ohio State player, supposedly Smith, who didn't work for the company. Then Baker allegedly added, "Now, I own him."

In an interview with the *Cleveland Plain Dealer*, Webster said it was upon hearing of that statement that he decided to come forth.

"I can't think of any way to make that a good statement," Webster told the newspaper. "I've spent thirty years as an attorney, word-smithing things. I have a real hard time coming up with anything else that he could have meant that could be a positive. I just can't. To say something like that is really wrong and really inappropriate."

The good news for Ohio State, and perhaps all of college football, was that Webster, a self-professed Buckeye fan himself, had turned in Baker in the hope that it would at least represent a small step toward helping clean up the program and maybe even college football in general. A "good booster" had turned in a bad one.

"Good boosters are terrific and exactly what you want," Geiger said. "The rogue booster is what you constantly worry about. That is what causes you to lose sleep."

Geiger wasn't going to lose sleep over it much longer. Less than one week later, the sixty-five-year-old Geiger announced his retirement. He explained his decision by basically admitting that it was no longer fun for him to come into work.

One day later, the Ohio State band marched to the front of Geiger's home in Upper Arlington and started playing. The last time anyone could remember them doing such a thing was years earlier after Earle Bruce had been fired as the head football coach, and the tunes they played hadn't changed one note. Geiger had to smile to himself as he listened to them perform "We Don't Give a Damn About the Whole State of Michigan."

Somewhere, Woody Hayes probably was smiling to himself, too.

Bibliography

Brondfield, Jerry. *Woody Hayes and the 100-Yard War.* New York: Berkeley Medallion Books, 1975.

Carpenter, Monte. *Quotable Woody: The Wit, Will and Wisdom of Woody Hayes, College Football's Most Fiery Championship Coach.* Nashville, Tennessee: TowleHouse Publishing, 2002.

The Columbus Dispatch. *A Season To Remember: Ohio State's 2002 National Championship.* Sports Publishing, L.L.C., 2003.

Greatest Moments in Ohio State Football History (foreword by Archie Griffin). Chicago, Illinois: Triumph Books, 2003.

Greenberg, Steve, and Zelina, Larry. *Ohio State '68: All the Way to the Top.* Sports Publishing, Inc., 1998.

Hooley, Bruce. *Ohio State's Unforgettables.* Sports Publishing, L.L.C., 2002.

Hornung, Paul. *Woody Hayes: A Reflection.* Champaign, Illinois: Sagamore Publishing Inc., 1991.

Natali, Alan. *Woody's Boys: Twenty Famous Buckeyes Talk Amongst Themselves.* Wilmington, Ohio: Orange Frazier Press, 1998.

Snook, Jeff, ed. *What It Means To Be A Buckeye: Jim Tressel and Ohio State's Greatest Players.* Chicago, Illinois: Triumph Books, 2003.

Index